REVELATION AND RESPONSE

REVELATION AND RESPONSE

THE KERR LECTURES FOR 1937

BY

EDGAR P. DICKIE

M.C., B.A.(Oxon.), M.A., B.D.(Edin.)

PROFESSOR OF DIVINITY, ST. MARY'S COLLEGE,
THE UNIVERSITY OF ST. ANDREWS

EDINBURGH: T. & T. CLARK, 38 GEORGE STREET

1938

PRINTED IN GREAT BRITAIN BY
MORRISON AND GIBB LIMITED
FOR
T. & T. CLARK, EDINBURGH

PREFACE

It is said that an aboriginal race in Borneo have a novel method for disposing of elderly members of the family. Periodically, they are invited to climb trees and, when they are established in the branches with the maximum of security, the trees are well shaken. If the aged relatives are able to hold fast, they are declared to be still immature ; if they drop off, they are pronounced ripe, and are ceremonially eaten.

The system of the Kerr Trust is so designed as to gather the fruit a little earlier. There is also a time-limit of twelve months between delivery of the lectures and their publication, in order to secure that the fruit will be rapidly prepared for the table. This means, first, that the lectures are written under considerable pressure and, second, that there must be a great deal which the writer will wish to develop and expand, but it is widely acknowledged that the provisions are wise, since they check the inevitable tendency, in enlarging and overloading, merely to obscure.

For permission to use some of the material of Chapters V and VII–X, already presented in my essays in *Religion in Life* (New York) and some of Chapter IV, taken from my article in *The Evangelical Quarterly* (April 1937), grateful acknowledgment is made to the editors and publishers of these widely honoured periodicals.

In revising the lectures, I received most valuable suggestions from Rev. James Brown, B.D., Arthur Melville Clark, D.Phil., F.R.S.E., Rev. Norman MacLeish, M.A., B.Phil., and A. J. D. Porteous, M.A. And I have tried, wherever possible, to indicate my indebtedness to other writers by references in the footnotes. I regret that the stimulating essays of Professor de Burgh's *Towards a*

Religious Philosophy appeared too late for me to consult them as I would wish to have done.

For the courtesy and kindness of the Very Reverend Principal W. M. Macgregor and the staff of Trinity College, Glasgow, I wish to express my gratitude. Those who have to operate the crowded time-table of a theological curriculum must often wish that extra-mural lecturers should be painlessly destroyed, or at least destroyed, but no vestige of such a feeling was allowed to come to the surface.

Rev. David Cairns, B.A., generously undertook the task of proof-reading, and through the great kindness of Mr. Wilfrid Meynell and the courtesy of the publishers I am able to quote the haunting verses on page 171.

EDGAR P. DICKIE.

St. Andrews.

CONTENTS

IN MEMORY
OF
MY FATHER AND MOTHER

CHAPTER I

REVELATION AND THE MOOD OF TO-DAY

SUMMARY

IT is commonly asserted that the mood of to-day is experimental. This is perhaps nearer the truth than to say that it is adventurous. We are seekers rather than finders. One feature of our time is the abundance of unresolved contradictions existing side by side. Intolerant of authority it has yet seen the establishment of totalitarian states. With a reputation for scepticism, it is hospitable to credulity in its most absurd forms. Self-reliance is curiously mingled with self-distrust. The exaltation of human reason is found alongside the purest irrationalism. Two factors are found at work among those who are outside denominational Christianity. (1) The unconscious and habitual Christian ethic. (2) The ineradicable religiosity of man ; at critical moments he turns to religion for sanction or consolation. Some are convinced that the worst possible way of treating the prevalent sickness of mankind is to admit revelation. Nature, it is argued, may choose for survival the natural man, who has shed his transcendental longings. Yet it is to be observed that these longings appear to be incorrigibly active and, still more, that the light may grow dim and disbelief triumph, because of man's sinfulness. The tendency to minimise the stress laid on sin would be justified only if (i) fellowship between man and God were perfect and complete ; or (ii) this fellowship were ignored and its possibility denied. A correct estimate of man sees in him an extraordinary dignity conjoined with an extraordinary distress. Religion encounters a double challenge : (1) It is affirmed that man has it in his own power to put himself right ; that he needs no help from outside since he carries the divine within himself. This is a superficial diagnosis. Sin is not an incident but a state. It destroys character, and that which man can so easily destroy he cannot by any human means restore. The power is not even immanent in man as an endowment given by God. It has been said that the higher man of to-day is not vexed by the problem of his sins. But, unhappily, hard facts persist, along with their bitter consequences, regardless of the amount of interest that men take in them. (2) From another side it is said that a righteous God and the necessity of redemption for man are only spectres of a diseased imagination. It is quite true that there may be cases where the sense of sin has ceased to be religious and has become a mental abnormality, but that is no more a sufficient reason for denying penitence its rightful place than the absurdities of some ascetics is a reason for denouncing self-control and sobriety.

As in the search for knowledge a primary condition of success is the rigid exclusion of presuppositions and prejudice, so the quest of spiritual truth demands the renunciation of sensuality, of pride, and of self-will. (1) The first requirement is obvious, and it includes not only the grosser sins but even more clearly the sinful attitudes and hidden indulgences of the mind. Only the pure in heart shall see God. (2) The second requirement is summed up also in words of Jesus : " Except ye be converted and become as little children." Men must put off all confidence in their own wisdom and wait on God in a purely receptive spirit. (3) The third is based on the fact that spiritual knowledge comes by the way of obedience. It demands the recognition of a superior will, in submission to which alone man can arrive at the truth.

CHAPTER I

Revelation and the Mood of To-day

Much is written in our time about "the modern mind." The real trouble is that there are so many minds, for the "man of to-day" will not be classified. It is impossible to pin him down with a neat label attached. He is not a butterfly but a hydra. If you think that you have transfixed one head, you discover that other two have appeared.

Thus more cautious writers prefer to speak of "the modern temper" (Joseph Wood Krutch), or "the modern mood" (W. M. Horton), indicating perhaps that the man of to-day has not yet *made up his mind*.

It is commonly asserted that the mood of to-day is experimental, and that is certainly nearer the truth than to call it adventurous. We are seekers rather than finders. But we are a little hectic in our search because we are not sure what it is that we are looking for. We redouble our efforts when we have forgotten our aim.

Disenchantment is part of the affliction. Mr. Walter Lippmann is probably as acute in diagnosis as any other, and he writes of those "who are perplexed by the consequences of their own irreligion"; who "have lost the certainty that their lives are significant." Modern man is aware of what John Stuart Mill called "the disastrous feeling of not worth while." "He may be very busy with many things, but he discovers one day that he is no longer sure they are worth doing. He has been much preoccupied; but he is no longer sure he knows why. He has become involved in an elaborate routine of pleasures; and they do not seem to amuse him very much. He finds it hard to believe that doing any one thing is better than doing any other thing, or, in fact, that it is better than doing nothing at all. It occurs to him that it is a great deal of trouble to

3

live, and that even in the best of lives the thrills are few and far between." [1] In this strange disease of modern life

> " Each strives, nor knows for what he strives,
> And each half lives a hundred different lives." [2]

It is perhaps wholesome for us to realise that this mood is not unique and unexampled. It will be good for those who are secretly rather proud of it to remember that it has manifested itself before, and for those who are troubled by it to know that it will pass. The writer of *Ecclesiastes* knew the mood, but he was wiser than our age in recognising that he was not the first to experience it. There is no new thing under the sun. Is there any thing whereof it may be said, See, this is new ? it hath been already of old time, which was before us.

There was a certain wisdom behind the street-orator's contemptuous reference to " This so-called twentieth century ! "

One feature of our time is the abundance of unresolved contradictions existing side by side. It is hardly possible to speak of *the* mood of to-day when it is in reality an amalgam of quite inconsistent moods. Ours is commonly supposed to be an age that is intolerant of authority, yet it has seen the establishment of totalitarian states. With a reputation for scepticism it is hospitable to credulity in its more absurd forms. The use of mascots is so common that the more lethal forms, carried on the front of motor vehicles, can provide a subject for legislation. A bone from an Egyptian tomb holds educated circles in terror. Innumerable persons, otherwise perfectly rational, will touch wood in order to avert the consequences of their boastfulness. [3]

---

[1] Walter Lippmann, *A Preface to Morals* (Allen & Unwin, 1931), pp. 3–4.

[2] Matthew Arnold, *The Scholar Gipsy*.

[3] The sacred wood of the Cross once received a worship similar to that offered to God Himself. See the account given by the Roman Catholic archæologist, Didron, in *Histoire de Dieu*, p. 531 (1843). A cross found in a Christian tomb in Rome has the magical inscription : *Crux est vita mihi, mors, inimice, tibi*—" The cross is life to me ; to thee may it be death, O enemy (the devil) "—de Rossi : *Bulletino di Arch. Crist.*, 1873, p. 138.

Revelation and the Mood of To-Day

It is an age, says Mr. Lippmann, which has sub
trivial illusions for majestic faiths. The modern
pated man does not believe the words of the Gospel but
he believes the best advertised notion.[1] Again, we see
self-reliance curiously mingled with self-distrust ; on one
side the exaltation of human reason, on the other the
purest irrationalism. It might be said and sometimes is
said, that there is one constant feature of the modern
temper ; it is subjective, brooding, introspective. There is
gaiety enough, but it is a screen for something not so gay.
Jazz is the perfect symbol of our mood, says one writer ;
our merriment is that of " one who plunges into revelry in
the endeavour to forget his mental misery." [2]

At the same time it must be remembered that the
noisiest elements are not often the best representatives of
the group to which they belong. A musical critic can write
that the twentieth century has come of age and it is going
to be a serious century. National crises in our own land have
revealed the unsuspected strength of the decent, industrious,
good-living people. The Christian Churches are quietly
carrying out vast historic achievements both in their
foreign mission fields and in their church-extension work at
home. Their social work is done quietly and without fuss,
for, like a happy marriage, it neither seeks, nor lends itself
to, publicity.

Of the temper of those who are outside denominational
Christianity we may take the analysis of one who has had
wide opportunities of gathering evidence, Dr. Albert
Mansbridge.[3] He underlines two factors which are sometimes forgotten. One is the unconscious and habitual
Christian ethic of many who profess no Christian allegiance.
" There is no court of appeal more readily admitted than
the teachings of Jesus." The other is the ineradicable
religiosity of man. " The bulk of people more or less out-

[1] *A Preface to Morals*, p. 8.

[2] W. M. Horton, *Theism and the Modern Mood* (Student Christian
Movement Press, 1931), p. 16.

[3] President of the World Association for Adult Education. See his
article, "The Demands of the Ordinary Man " (in the symposium, *Christianity and the Crisis* (Gollancz, 1933)).

side the Churches are where they are because of preoccupation with the affairs of this world, a preoccupation forced
upon some by poverty and others by riches." Yet he
observes that " at critical moments the majority of men
turn to religion for sanction or consolation." [1]

I prefer to call the second " religiosity " because, as
every Christian minister knows, the ordinances of the
Church are sometimes sought on unworthy grounds. The
wish that marriage may be celebrated in a church may be
prompted by considerations of social prestige ; the sacra-
ment of baptism and the last Christian rites may be desired
because of motives that are little more than superstitious.
But, when that caution has been made, we know that deep
down in the hearts of men there is something more stable.
In cases where Christian burial has been refused because
it was being looked upon as a magical ceremony, the result
has not infrequently been the awakening of a much nobler
sense. Along with the most irrational superstition there is
found at work a real longing, however dim or embryonic,
for the sound of a voice from above, some authentic word
of God. Where a man has been concentrating his attention,
in moments of pride, on the possibilities of his own human
endowment, or, in time of perplexity and agitation, on
his own desperate state, the first thing which the certainties
of religion will accomplish is probably the suggestion of
new and unsuspected needs, in comparison with which the
others are trivial and ephemeral.

It is not strange that such contradictions should be
found in the temper of an age, when they may exist in the
same individual. And it may be that the real characteristic
of our time, if it is possible to isolate one, is just this fluctua-
tion, this tendency to vacillate from one mood to another.

Perhaps the reason is to be found in the enormous mass
of specialised knowledge which is available ? Acquaintance
with its innumerable branches must for most men be vague
and patchy, yet that does not prevent us deducing from
it the most confident though erroneous conclusions. An
investigator has recently made a collection of the items of

[1] *Op. cit.* p. 46.

knowledge possessed by the average layman (wisely allowing the word "knowledge" to cover the most profound
depths of ignorance). This is part of his discovery : " People
are descended from ' monkeys ' ; the sun is made of radium ;
Mars is inhabited by a race of canal-diggers ; the ancient
Mayas knew all about relativity ; the earth is getting
hotter ; the earth is getting colder ; the earth will be
smashed up by running into a comet ; the average mental
age of Americans is thirteen ; all progress comes from a
superior Nordic race ; mankind is losing all its teeth and
hair ; the world is going to starve to death from over-
population ; the world is going to die off from race-suicide
. . . there is no soul ; everybody has two or three souls ;
according to Freud you must give rein to every impulse
or die of a complex ; all rheumatism comes from bad
teeth." [1]

It cannot be denied that to-day the omnivorous mind
is certain to suffer a considerable amount of mental indi-
gestion, but it is also quite clear that the real trouble lies
elsewhere. The alarming distraction is not without but
within. The familiar oscillation between an exalted view
of reason and pure irrationalism, between human pride
(titanism) and self-distrust, between scepticism and credulity, is a more disquieting symptom than the possession
of even a rich store of woolly and inaccurate knowledge ;
and it is the symptom of an incurable disease in the natural
man. " Science, philosophy, and culture," writes Emil
Brunner, " are man's creations. Hence man himself is the
problem of all problems and the greatest of all riddles. It
is a characteristic of the man of to-day that he is not aware
of this self-evident truth. He makes himself a part of his
own science, whereas science is really a part of his own real
self. Opposition to faith in revelation does not grow out
of science, philosophy, or culture, but out of false thinking
about science, philosophy, and culture." [2]

[1] E. E. Slosson in *The New Republic*, vol. xxxvii. p. 296, quoted by
M. C. Otto in *Things and Ideals*, p. 237.
[2] Brunner, *The Philosophy of Religion* (E.T.) (Nicholson & Watson,
1937), p. 183.

Religious people are well aware that the one thing needful is that the world should take revelation seriously. Nevertheless, there are those who are convinced that to admit revelation is the worst possible way of treating the prevalent sickness. We must briefly examine the alternative which they suggest. They agree that some really violent readjustment is necessary if the human spirit is not to be threatened with final extinction. But revelation is not for them. Instead, they see a vision of natural man becoming still more natural. Already they notice adumbrations of the ideal type. " Among those of keener intellect there are scientists to whom the test-tube and its contents are all-sufficient, and among those of coarser grain, captains of finance and builders of mills, there are those to whom the acquirement of wealth and power seems to constitute a life in which no lack can be perceived. Doubtless they are not new types ; doubtless they have always existed ; but may they not be the strain from which Nature will select the coming race ? Is not their creed the creed of Nature, and are they not bound to triumph over those whose illusions are no longer potent because they are no longer really believed ? " [1]

The author believes that Nature may very well choose for survival the natural man, who has shed all transcendental longings. Yet, strange as it may seem, Nature, we believe, has shown in the past no sign of doing any such thing. She has gone on insisting that men shall be born with all their transcendental longings incorrigibly active.

Shelley, in his preface to *Alastor*, indicates the profound dissatisfaction with which the youth of the poem turns from the contemplation of the universe. The wonder and beauty of the external world at first bring him tranquillity and joyousness. But the time comes when these fail. His mind is suddenly awakened. He thirsts for intercourse " with an intelligence similar to himself."

It begins to appear that the last word in this matter does not lie after all with Nature. In a sense, Mr. Krutch is conscious of this. Many of the lost illusions, he admits,

[1] J. W. Krutch, *The Modern Temper* (Jonathan Cape, 1930), p. 21.

had survival value. Individuals and societies whose aim is clear, and whose outlook is hopeful, live their lives with an energy that is unknown to the sceptic and the pessimist. This he grants, and this, he thinks, is all.

It is not all. Let it be admitted that spiritual hopes contribute to survival. But these must not be hopes that are for ever deferred. If we are to take this analogy from the field of evolution, we must be faithful to its terms. The equipment of living organisms has survival value only in so far as it corresponds to the facts of the world in which survival is to be achieved. Let that equipment consist largely of illusions concerning the laws of the physical world and the organism will not be long in dying out. If man's transcendent longings have no relation to the ultimate nature of reality, they have no survival value, but the reverse. Had they found nothing to satisfy them, they must long ago have perished. Nor can it be said in reply that they have brought their own satisfaction. For, if there is illusion here, and self-deception is in no way injurious to the evolving life, there is no possibility of finding truth anywhere. If the activity of the mind can thus deceive at its highest and clearest and most satisfying, then indeed there is no human thought to be trusted. Mr. Krutch is right in speaking of " The Disillusion with the Laboratory " and intelligible when he refers to " The Phantom of Certitude," but the conclusion of his book is quite unwarranted. He prefers that we should die as men rather than live as animals. "Our human world," he writes (p. 249), "may have no existence outside of our own desires, but those are more imperious than anything else we know, and we will cling to our own lost cause, choosing always rather to know than to be." *To know* is precisely that which is impossible for him, if there is no guarantee that it is truth and not illusion which will prevail. We are to go down, if that is our end, consciously deceiving ourselves to the last, and defiant in our self-deceit. It may seem the only possible way on the presuppositions, but somehow it does not look very noble. We are to say, " Psychology has taught me that my desire sometimes influences my belief ;

therefore nothing can be true that I would wish to be true."

Admittedly it does not follow that, because a thing is desirable, it is therefore true.[1] But neither does it follow that the desirable thing is untrue. Still less is it good reasoning to argue that a belief is necessarily well founded *because* it is depressing or repellent.

This type of argument is always two-edged. It may work the other way, and our real safety may lie in asking whether our disbelief is not in fact caused by some unwillingness to decide for the truth because the truth is unpalatable.

> " For, though I knew His love Who followèd,
>   Yet was I sore adread
>   Lest, having Him, I must have naught beside."

Mr. Krutch thinks that man has been spared the worst shock of disillusionment because it has not come all at once. " Illusions have been lost one by one. God, instead of disappearing in an instant, has retreated step by step and surrendered gradually his control of the universe. Once he decreed the fall of every sparrow and counted the hairs upon every head ; a little later he became merely the original source of the laws of nature, and even to-day there are thousands who, unable to bear the thought of losing him completely, still fancy that they can distinguish the uncertain outlines of a misty figure. But the rôle which he plays grows less and less, and man is left more and more alone in a universe to which he is completely alien." [2]

The mistake which vitiates this reasoning is that of supposing that faith consists in making an intellectual survey of the universe or a philosophical analysis of man, when it is really a question of taking sides, of making a personal decision. A God of love, Who claims men for His

---

[1] And no religious man ever bases his faith on his own desires. It is true, perhaps, that the irreligious man may do so, believing that there is no God because he would prefer that it should be so.

[2] *Op. cit.* pp. 9–10.

own, Whose redeeming love I am called upon freely to accept, does not by any means play a smaller rôle than the divine figure which is here portrayed.

There are other reasons besides the one suggested for the fading of the thought of God. Ruskin, for example, describes his experience.[1] He had a continual perception of sanctity in the whole of nature, from the slightest thing to the vastest. He could not explain it to others, any more than he could describe the sense of bodily hunger to a person who had never felt it. Indeed, it seemed to him like a sort of heart-hunger, satisfied with the presence of a Great and Holy Spirit. " These feelings," he writes, " remained in their full intensity till I was eighteen or twenty, and then, as the reflective and practical power increased, and the ' cares of this world ' gained upon me, faded gradually away, in the manner described by Words-worth in his ' Intimations of Immortality.' "

As we well know, the " cares of this world " are a very small part of the influences at work leading to the obscura-tion of the thought of God. The case of Darwin is frequently quoted. Having given many years of his life to the collec-tion of scientific facts as data for his investigations, he found, on turning back to his early interests in other fields, that his love for music and literature had died. He knew then that he ought to have devoted some part of every day to poetry and music, so that his taste for them might be preserved. It is not very different with the practice of the presence of God. I have spoken with a scientist who declared that belief in God was absurd, but who admitted that for fourteen years he had not attended church and for ten years had not read the Bible. Had I accused him of speaking dogmatically in his own sphere after studying the evidence for only one side, he would have been justly indignant. In his own sphere he was open-minded, cautious, and impartial. Nevertheless, in the matter of religion, he had deliberately shut himself off from those sources where he might reasonably expect to hear the evidence for the other side, yet he believed himself here also to be an unbiased

[1] *Modern Painters*, Popular Edition, vol. iii. p. 309.

observer. To quote again the experience of Francis Thompson :

> " The angels keep their ancient places ;—
> Turn but a stone, and start a wing !
> 'Tis ye, 'tis your estrangèd faces
> That miss the many-splendoured thing."

Most important of all, the light may grow dim, the vision perish, and disbelief triumph, because of man's sinfulness. It is commonly supposed that the modern world finds this conception somewhat unreal. However we are to account for it, says Dr. J. S. Whale,[1] " a louder and more articulate expression is being given in our day to the unanalysed notion (it is no more !) that a lot of un-necessary fuss can be made about the mystery of iniquity ; that to bother much about one's sins is morbid, while to bother at all about the sins of others is impertinent."

In a modern (or would-be-modern) play, one of the characters says lightly, " That is what we used to call sin." I believe that flippancy is the vice of an evil old age, in persons or in nations. The child is never flippant. But I believe that we are right in assuming that such flippancy is not at all characteristic of our age. Personal sense of sin may frequently be obscured, but the social sense is present as perhaps never before. Wherever there is poverty and wretchedness and vice in the land, good men and women feel, as never before, a certain shame at the facts, and a real responsibility for the removal of them.

It seems that there may be two reasons for regarding " sin " as a word that is unreal and irrelevant. They are deduced from the further fact that sin is known in its real nature only by contrast with the fellowship of blessedness in which man is at one with God. The word may be considered out of date, and we may speak of " what we used to call sin," if, in the first place, the fellowship between God and man is perfect and complete ; if all men are good and all men are blessed. No one, presumably, would claim to-day that we have reached that stage. In the second place, then, the word may be discarded if fellowship

---

[1] In *The Christian Faith* (Eyre & Spottiswoode, 1936), p. 186.

between God and man is ignored and its possibility forgotten. And, where the word has actually been abandoned, this is usually the reason. Man is regarded as in no way essentially different from the beasts that perish.

A correct estimate of man sees in him an extraordinary dignity conjoined with an extraordinary distress. He can rise to such heights as to justify our belief that he is made in the image of God ; and he can descend far lower than the brute creation. The angel has him by the hand and the serpent by the heart.

Once again, however, this whole line of approach may be challenged from one or other of two standpoints. (1) It is affirmed that man has it in his own power to put himself right ; and therefore brooding on his own sinfulness is nothing but a stultification of his ability to redeem himself. The old protest against man's need of divine salvation has recently become articulate again in a new form. Karl Heim [1] quotes some typical utterances (by Ernst Bergmann and others) from the side of German racial faith : " Original sin and the depravity of guilt are delusions of the synagogue." " The Indo-Germanic peoples had no acquaintance with the idea of sin at all." " The classical expression of German-Nordic ethics is the ethic of moral imperatives, propounded by Kant and Fichte— an ethical optimism . . . namely, a faith in the goodness, nobility, strength, and heroism in men." We need no help from outside, it is argued, to cleanse us of stains ; for we carry the divine within us.

It is true that sin may appear at first to the untutored and undeveloped conscience as simply an incident. It is of one evil act that a man at first accuses himself ; he regards it as a stain, a blot, an exceptional phenomenon, to be dealt with by himself. But he soon finds that it is an incident which cannot be altered and one which has unlimited consequences. The river cannot revoke its waters and run upward to the holy hills. The first step includes all sequent steps. In a primitive stage of develop-

[1] *The Church of Christ and the Problems of the Day* (Nisbet, 1936), p. 76.

ment, just as in childhood, men repent of what they have done ; but at a more mature stage they repent of what they *are*.[1] Sin has passed from incident into state. It has destroyed character. And that which man can so easily destroy, he cannot by any human means restore. The power is not even immanent in us as an endowment given by God. Heim writes in this connection : [2] " I do not bear God within myself as the kernel of my inmost being in such a way as to be able to restore the disturbed relationship to Him, of myself. God is rather wholly and entirely outside of and beyond me. The relation existing between God and me is not under my control ; I cannot alter it from my side, because I do not have God in my power."

It has been said that the higher man of to-day is not vexed by the problem of his sins. But, unhappily, hard facts persist, along with their bitter consequences, regardless of the amount of interest that men take in them. There was once a large group of the higher men, who were not troubling about their sins. They are well known in history. They crucified Jesus.

(2) From another angle, objection is taken to our whole treatment of this subject by those who regard a sense of sin as a hindrance in the search for truth. A righteous God, they say, and the necessity of redemption for man are only spectres of a diseased imagination.

This is the familiar plan adopted by those who wish to throw discredit on an inconvenient principle, but it is too superficial to carry any weight. There may be pathological cases where the sense of sin has ceased to be religious and has become a mental abnormality, but that is no more a sufficient reason for denying penitence its rightful place than the absurdities of some ascetics would be a reason for denouncing self-control and sobriety. " Against the charge of morbidity it should be enough to reply that, if you allow yourself to dismiss any *universal* characteristic of life as ' morbid,' you lose the very basis for an intelligible distinction between health and disease. If we cannot take

---

[1] Cf. Denney, *Studies in Theology*, Lecture IV.
[2] *Op. cit.* p. 80.

quod semper, quod ubique, quod ab omnibus as the standard of health and normality, what is to be our criterion of the normal and the morbid ? If all men without exception are mad, how are we to draw the distinction between the sane man and insane ? " [1]

Nor is it any more difficult to turn the argument against those who put it forward. We find that it is by the way of self-abnegation and precisely *not* by that of self-glorification that spiritual truth is discerned. Just as in the search for intellectual knowledge a primary condition is the rigid exclusion of presuppositions and prejudice, however dear, so the quest of spiritual truth demands the renunciation of sensuality, of pride, and of self-will.

The first of these requirements is obvious, and it includes not only the grosser sins but even more clearly the sinful attitudes and hidden indulgences of the mind.[2]   Only the pure in heart shall see God.

The second requirement is summed up also in the words of Jesus. " Except ye be converted and become as little children ye shall not enter into the kingdom of heaven." [3] " I thank Thee, O Father, Lord of heaven and earth, because Thou hast hid these things from the wise and prudent, and hast revealed them unto babes." [4]   Men

---

[1] A. E. Taylor, *The Faith of a Moralist* (Macmillan, 1932), vol. i. p. 176.

[2] Professor H. H. Farmer puts the matter cogently in dealing with sin as *insincerity* (*The World and God* (Nisbet, 1935), pp. 190–195). " That sin is thus at its heart and centre insincerity most sensitive natures have felt. It is going against the light, such light as one has, not in the sense of snuffing it out as a man might a candle-flame between his fingers, for that no one can do, but in the sense of screening it under a veil of excuse and subterfuge. It is ' holding down the truth in unrighteousness.' " The result of " tampering with the truth " is that the personality " grows less and less capable of discerning what the will of God is, or even that there is a will of God at all. . . . Insincerity swiftly becomes a habit, continually creating fresh opportunity and occasion for its exercise ; until it ends by being almost a necessity, for the longer this way is persisted in, the more the monitions of God—if indeed they can break through the increasing dimness and insensitivity of the soul—lose their quality of being an invitation to blessedness and become instead a condemnation threatening the whole structure of the life in a way too disturbing to be faced."

[3] Matt. xviii. 3.   [4] Matt. xi. 25.

must put off all confidence in their own wisdom and wait on God in a purely receptive spirit.[1] It is hard for them that trust in intellectual riches to enter into the kingdom of God.

The third requirement is the most important. Spiritual knowledge comes by the way of obedience, the renunciation of self-will. It demands the recognition that there may be something in the universe more important than I ; that there may be a superior will in submission to which alone I can arrive at the truth. " If any man shall do His will he shall know of the doctrine." First must come the acknowledgment that there *is* His will, very often antagonistic to our own. Many to-day would deny this. The highest I can get out of life, they would say, is to be had by " self-expression." But, if we are frank with ourselves, we cannot imagine the world being very much better for the expression of our self. When St. Paul tried this way he discovered that the self which he succeeded in expressing was usually the worse one. " The good that I would, I do not : but the evil which I would not, that I do." But what concerns us more nearly at the moment is the tendency of self-will to seek safety first. The desire for some form of security may be more important to it than the desire for the truth. The sense of security may be purchased at too great a price if it means the death of the adventurous spirit and the impossibility of progress towards a larger truth.

" ' Wait ! ' said Bagheera, and flung himself forward with one superb bound as far as ever he could. The first thing to do when a trail ceases to explain itself is to cast forward without leaving your own confusing footmarks on the ground." [2]

It is a common enough thing for the signs of grace to be obliterated, before even they are perceived, by the heavy blunderings of self. If it is said that the cultivation of the self offers at least something that is certain and tangible, a sphere circumscribed, it may be, but definite

---

[1] See further, E. F. Scott, *The New Testament Idea of Revelation* (Nicholson & Watson, 1936), chap. vii.

[2] Rudyard Kipling, " The King's Ankus " in *The Second Jungle Book*.

and manageable, it may be sufficient to reply that the
achievement will be limited by the aim. It is not likely on
the face of it that the wealth of the universe is so meagre
that it can be caught within the confines of a prosaic and
timorous self-complacency. It is only by venturing that
knowledge is to be gained.

A man is carrying a lantern. The light in it is dim.
When he stands still, there is just sufficient to see the
ground. He is safe, certainly, so long as he remains
stationary. But, if he will venture to go forward, the
draught of air is enough to make the wick burn up brightly.
The man who stands waiting for proof before he ventures
will never have the light. The light to walk by comes as
he advances. The nature of God is revealed only to those
who trust and act on their trust.

When the colony of Pennsylvania was founded, William
Penn's " Frame of Government " visualised a country ruled
by love instead of by force. It was to have the mildest of
penal laws and the least rigorous forms of prison discipline
conceived up to that time. Treason and murder alone were
subject to the death-penalty. Writing of the grant of
territory, Penn said : " I eyed the Lord in obtaining it.
. . . There may be room there, though not here, for such
an holy experiment." [1] There was adventure and there
was risk in the design. But the Quaker principles prevailed.
Faith is " an holy experiment," for spiritual truth can be
achieved only by the devotion of the whole personality to
the leading of God, and that on His bare promise that this
is the way by which light will come.

[1] Letter to James Harrison ; see Janney, *Life of Penn*, p. 175.

CHAPTER II

REVELATION OR DISCOVERY?

SUMMARY

It is probably true that the chief concern of the average decent but non-believing man of to-day is personal self-realisation. Where faith is lacking, there rises the unavoidable doubt whether pure altruism has any legitimate place in human life. The doctrine of self-realisation may lead in either of two directions : (1) To naturalistic ethics, which is the equivalent of no ethics at all. It is said that our chief duty is to ensure that self-realisation is nowhere endangered by the sense of duty. But this type of anthropology is already out of date. It cannot account for the difference between the convenient and the obligatory, and it cannot provide a sufficient reason for the survival of ethical ideals. (2) Man discovers the need of some loyalty other than that demanded by self. He may find it in some form of the totalitarian state. Others find the highest object of their admiration in the spirit of man. The achievements of human discovery suggest to them that there is no need to believe in that which is superhuman or supernatural. The real lesson to be learnt from the present position in science is that of the inadequacy of the observational and experimental method to interpret ultimate reality. The attitude described as "disillusion with the laboratory" grows out of the discovery that science deals with abstractions and generalities, and that reality, which may be the individual, may therefore escape through its net.

In Psychology, there are two movements which are supposed to be specially inimical to theism. (1) *Behaviourism.* Just when materialism has vanished from its place among plausible theories, it appears that mechanism breaks out once more—in the soul of man and in human conduct. Mental states are studied as physiological changes, and the behaviourist may end by denying the existence of mental states and reducing all behaviour to "conditioned reflexes." Philosophically, the theory is, if not absurd, at least absurdly vulnerable. On its own principles, it is the outcome of conditioned reflexes and nothing more. It cannot claim to be a statement of truth, nor, if there is no consciousness and no reason, can it appeal to these for acceptance. Furthermore, even if it is true that the self is in large measure determined through *being acted upon* by the environment, the question must still be raised, What is the environment which acts upon it ? The answer of the religious man is in the doctrine of creation. The self has only secondary reality. It was created and is preserved in being from moment to moment by the divine activity. (2) *The Psychology of the Unconscious.* Believing that religion is the outcome of neurosis, wish-fulfilment, or illusion, these theories have failed to account for its survival. Fantasy and imagination can be of value in the process of survival only if they successfully anticipate experience. If they fail to do this, they will speedily be shattered on the hard facts of reality. And it is not solely with the fact of the experience that we have to deal, but also with the nature of it. We find that what all men have in some degree the best have in the highest degree. It is the saints who have the first claim to be heard on this matter. And the unanimous testimony of the saints is that the experience is a valid one. It is here, they say, with one voice, that we have the truth about the universe.

CHAPTER II

REVELATION OR DISCOVERY?

IT is probably true that the chief concern of the average decent but non-believing man of to-day is personal self-realisation. The motto "Service not Self" has failed to satisfy him, and it must inevitably fail where there is not the religious urge to sacrifice self for the sake of a divine kingdom. Where faith is lacking, there rises the unavoidable doubt whether pure altruism after all has any legitimate place in human life. If it has no sanction in the nature of the universe, it must have it in the nature of man. But it is then discovered that a command which is laid by the self on the self cannot be absolute and unconditional. That which the self has imposed the self may abrogate. Service is found to be obligatory only because, and only in so far as, it is a form of self-realisation.

Then it is speedily recognised that the matter cannot rest there. Problems are at once suggested. Which is the *true* self? What is to be its relation to others—in the family, the industrial group, the state, the world? The doctrine of self-realisation may lead in either of two directions:

1. To naturalistic ethics, which is the equivalent of no ethics at all. It is said that nature is all; morality is nothing; our chief duty is to ensure that self-realisation is nowhere endangered by duty. "In pursuing its own interests," it is declared,[1] "every organism constantly finds itself in the presence of other organisms whose interests and welfare cannot but conflict with its own; whence results a struggle wherein the inferior organism must

[1] Mr. Antonio Llano in an essay, "Morality the Last of the Dogmas," *Philosophical Review*, vol. v. pp. 377, 379; quoted by M. C. Otto, *Things and Ideals*, p. 98.

succumb and the superior organism survive and propagate.
Whether this condition of affairs be repulsive or shocking,
and whether it ' ought ' to be different from what it is, are
questions no longer to be asked, once we have discarded
the old idea of an arbitrary will governing the phenomena
of nature. . . . If I consult or scrutinise my conscience,
I find that it is a sort of ghost whose authority is derived
from the servility and slavery of my ancestors and whose
' imperative dictates ' are the echoes of a state of oppression
and superstition against which my present feelings of
freedom protest and revolt. I recognise no claims of others
on me, no conscience, no obligation. I am my own master."
This type of anthropology is already out of date, and need
not delay us. "An authoritative ghost" is not an adequate
description of conscience. It cannot account for the
difference between the convenient and the obligatory.
And it cannot provide a sufficient reason for the survival
of ethical ideals. " It is an old topic of ethical argument,"
says the Dean of St. Paul's, " that the appearance of virtue,
on a naturalistic view, is more useful than the reality ;
and a purely biological account of evolution would appear
to throw more light on the persistence of hypocrisy than
on the advance of ethical ideals." [1] Adaptation to environment cannot be invoked for the survival of moral impulse
unless the environment is believed to be congruous with
the ethical beliefs of man ; unless, that is, the purpose
which man seems to discern in his moral ideals is in fact a
part of objective reality. Survival of moral impulses can
be accounted for only if God is the ultimate environment.

We may pass to the other side on which the doctrine
of self-realisation may develop.

2. Man discovers the need of some loyalty other than
that demanded by self. (*a*) He may find it in some form
of the totalitarian state. We notice the almost religious
quality in the devotion of the Communist to his society.
The Communist morality, says Nicolas Berdyaev (who knew
it from personal experience), " demands of man great

[1] W. R. Matthews, *Studies in Christian Philosophy* (Macmillan, 1928),
2nd ed. p. 127.

sacrifices, but it offers an almost mystic joy of submergence
in the collective life. . . . Not man is deified, but the
collective in which the individual is dissolved." [1] In
Germany we have seen a mystical enthusiasm gather
round the idea of the holy race. Ernst Bergmann writes
(in *The German National Church*) : " No one comes to our
aid save the divine that is in us, namely, ourselves and our
sacred will." [2]

(b) Vast multitudes of people cannot be satisfied by the
claims of the nation to be the supreme object of loyalty.
Yet they are not content with the aim of self-realisation.
They are profoundly aware of a sense of impotence and
self-distrust. They compare the self as it is with the self
as it might be and ought to be ; and, if this is not yet a
" sense of sin," it is at least the realisation that they must
find something other than self in which to trust. Dr. W. M.
Horton diagnoses the situation as it exists in America,
particularly among students of the universities. " This *is*
an age of scepticism, cynicism, and disillusionment ; but
it is also, and simultaneously, an age that is wistfully in
quest of religious sustenance and religious certitude, and
almost pathetically credulous when given half a chance.
. . . It is precisely the most sceptical students who are

[1] Essay on " Communist Secularism " (in *Christianity and the Crisis*).
" Communism as a Religion " is the title of the first chapter in Dr. H. G.
Wood's *The Truth and Error of Communism* (Student Christian Movement Press, 1933). Dr. Hans Lilje speaks of " the immense religious
passion which is behind this theoretical façade, explaining itself in the
overwhelming demand for self-sacrifice, self-forgetful enthusiasm, and
fanatical belief " (*The Christian Faith To-day* (Student Christian Movement Press, 1933), p. 48).

[2] See Alfred Rosenberg, *Der Mythus des 20 Jahrhunderts*, 3 Aufl. 1932,
p. 129. Bergmann, *Die deutsche Nationalkirche*, 1933, p. 15 ; cf. p. 368.
Professor Anders Nygren writes (in *The Church Controversy in Germany*)
(Student Christian Movement Press, 1934) : " A new religion has appeared
on the stage by the side of, and in opposition to, Christianity—a religion
founded on blood and soil, or race-idealism—or should one not rather
say race-materialism ? . . . It cannot be denied that to great multitudes
the deification of their own race is taking the place of religion. . . . The
God who is *really* worshipped is the idol of the nation " (pp. 86–89).
Cf. also Karl Heim, *Glaube und Denken*, 3 Aufl. 1934 ; English Translation, *God Transcendent* (Nisbet, 1936), pp. 7 ff.

the most apt to yield to a sudden attack of credulity, for the simple reason that it is they who feel the lack of religious certitude most painfully. The attitude of complete incredulity is in fact inconsistent with the quest of self-realisation. To demand everything of life without trusting life, to seek a full, rich, colourful existence without yielding to any enthusiasm, is a psychological impossibility. . . . The quest of self-realisation is simply a modern equivalent for the evangelical quest of personal salvation." [1]

There is therefore a real truth expressed by present-day dissatisfaction with " service " as the watchword of good men and women. Even where it is a case of the social sense of sin taking the place of a sense of personal unworthiness, it may very well be that we are sheltering ourselves behind the defences of " social service," and assuming that *we* are able to set things right in the world ; that all we need is the better distribution of wealth, or better houses, or lighter conditions in industry ; that education and social amelioration can take the place of personal salvation : whereas what men most need may not be what they desire, or even what the best men desire for them. The discovery and satisfaction of our own needs is not enough. We require revelation to show what ought to be desired. When Mr. J. W. Krutch proceeds to show that human values are equally involved in the dismissal of divine objective values ; that man " is never strong enough in his own insignificant self to stand alone in a universe which snubs him with its indifference " ; that " living is merely a physiological process with only a physiological meaning, and that it is most satisfactorily conducted by creatures who never feel the need to attempt to give it any other," [2] he does not in fact arrive at the right conclusion, yet he makes it abundantly clear that man's lack of apprehension of spiritual reality is not due to any temporary limitation but to radical unfitness to achieve unaided any such knowledge.

The apprehension of spiritual truth is made possible

---

[1] *Theism and the Modern Mood*, pp. 18–20.
[2] *The Modern Temper*, pp. 136 and 235.

only by revelation : human discovery can never arrive at
it. Discovery can do no more than convince itself of its
own impotence in this sphere. It follows therefore that the
agnosticism of the scientist may be the right attitude for
the scientist as such. " It is the admission that beyond
the material things which can be measured and explained
there is another sphere of reality. When knowledge has
been pushed to its limit we find ourselves confronted with
a closed door. The agnostic perceives the barrier, and
holds that it can never be penetrated ; and this attitude,
if the fact of revelation be denied, is the only one now
possible to reverent and thoughtful men." [1]

Thus Dr. Julian Huxley is quite wrong when he writes
a book with the title, *Religion without Revelation.* He
desires to have that which cannot be secured and does not
follow from the premises with which he begins. He takes
his stand on the theological principles of Rudolf Otto
(apparently quite unaware that they have ever been
criticised), and proceeds to argue that the attribution of
personality to God implies thinking which is anthropomorphic and therefore bad. Now it may readily be admitted
that a great deal of anthropomorphic imagery is misleading.[2]
But it is equally necessary to insist that *all* our thinking is
anthropomorphic—simply because we are men. Dr. Huxley
(p. 18) declares that the concept of a personal God is anthropomorphic, whereas the idea of sacredness is not so. The
truth is that the latter is a notion derived from a primitive
stage of human thought, and the former one which is
developed at a more mature level ; and when we come to
consider the essence of religion we shall be nearer the truth

---

[1] E. F. Scott, *The New Testament Idea of Revelation*, p. 4.

[2] Indeed, no better example of it could be found than that on page 40
of Dr. Huxley's book: We are to " see God, under one aspect as a number
of vital but separate facts, some material and some spiritual, but, regarded
as a unity, as a creation of the human soul (albeit a necessary and fruitful
one), compounded of the hard facts of soulless nature and the spiritual
and intellectual aspirations of the nature of man, the two organised into
a single whole by the organising power of the human mind." I do not
think that there is very much meaning in that passage, but, so far as
there is any, it is drenched in anthropomorphism of the worst type.

if we examine its best manifestations than if we are guided solely by its origins and its primitive forms. But of course the choice does not lie between thinking which is anthropomorphic and thinking which is not, but between good thinking and bad thinking. It is meaningless to say that we choose to *worship* the impersonal, the unknown, the unknowable. The conclusion at which Dr. Huxley, on his premises, ought to arrive is that, if there is such a thing as religion, science is not capable of reaching it by its own methods. Science can deal with the impersonal; and the scientist with a metaphysical bent may also surmise that there is a reality (possibly the ultimate or even the sole reality) lying behind the impersonal with which he deals; but the one thing which science clearly cannot do is to *know* that the unknown impersonal is an object suitable for worship. There is not such a thing as " Religion without Revelation." " All religion is by its very nature revealed; this is what makes it religion, as contrasted with ordinary knowledge. . . . The animals never arrive at religion; neither do the philosophers and men of science. The facts of religion lie apart from the natural order, and can only be known through revelation." [1]

Nevertheless it may fairly be asked whether the successes of human discovery do not indicate already that there is no need to seek for more. At one time it was felt that such an indication was given by the comprehensive achievements of science; more lately a similar claim has been made for psychology. If all the facts of which we have cognisance can be adequately explained in natural terms, it may be unnecessary and misleading to seek knowledge of the supernatural.

In some ways it might appear that science is to-day throwing the door wide open to the entrance of idealist theories. But it may be questioned whether that is a proper account of the situation. It is true that materialism is dead. Even in an age when the vastness of the material universe has been brought home to men as never before, when it is realised that, in the poet's phrase, this world,

[1] E. F. Scott, *The New Testament Idea of Revelation*, p. 2.

seen from the walls of heaven, must be no more than a fretful midge, theories of materialism will not suffice. We refuse to be intimidated by size, acknowledging that there is a realm in which size is irrelevant.

We realise also that materialism cannot take account of consciousness. (Materialism, Kant said, is shattered on the humblest earthworm.) It may say that conscious-ness is nothing but a passive shadow which accompanies material processes, but then the awkward conclusion is that science itself and the theory of materialism are illusions. "A piece of nature could never form the conception of nature, could never interpret and use nature." If there were nothing but matter, there would be no materialism ; if there were nothing in man but what the chemist and the biologist can discover, there would be no chemistry and biology. The fact that there *is* more than they can dis-cover leaves the field open to the metaphysician and the theologian.[1]

We recognise, moreover, that the conception of matter has itself been fallacious. There is no such thing as an irreducible brute material spread throughout space in a flux of configurations. " It is an assumption," says Professor Whitehead, " which I shall challenge as being entirely unsuited to the scientific situation at which we have now arrived. It is not wrong, if properly construed. If we confine ourselves to certain types of fact, abstracted from the complete circumstances in which they occur, the materialistic assumption expresses these facts to perfection. But when we pass beyond the abstraction, either by more subtle employment of our senses, or by the request for meanings and for coherence of thought, the scheme breaks down at once." [2]

But the importance of this conclusion is somewhat reduced when we discover that there is grave doubt as to what should take the place of matter. It is well to have it said that there is no point in being a materialist when no one knows what matter is. But this ignorance itself raises

[1] See Denney, *Studies in Theology*, p. 77.
[2] *Science and the Modern World*, p. 22.

serious problems. Matter is certainly not what it once was thought to be. "We have suffered," says Sir Arthur Eddington,[1] "and we still suffer, from expectations that electrons and quanta must be in some fundamental respects like materials or forces familiar in the workshop—that all we have got to do is to imagine the usual kind of thing on an infinitely smaller scale. It must be our aim to avoid such prejudgments, which are surely illogical; and since we must cease to employ familiar concepts, symbols have become the only possible alternative." But, when we ask what lies behind the symbols, we are met with the disconcerting reply that physics has no means of probing beneath the symbolism.[2]

The disappearance of matter, or its dissolution into mystery, is not, after all, a very helpful move in the direction of a spiritual conception of the universe, if it implies that, so far as science can tell, nothing is left except symbols of an algebraic unknown.

The same may be said of the breakdown of the mechanical interpretation of the universe. Just as the gain suggested by the dissolution of matter is offset by the discovery that we are left apparently with symbols symbolising an unknown, so the announcement that indeterminacy within the atom seems to leave the door open for the entrance of transcendent causality cannot be received with undiluted satisfaction if this means the acceptance of a principle of uncertainty and a universe dominated not by law but by chance, contingency, crass casualty.

The real lesson to be learned from the present position in science is that of the inadequacy of the observational and experimental method to interpret ultimate reality; of " disillusion with the laboratory "; the lesson that science deals with abstractions and generalities, and that reality may escape through its net.

It is, however, in psychology rather than in science that many people see the real attack on the supernatural and on the idea of revelation. There are two movements in

[1] *The Nature of the Physical World*, chap. xii.
[2] Cf. Eddington, *Science and the Unseen World*, p. 20.

particular which appear inimical to theism, Behaviourism
and the Psychology of the Unconscious.[1]

1. *Behaviourism.*—When materialism is quickly vanish-
ing from its place among plausible theories, it appears
that mechanism breaks in once more, not this time in
the account given of the material world, but in the characterisation of the human soul or of human conduct. It
has disappeared from physics—because the "machine"
appears to be without ultimate parts ! It has disappeared
from biology, because the "machine" is found to adjust
itself in a way that makes the use of the name absurd.[2]
An organism which is "self-stoking, self-repairing, self-
preserving, self-adjusting, self-increasing, self-producing"[3]
is not appropriately described as a mechanism.

Now the mechanistic theory rears its head again.
Psychology, for the Behaviourist school, is to be regarded
as an exact science, purely objective and experimental.
The time has come, it says, to discard all reference to
consciousness, and to deal simply with stimulus and
response. Introspection is looked upon as an illegitimate
method of study. Mental states are to be studied as physiological changes in the brain and nervous system, and the
behaviourist not unnaturally ends by denying the existence
of mental states and reducing all behaviour to "conditioned
reflexes."

Philosophically, the theory is, if not wholly absurd,
at least absurdly vulnerable. On its own principles, it is
the outcome of conditioned reflexes and nothing more. It
cannot claim to be a statement of truth. If there is neither
consciousness nor reason, it cannot appeal to these for
acceptance. Its importance lies therefore not so much in

[1] The latter is sometimes known as psycho-analysis, but this term,
when used of a *method*, should be confined to the Freudian school alone
(cf. William Brown, *Mind and Personality*, p. 9; and David Yellowlees,
Psychology's Defence of the Faith, p. 57), and it is perhaps better therefore
to avoid also the use of it as a name for a psychological theory.

[2] See especially Hans Driesch, *The Science and Philosophy of the
Organism.*

[3] J. A. Thomson in Hastings' *Encyclopædia of Religion and Ethics,*
vol. viii. p. 7 b.

its attitude to revelation as in its attack on reason. But for our purposes it may be worth noticing that there is some truth in its discarding of the method of introspection. The spectator-attitude can never see the self as it is, since every attempt to look at the object in this case inevitably *changes* the object. The mistake of the behaviourist lies in his conclusion—that there is *no* conscious self. The right inference is that another method is needed to achieve awareness of the true self. When Professor J. B. Watson writes,[1] " I have never replied to a criticism," we may surmise that one of the reasons is that much of the criticism is unanswerable.

In order to establish itself as an exact science, this school of psychology has been forced to minimise the importance of reason. Behaviourism regards conduct as the result of " conditioned reflexes," fully explicable without any regard of the mind or of reason. But it is in fact quite incredible that consciousness should have survived if, as the behaviourist maintains, it has never exercised any function, and has been only a kind of shadowy accompaniment of the processes of conduct, running parallel to these but exerting no influence upon them.

It is not surprising that Professor Watson roundly declares that the behaviourist finds no evidence for mental existences or mental processes of any kind. But there is, in fact, quite a valid reason why psychology is unable to take account of the mind. The mind is not something which can be observed, examined, weighed, and measured like the accomplished facts and states of the world. If the mind is to be known at all, there must be another way of knowing it than the scientific way, the way which is characteristic of the spectator-attitude. " The Behaviourist position is the only possible one, so long as it is assumed that no knowledge is valid unless it is reached by the methods of pure science." [2] It is the *reductio ad absurdum* of the claim that the spectator-attitude is the sole legitimate one.

[1] *Behaviourism* (Norton, New York, 1930), p. x.
[2] B. H. Streeter, *Reality*, p. 106.

The *existence* of the self is known in thinking and in acting. (It cannot be argued away, since in the very process its existence is established.) And the *value* of the self is also known in thinking and in acting. We shall see later that the very desire to know, the disinterested " search " for truth is the sign of a challenge from Beyond. And in the sphere of action it is rightly affirmed that the self is most truly a self when it is surrendered to the will of the Beyond.[1]

Even if it is true that the self is in large measure determined through *being acted upon* by the environment, the question must still be raised, What is the environment which acts upon it? Is there an environment which is above and beyond the natural world? The answer of the religious man is in the doctrine of creation. The self has only secondary reality. It was created, and is preserved in being from moment to moment, by the divine activity. Knowledge of self is not acquired but given. It is never complete because there are barriers of will, as well as of finitude, between us and God. Professor Karl Heim, summing up his epistemological conclusions in *God Transcendent* (p. 213) writes that " We are estranged from Him in Whom nevertheless ' we live and move and have our being.' For this reason the form in which our perceiving, our concept-making, our cognising goes on inevitably hides

[1] The sovereignty of God is not incompatible with man's freedom. God has to deliver men (1) from temptations, which destroy freedom ; (2) from the wrong emphasis on self, which equally destroys freedom. But the deliverance takes place without impinging on man's moral responsibility. The freedom which we are concerned to assert, in the interests of religion and morality, is not the terribly imperfect thing which we see in man. If freedom such as ours were regarded as the highest or perfect type of freedom, then the scientist might despair of life in such a " chancy " universe (cf. Leonard Hodgson, *Essays in Christian Philosophy* (Longmans, 1930), p. 43). Behind all is the freedom of God, the rational ground of the " dependableness " of the natural order and of our hope that one day we shall attain to the liberty of the sons of God (*ibid.*). There are two obligations laid on man : (1) Thou shalt do right ; (2) Thou shalt be free. The ideal is, Thou shalt freely do the right. In actuality, it may sometimes be more important that man shall do the right thing than that he shall practise freedom. Man's will may be overruled by divine grace.

from us our own true nature. I cannot know myself as I really am. I could know myself only if I first knew God, upon Whom my being is based."

2. *The Psychology of the Unconscious.*—Behaviourism turns away from consciousness to action : it studies not the soul but behaviour. The other recent trend in psychology has turned attention from the conscious to focus it on the unconscious. The conscious motive of an action is frequently not the real motive : that lies deep in the unconscious. That which we imagine to be the considered verdict of reason is only " rationalisation." We find reasons to justify what we have done, but remain unaware that it is we who have invented them.

It is clear that these theories, while contributing much to our understanding of certain phenomena, will not carry the weight which is frequently placed on them. " Reason and intelligence are perhaps less supreme than some of us like to think, but they are not so entirely negligible and delusive as Freud would imply." [1] Indeed this uncompromising disparagement of reason, in which many psychologists indulge, would prove fatal to the reliability of their own pronouncements. In order, for example, to demonstrate that rationalisation has been at work, the psychologist himself must be able to distinguish real from imaginary motives. He must trust the analysis made by his own reason. And it would be easy to argue that the belief in rationalisation held by any psychologist is in fact induced by an unrecognised desire : he is afraid to face reality as it is and to admit that situations in which he is placed are such as demand rational solution or moral decision.

When we turn to the theory of religion which springs from these presuppositions we discover, as we might expect, that faith is dismissed as illusion, the product of suggestion or of neurosis. God is nothing but a projection, a thought which humanity in every part of the world and in all ages has brought forth from itself and always in similar

[1] Yellowlees, *op. cit.* pp. 45–46.

forms.[1] God is a projection due to the activit〉 mind in its tendency to idealise and personify.[2] 〈 is a neurosis, a perpetuation of the infantile attit life ; nothing more than a nervous disease. The 〈 found protection and security in his father : now he projects and objectifies, in the figure of God, his continual craving for security and peace.

(*a*) Consider first the declaration that religion is a

---

[1] Jung, *Psychology of the Unconscious*, chap. iii. Jung and others of the Zürich school make considerable use of the religious motive in thera- peutic practice, but this does not mean that they regard religion as any- thing other than a mode of harmonious self-expression ; there need be no reference to any objective ground, in the " Beyond," of the satisfying experience. Jung's position is stated somewhat ambiguously in his more popular volume of essays, *Modern Man in Search of a Soul* (Kegan Paul, Fifth Impression, 1936). He uses the phrase, " We Protestants," and states, " My own position is on the extreme left wing of the congress of Protestant opinion " (p. 281). The medicine man is also the priest ; religions are systems of healing for psychic illness. This is true most of all in the two greatest religions of man, Christianity and Buddhism. " Man is never helped in his suffering by what he thinks for himself, but only by revelations of a wisdom greater than his own " (p. 278). Unlike Freud, who would declare that the religious symptoms are only a screen for sexual disharmonies, Jung finds very frequently that the religious trouble is the primary one. And he considers that " it is indeed high time for the clergyman and the psychotherapist to join forces " (p. 265). One would imagine that it would be necessary next to affirm the objective reality of that in which the patient is encouraged to believe, since there is neither consolation nor healing save in the truth. And we should welcome a clear statement from Jung as to his own opinion in this vital matter. In this also it is indeed high time for the clergyman and the psychotherapist to join forces. But such statements as we have are tantalisingly meagre and ambiguous. He speaks, it is true, of ' un- prejudiced objectivity ' (p. 271), but this refers to the attitude of the physician (who, it appears, is to be neither partial on the one hand nor impartial on the other !) and there is a curious passage (p. 274) about egoism being the true will of God for a man. But when he writes, " Healing may be called a religious problem. . . . Modern man has heard enough about guilt and sin. He is sorely enough beset by his own bad conscience, and wants rather to learn how he is to reconcile himself with his own nature—how he is to love the enemy in his own heart and call the wolf his brother " (p. 274), he appears merely to hold that religion is useful as one element in the cure and that this is the sole function of religion and the only sense in which we may claim that faith is anchored in reality.

[2] Tansley, *The New Psychology*, chap. iv.

3

form of *neurosis*. Those who desire to see in religion only a manifestation of the neurotic temperament are involved in a process which will carry them much farther. Neurotics have often made great saints ; but they have also made great poets, musicians, artists, scientists, inventors. It is recorded of Beethoven that, after the battle of Jena, he said of Napoleon : " I wish I knew the art of war as I know the art of music : I could have beaten him." Here is one reason for the association of neurosis with genius. Genius has a surplus of endowment over the opportunities offered by a brief life to develop it. The late Dr. B. H. Streeter suggests two other reasons. First, genius is sensitive. It is the tip of the flame which is most tremulous. " A razor is more easily notched than an axe, and enhanced sensitiveness cannot but be accompanied by increased liability to injury." Genius is not the result of neurosis ; they are parallel results of unusual sensitiveness. Second, though genius is not the result of neurosis, neurosis may give to it the opportunity of developing. There is a grain of truth in the description of genius which sees in it, first of all, a " transcendent capacity of taking trouble." [1] Perfect *bodily* health is frequently an obstacle to intellectual achievement. Life is too full of interest to allow of concentration. The same may be true of perfect psychic health. " The effort of the psyche to over-compensate for a sub-conscious feeling of inferiority often leads the individual to concentrate exceptional energy upon some pursuit for which he has a natural aptitude." [2]

If the aberrations of religion exhibited in the cloisters of the Middle Ages are quoted on the other side, we must remember, says Dr. Streeter, that this consideration is double-edged. " The austerities endured, and the lives lived year after year by some of the saints, were enough to kill any ordinary person in six months. Somehow and somewhence these people must have secured some special enhancement of vitality ; and this at least suggests the possibility that in Religion itself there is a health-creating

[1] Carlyle, *Frederick the Great*, IV. iii.
[2] Quoted from Adler in *Reality*, p. 276, by Canon Streeter.

power which may go some way to counteract a psycho-neurosis which has originated from some other cause. Pursuing this suggestion, we soon come across evidence which points towards the conclusion that Religion, so far from being a pathological symptom, is, psychologically considered, a phenomenon characteristic, not of disease, but of health." [1]

(b) Turn next to the theory that the objects of worship and religious experience are *projections*. Dr. T. Hywel Hughes [2] makes the point that there are two types of projection, one a perfectly legitimate operation of man's reason, the other an activity of the unconscious self, spring-ing from repressed emotions. We may admit at once that the idea of God is a projection, since in no other way could we have an idea of Him. The mistake made by the psycho-logist is to suppose that because the idea is projected there is no Being that corresponds to it ; that because it is born in man's experience it is an illusion. It would not be hard to show, on the same principles, that the universe whose laws and processes are investigated by science is also a projection of man's mind. The uniformity of nature and the principle of causation are both projections. Like the idea of God, however, these ideas are produced in response to an appeal from without. The fact that they persist and that they are verified by experience indicates that they are valid projections ; there is that in reality which corre-sponds to the ideas evolved in men's minds.

Dr. William Brown [3] makes another important point. Where neurosis and illusion are to be dealt with, it is found that treatment by deep analysis removes the projections which have been pathologically produced ; whereas the effect of such treatment is not to remove but to strengthen religious convictions. " According to one's experiences of the pathological processes of projection and regression and the influence of the Œdipus complex in a patient, these

---

[1] *Reality*, pp. 277–278.

[2] *The New Psychology and Religious Experience* (Allen & Unwin, 1933), chap. ii.

[3] *Mind and Personality*, chap. xx. *sub fin.*

are usually diminished or eliminated by a course of psycho-
analysis. If, therefore, the typical religious attitude
towards life is explicable in these terms, the religious consciousness would be altered by analysis in the direction of
elimination." The reverse is the case. The analysis has a
purifying effect on religious feelings ; it sets them free
from much that is merely infantile or sentimental, but it
indicates most clearly that religion is the most important
thing in life and that it is essential to mental health. " Although mere emotionalism and religiosity is diminished,
the essentially religious outlook on life remains unim-
paired." [1]

It is true that psychologists have suggested other
reasons to account for the troublesome persistence of the
" illusion." Professor Leuba, for example,[2] argues that
belief in a personal order has biological value. It gives
the impression of powerful support which can be called in
to help in gaining the victory in the battle of life. Having
this value in the struggle for existence, it is not surprising
that it has been perpetuated, and is found almost univer-
sally. Leuba feels that he has thus accounted for the
persistence of the illusion.

It is not so. An erroneous idea, it is true, may possess
survival value because it protects the mind from the shock
of reality. But neither the idea nor its value will outlast
its power to deceive. It loses its efficacy whenever it is
found out.[3] Fantasy and imagination can be of value in
the process of survival only if they successfully anticipate
experience. If they fail to do this, they will speedily be
shattered on the hard facts of reality. " If a type of
behaviour which works with meaning and assumes its
environment to have qualities of knowledge, wisdom, and
justice which give meaning, succeeds so well in the battle
of life, how are we to know that any power is real if this

---

[1] *Op. cit.* p. 268.   [2] *A Psychology of Religion.*
[3] So it might be argued that, in the early Christian Church, the expectation of a speedy Second Coming helped many Christians to endure
persecution. But it cannot be argued that the Church survived because
of that mistaken expectation. It survived *in spite* of its disillusionment.

kind of power is unreal ? Were paper money thus honoured day by day in life's business, with nothing behind it, the problem of how to live at the rate of ten thousand a year on nothing would be solved. And what would such a religion be but money that is nothing save paper ? " [1] And this cannot apply to religion alone. " If mind is developed in the struggle for life and if, in this struggle, illusion will serve as well as truth, what assurance is left of any reality ? Why, for example, in spite of the utility of science, is not the object of it as much an illusion as the object of religion ? Pragmatical grounds are worthless, for the assumption of Pragmatism is that reality alone will work in the end, and that even illusion only works up to the measure of reality it contains." [2]

Further, and more important still, it is not solely with the fact of experience that we are concerned, but with the nature of it. It *is* significant that the religious experience has found satisfaction ; that pragmatically it has been justified. This leads to the confident expectation that there is a reality, corresponding to it, which has brought that satisfaction. But what is still more significant is this, that what all men have in some degree, the best have in the highest degree. It is the saints who have the first claim to be heard on this matter. And the unanimous testimony of the saints is that the experience is a valid one. It is here, they say with one voice, that we have the truth about the universe. If we disagree with the good people about religion, we may be sure that it is we who have missed the truth ; that they are seeing something which is up to now hidden from us.

To all who seek to explain away religion as illusion, and the idea of God as wish-fulfilment, and in particular to Feuerbach, the most consistent illusionist, the late H. R. Mackintosh says : " Derive religion, if you choose, from the glories of nature or the sublimities of the moral order, or from any other source where you suppose the transcend-

---

[1] John Oman, *The Natural and the Supernatural* (Cambridge, 1931)ʼ p. 39.

[2] *Ibid.* p. 40.

ent powers of destiny have their seat. But pray, whatever
happens, do not ask us to believe that poor mortals,
confined to their own experience, have found in what they
are, as sinners fated to sink into the grave, the content
out of which they have built the conception of the Lord
God, eternal and high and lifted up, Who is of purer eyes
than to behold iniquity." [1]

It is well to recognise that psychology must renounce
the right to adjudicate on the validity of religious experience.
The purely empirical view which it must take in dealing
with origins can give only a fragmentary picture of the
universe. It is true that psychology, as an empirical
science, must be loyal to its own nature. For it to have
recourse to the theory of a divine origin of these experiences
is equivalent to abandoning the attempt at scientific
description. Nevertheless, those who have the experiences
believe that they can be explained only as the spiritual
effects of divine grace, the workings of the Holy Spirit. [2]

The experiences of which we speak may indeed be
called subjective experiences—if by this is meant that they
are *in the mind*. But not all that is subjective is unreal.
Where else could they be than in the mind? All the rest
of knowledge is there also. You cannot therefore deny
validity to the one, without denying it to the other. Dr.
John Oman rightly draws attention to another verdict of
psychology. It admits that belief in the supernatural is
practically as wide as humanity ; that it has been held by
all the sanest minds ; and that it has had a very deep and
continuous influence on human affairs. " This type of
theory is, therefore, compelled to derive the illusion from
the ordinary working of the human mind under the actual
conditions set by the universal experience. Psychology,
therefore, so far as it can determine validity at all, would
seem to be on the side of a belief that has arisen from the
normal mind, dealing with a universal experience. . . .
Wherefore, if what the mind takes to be objective knowledge

---

[1] See an article in *The Expository Times*, February, 1932.
[2] See further W. P. Paterson, *The Nature of Religion* (Hodder &
Stoughton, 1925), pp. 36–37.

can, from the nature of the mind itself, be shown to be illusion, all knowledge must be suspect." [1]

The truth is that not everything which can be called subjective is necessarily therefore untrue or misleading or without foundation. There is an ambiguity in the use of the word " subjective," which has been very clearly exposed by Professor John Baillie. " The fashionable modern distinction, introduced by Kant, between the objective and the subjective is a highly confused one and needs to be broken up into at least two separate distinctions, that between significant and merely illusory experience, and that between public and private experience. There is no reason to suppose that all private experience must be illusory." [2]

The mistake made by some psychologists is to suppose that these experiences, because they are in the mind and follow the laws of the mind (as they must surely do, while they *are* in the mind !) are for that reason not significant but illusory. All that they are able to say is that they are private experiences : they still leave open the vital question, Is there a reality to correspond with them ? Are those experiences experiences of God, or do they begin and end in the mind ?

A scientific proof of the existence of an unseen spiritual world is as much a chimera as a scientific proof that an objective world exists behind phenomena. But the absence of a scientific demonstration does not, in either case, prove the falsity of our belief in that which is unseen. Man has to choose. Nevertheless, it is not *blind* choice. Certain propositions may be formulated out of the religious experience at its highest—for example, That God exists ; that He is seeking the souls of men ; that He is wise, personal, loving. " These propositions," it has been said,[3] " come to us by way of a Voice. If I chose to believe—and choose one way or the other I must—that that Voice is the Voice

---

[1] *The Natural and the Supernatural*, p. 46.

[2] *And the Life Everlasting* (Oxford, 1934), p. 155.

[3] Edwin Lewis in *Religion in Life* (New York), Winter Number, 1936, p. 141.

of God, mediated by a process called ' revelation ' through
a historic body called ' the Church,' a Voice, one admits,
sadly muffled at times by reason of the unresponsiveness
of the medium, but nevertheless authentically divine even
when least clearly heard—if I choose to believe that, I
submit that the choice does not mean that I am childishly
credulous.   I choose *because*—— !   Here are affirmations,
meaningful, overwhelming, revolutionary—and   *testable*.
For they are testable in the arena of life itself.   They invest
existence with a certain dread solemnity.   They release
man from the grip of coldly impersonal law.   They challenge
to high endeavour.   They keep hope alive even in a day so
dark as this.   They supply motivation for the pursuit of
a ' Supremely Worthful ' which is that indeed."

It is of course necessary that these empirical studies,
in the field of science and psychology, should be followed
to their conclusion.   We shall see later that even they are
not independent of faith and revelation ; but in the meantime it is to be noticed that these disciplines point forward
to another type of knowledge.   Their most valuable contribution to epistemology is their testimony that of themselves they are unable to give a satisfactory account of
experience.   They do not deal with that which is ultimately
real.   Dr. Karl Heim writes that the form of the present
world is a veiling of the true nature of reality.   " Certainly,
it presents Reality from one side with great wealth of
detail, and it is indeed worth while to appease our thirst
for knowledge by investigating and drawing out all we
can see of Reality in this way.   But what is here presented
to our eyes is nothing more than a surface-view." [1]

At this stage, discovery is at a maximum, revelation at
a minimum ; but, when we come to consider religious
knowledge, the reverse is true.   The whole initiative lies
with God.   " The bare emergence of the Idea of God
confronts us with an ultimate Either/Or.   *Either* our Forms
of Intuition and Forms of Thought have final validity for
the understanding of Reality, and then we must either

[1] *Glaube und Denken*, 3rd edition ; in English, *God Transcendent*,
pp. 212–213.

interpret the Idea of God in the way Idolatry does, by giving absolute value to some only relative reality, or, as Pantheism does, by deifying the infinite Whole of things ; *or*, on the other hand, God is the *ens realissimum*, and then our intramundane Forms of Intuition have the effect of veiling the ultimate deeps of the ' I,' the ' Thou,' and the World, because God, the Giver of all existence, cannot be apprehended in these Forms.

If God is a Reality and not to be explained away in the manner of Idolatry and Pantheism, then it is impossible for us, by any observation or any thinking of our own, to reach what He is and what He wills. We are thrown back on God's own revelation." [1]

[1] *God Transcendent*, p. 231.

CHAPTER III

REVELATION AND MORAL VALUES

SUMMARY

MORALITY is the proper science and business of mankind. May we not claim that here the initiative lies with man himself ? Naturalistic theories of ethics reduce obligation to expediency. Man is to be praised because he is clever, not because he is good. Psychology has slightly improved the position of naturalistic ethics by calling attention to altruistic, social instincts which must be satisfied if man's well-being is to be secured. But if love is described as *selfishness for two*, the distinction is not removed. It is still something quite different from selfishness for one. Others have widened the circle, so that morality becomes " selfishness for the tribe " ; an act is good according as it tends to the preservation of the race. But it is clear that such a " conscience " loses its power as soon as it is found out. Kant is justified in maintaining that the sense of obligation cannot be minimised nor evaded. Yet, even in Kant, the sense of obligation is not the basis of religion, as is sometimes said, but a derivative from it. Moreover, a theory which finds the principle of right conduct in Reason and its autonomy is unable to deal adequately with the phenomena of the evil will. There are profound difficulties also in ethical theories of self-realisation. The use of the term " realisation " points to an ideal self not yet actualised. Man is called to the realisation of something other than the self as it is, that which the religious man knows as the will of God. Otherwise the quest of self-realisation is faced with the grim reality of self-deception.

Moral values are personal in two respects : (1) Persons are the bearers of individual values. (2) The system of values must have a personal source and sustainer. Though values are known by our appreciation of them, they are not brought into being by that appreciation. This theistic completion of ethical theory has been challenged from time to time. Nicolai Hartmann holds that God is not the highest and absolute person but the absolutely impersonal being. The weakness of his argument lies in the supposition that in man we have an example of complete personality. The truth is that in man we have only the adumbration of that which we believe finds its actuality in God alone. Hartmann disallows also the claim that God is the source and sustainer of moral values. But he is himself involved in fatal difficulties when he comes to speak of the critique of values. This is inevitable in a theory which speaks of love as if it were only one among a number of other values. The place of love is unique.

The personality of God is also a critical point in Bergson's *The Two Sources of Morality and Religion*. He argues that divine love is not an attribute of God : it is God Himself. Bergson's weakness is in the inter-relating of morality and religion. The facts of right conduct would appear to be more readily explained by the work of the Divine Spirit than by the difficult concept of an impersonal biological force. And the " life-impulse " does not allow to failure and sin the place which is actually occupied by them in human experience.

Morality flows, not from the nature of man, but from the nature of God. The divine indicative precedes the divine imperative. The moral imperative is not based on a possibility but on an order of reality. In the experience of redemption, man is made capable of seeing the good and of doing it.

44

CHAPTER III

REVELATION AND MORAL VALUES

MORALITY is the proper science and business of mankind. Here, then, may we not claim that the initiative lies clearly with man ? In the realm of conduct have we not one field, and that the most important in human life, which we can characterise as *our own* ?

So the natural man might inquire. And in doing so, he would be seeking to conserve a real truth, our conviction that we are responsible for our own acts. Man is prepared to admit that his failures are his own : he wants also to claim credit for his virtues. He feels that he is not obeying a transcendent law but fulfilling an immanent purpose. He is autonomous. In this sphere he is both subject and legislator.

If, however, he is to insist on this claim, he must realise that *merit* is out of place. A legalistic system might leave room for meritorious acts. Once the law was satisfied, there might be scope left over for a surplus of good conduct.[1] But the claim we have stated demands more than this. The rules, it insists, are laid down by man himself, for himself ; and the self which is the legislator will not be satisfied with anything but the highest. He will not be content with any actual achievement, but only with the attainment of the ideal, which yet can never be realised.

If it is truly autonomous morality, it is the challenge of an obligation felt to be absolute and unconditioned. If anyone desires to discard the theistic completion of ethics, but nevertheless to conceive the moral code as other than

---

[1] I am told that elephants which are trained to carry timber become quite human in their habits. If the siren sounds when they are in the middle of the compound, they will drop the log and trot off duty. Presumably, the elephant which completes the journey has done his duty *and more.*

a legalistic system, he is compelled to find its sanctions in ideals which are native to man. He may say, it is true, that he observes certain actions to be right actions ; that they are performed freely, and in face of real resistance ; and therefore that they are praiseworthy, meritorious actions. And in fact nothing is more common, at the merely moral level, than pride and self-righteousness. Yet the fact that these terms are generally used in depreciation of the moral character, indicates that they can be employed only where the ethical level is not particularly high. It is implied either that a man is taking too narrow a view of the ideal or that he is looking with too much complacence on his achievement. He is content with the good when he ought to be seeking the better. The concept of merit involves a restricted and inadequate view of human obliga- tion. And, where the best human experience is taken into account, it appears to be entirely out of place. Children do not feel that they have *merited* the love and protection of their parents, and the parents—unless they are like the subjects of the cartoonist who made it plain that they had both "married beneath them"—do not claim that they have *deserved* the love which they receive from each other. The idea of merit is, in fact, foreign to the genuinely moral consciousness. " So far from the term ' meritorious ' pointing to that which is dutiful *and more*, it suggests an attitude of mind that has positively failed to rise to the level of true obedience." [1]

We must inquire much more closely into the nature of this sense of obligation.

Is it to be *explained away* ? That is the outcome of every naturalistic theory of ethics. Obligation is reduced to expediency. Morality is explained by natural fact.[2] The man who is lauded for his right conduct wins this eulogy because he is clever, not because he is good.[3] His

[1] H. R. Mackintosh, *The Christian Experience of Forgiveness* (Nisbet, 1927), p. 139. Cf. Pringle-Pattison, *The Idea of Immortality*, p. 179.

[2] " Here is the earthquake rent which passes across the whole natural- istic construction of the world." D. S. Cairns, *The Riddle of the World* (Student Christian Movement Press, 1937), p. 102.

[3] Cf. Emil Brunner, *The Divine Imperative* (Lutterworth Press), p. 36.

conduct is aimed solely at the production of his own well-being.

Psychology has slightly improved the position of naturalistic ethics by calling attention to certain altruistic, social instincts, which require satisfaction. If they are neglected or starved, a man's own individual well-being is not yet secured.

Quite clearly, however, not even this can account for the sense of obligation. It is not explained, but explained away. We cannot pass from the sense that " I do this because it suits me " to the sense that " I do this because it is right. You may describe love as " selfishness for two," [1] but that does not remove the distinction. It is still something quite different from " selfishness for one."

Suppose, then, that we widen the circle and take in the possibility that love may be " selfishness for the tribe." It may be argued that there is no divine authority, but only human. " Custom," says J. W. Krutch, " has furnished the only basis which ethics have ever had, and there is no conceivable human action which custom has not at one time justified and at another condemned." [2] The ethical is resolved into the biological. The compulsion felt in duty is simply the compulsion of instinct. An act is good according as it tends to the preservation of the self, of the tribe, or even of the race. There is therefore no such thing as duty. The criterion of conduct is found solely in the consequence of an action, and never in the motive.

Such a theory of conscience is, however, quite unable to bear the strain placed upon it. It might indeed be true that, in the course of evolution, man acquired a strong and confident sense of that which is expedient for the survival of mankind. But it could not also be a sense that he is *obliged* to follow its dictates when they lead to the sacrifice of his own interests. Such a " conscience " loses its power as soon as it is " found out." The first man who was clever enough to discover that there is no such thing as goodness, but only expediency, would cease to obey conscience.

[1] Cf. M. C. Otto, *Things and Ideals*, p. 39.
[2] *The Modern Temper*, p. 13.

Thus it has frequently been noticed that the exponents of evolutionary ethics do, in fact, change their ground unwittingly. They move from fact to value. It may be by adopting unexamined the assumption that pleasure and pleasure alone is good, or some other assumption which is not logical but ethical. One truth at least is apparent : that " as long as the argument is logical, it has no ethical consequences ; and that, when ethical propositions enter, they have not been reached by any logical process." [1]

Kant is therefore perfectly justified in maintaining that the sense of obligation cannot be minimised nor evaded. He is the first to make it quite plain that a metaphysical theory must take cognisance, not only of the realm of nature, but also of the realm of ends. " Nothing can possibly be conceived, in the world or out of it, which can be considered good without qualification, except a good will. Intelligence, wit, judgment, and the other talents of the mind, however they may be named, or courage, resolution, perseverance, as qualities of temperament, are undoubtedly good and desirable in many respects, but these gifts of nature may also become extremely bad and mischievous if the will which is to make use of them, and which therefore constitutes what is called *character*, is not good." (A scoundrel is bad enough ; worse still is a *perfect* scoundrel !) " A good will is good not because of what it performs or accomplishes, not by its aptness for the attainment of some proposed end, but simply in virtue of its volition, that is, it is good in itself." [2] Elsewhere Kant says : " Two things fill the mind with ever new and increasing admiration and awe, the oftener and the more steadily we reflect upon them—the starry heavens above and the moral law within." [3]

Because of the form which the argument takes in Kant, we might easily underrate its importance. Actually, what is vital to it is the belief in a real moral order. If I live in

[1] W. R. Sorley, *Moral Values and the Idea of God* (Cambridge, 1921), 2nd ed. p. 14.
[2] *Fundamental Principles of the Metaphysic of Morals*, First Section.
[3] *Critique of Practical Reason :* Conclusion.

a non-moral universe, I cannot be obliged to be moral.
But I am aware of this obligation : therefore the universe
is moral.   Our sense of value is not a matter of selfish
preference ;   " the judgment of value is as impartial as it
is unhesitating." [1]   Now it might be said that it is precisely the *givenness* of the moral law which requires examination.   Men may readily admit that the postulates of freedom,
immortality, God are involved in it, but many ask for a
more convincing justification of the premiss.   Yet there is
this to be said :   There are three stages in Kant's argument.
(1) He notices that reverence for the moral law is found
wherever mankind is found.   At this stage it is an unreflecting, unquestioning recognition.   The thing, however,
is there :   it must be explained.   (2) At the second stage
Kant offers the explanation.   It lies in the belief that
goodness is objectively grounded.   It is not a convention,
not a parochial prejudice, as those must say who wish to
explain it away.   The best human endeavour is in line
with the eternal purpose of God.   This second stage is the
vitally important one.   It is here that Kant passes from
morality to religion ;   not, as is sometimes supposed, at the
third stage.   (3) Here, Kant simply indicates the postulates
which are involved if the second stage is legitimately
reached.   " Despite the elaborate display of demonstration
which the *Critique of Practical Reason* makes, the really
crucial step—the step marking the actual transition from
morality to religion—is not bridged by anything which
can claim to be an adequate logical deduction." [2]

That is the first observation that must be made on
Kant's conception of the autonomy of the will—the sense
of obligation is not the basis of religion but a derivative of
it.   " The Christian believes that the ideal of love is real
in the will and nature of God, even though he knows of no
place in history where the ideal has been realised in its
pure form.   And it is because it has this reality that he feels
the pull of obligation.   The sense of obligation in morals

---

[1] Pringle-Pattison, *The Idea of God* (Oxford, 1917), p. 41.

[2] John Baillie, *The Interpretation of Religion* (T. & T. Clark, 1929),
pp. 275–276.

4

from which Kant tried to derive the whole structure of
religion is really derived from the religion itself. The ' pull '
or ' drive ' of moral life is a part of the religious tension of
life." [1]

Secondly, a criticism is suggested by the fact of moral
wrong-doing. A theory which finds the principle of right
conduct in Reason and its autonomy is unable to face this
fact. Wrong-doing is more than a hindrance, more than a
" not-yet " : it is the outcome of an evil will. We are
confronted with a dilemma. " Either the moral law is
God's law (in which case we are not autonomous, not law-
givers, not even co-lawgivers), or the moral law is really a
law given by ourselves, and the intelligible ego is our own
deepest ego, in which case we have no serious knowledge
of either evil or God." [2]

Serious difficulties also beset ethical theories of self-
realisation. It is suggested, for example, by the idealist
school of T. H. Green, that the *summum bonum* is the
development of a harmonious personality ; the baser
impulses are to be abolished and the whole is to be rationally
controlled and co-ordinated.

The thought of a harmonious personality might provide
a clue, but it raises immediately the question, What is the
self that is to be realised ? The use of the term " realisation "
indicates that it is an *ideal* self, not yet actualised, which is
thought of ; a self, that is, which *ought* to be, yet never
completely *is*.[3] We are called therefore to the realisation
of something *other* than the self as it is, something, in fact,
which the religious man knows as " the will of God for me."
Unless this is so, the quest of self-realisation is faced with

[1] Reinhold Niebuhr, *An Interpretation of Christian Ethics* (Student
Christian Movement Press, 1936), p. 19.

[2] Emil Brunner, *The Philosophy of Religion*, p. 72.

[3] Green was always aware of the difficulty. See, for example, his
Prolegomena to Ethics, section 288 : " If the idea, as it actuates us, carried
with it a full consciousness of what its final realisation would be, the
distinction between idea and realisation would be at an end. But while
for this reason it is impossible for us to say what the perfecting of man,
of which the idea actuates the moral life, in its actual attainment might
be, we can discern certain conditions which, if it is to satisfy the idea, it
must fulfil."

the grim reality of self-deception. Sin can mislead the self and can do so the more disastrously because the self is unaware of its own most profound limitations. There is, in fact, no power in an ideal which is no more than an ideal, in a value which has no relation to actuality. " If God is not only the goal, but the author and sustainer of moral effort, the whole moral endeavour of man must be a response to what we can only call a movement from the other side. It is, indeed, our own because it is the response of such moral personality as we already possess, but none the less it is a *response* to a divine initiative." [1] A self which deceives at least as easily as it guides cannot be the ultimate criterion of that which is right. The self's inspection of itself will not carry us very far.

How, then, are we to interpret the objective reality of moral values ? Are they in fact objectively real ?

It is true that values must apply to a person (moral predicates do not belong to *things*) ; and, if they are to be known *by me*, they must at some point touch *my* personality. Our standard of worth is an ideal of *personal* worth. Moreover, we cannot speak of values or disvalues inherent in the order of nature except in so far as nature is personified. As it has been pointed out in connection with J. S. Mill's indictment of the processes of nature, the language of denunciation has cogency only because the writer is arguing against the view that the natural order is the result of an omnipotent benevolent will. " The moral judgment upon nature—whether it be a judgment of approval or of disapproval—becomes appropriate when nature is contemplated as the work of a supreme being or person ; and it is only when nature is thus contemplated that the judgment is in place. It is to persons, therefore, and not to mere things that the moral predicate can apply." [2]

Moral values are personal in these two respects. (1) Persons are the bearers of individual values. (2) The system of values must have a personal source and sustainer. The first of these statements is not to be taken, therefore, as

---

[1] A. E. Taylor, *The Faith of a Moralist*, vol. i. p. 239.
[2] W. R. Sorley, *Moral Values and the Idea of God*, p. 123.

meaning that man creates his values from his own reason. Though they are known by my appreciation of them, they are not therefore brought into being by that appreciation.

The second statement belongs to theism rather than to ethics. It declares that the divine will is the source of moral values ; that the universe is grounded in the will of creative Deity ; that this divine will determines for each individual his special place within the order, his " vocation." [1]

This theistic completion of ethical theory has frequently been challenged. Fichte, for example, exalts the thought of vocation but finds no need for a Person behind the moral order. To listen to conscience, he says,[2] " to obey it honestly and unreservedly, without fear or equivocation—this is my true vocation, the whole end and purpose of my exist-ence. . . . That which conscience demands of me in this particular situation of life it is mine to do, for this only am I here ; to know it, I have understanding ; to perform it, I have power." But we must, he adds, be content with this. It is pure imagination to base the moral order on a holy will, to personalise it in a superhuman being. This is simply to throw our tiny human shadow on existence. We make this superhuman being only by predicating of Him our own attributes.[3]

[1] See William Temple, *Nature, Man and God*, Lecture XVI.

[2] *Vocation of Man*, Book III. i.

[3] In his later years, Fichte modified his views considerably—in the direction of a kind of philosophical mysticism. We need faith in the Infinite Being and in His reason and faithfulness. Only the infinite reason can limit the finite reason. Self is the great negation of God. Only in God do we find ourselves. Instead of self and duty, he now lays the emphasis on life and love. Man must not try to become something of himself, but, annulling himself, will find that God has entered to become all in all.

It is interesting to notice that, during the War of Liberation, one of Fichte's students revealed a plot to blow up the French powder-magazine in Berlin and asked for his teacher's advice. Was it an honourable way of achieving their purpose ? Fichte replied that it was not, and himself conveyed news of the plot to the French commander. This same student, during a battle, was struck by a musket-ball and owed his life to the fact that he was carrying a copy of Fichte's *Religionslehre*. (It seems a good reason for young men buying their professors' books.) The ball stopped at the passage : " For everything that comes to pass is the will of God and therefore the best that can possibly come to pass."

In our own time the chief challenge to theism in this respect has come from Professor Nicolai Hartmann, of Berlin.[1]

1. He will not allow the conception of a personal God. In Volume I. of the *Ethics*, he speaks of the fundamental presupposition that the universe requires a correlate ; that to be a world for someone inheres in the very mode of the world's existence. " But this presupposition has been shown to be erroneous. There is no such essential law. It contradicts the plain and evident meaning of all objectivity, theoretical as well as practical. Just as little does the concreteness of the world depend upon the concreteness of a personal counterpart. Conversely, a personal being which was not a member of a concrete, real world would itself be an abstraction. . . . It is necessarily set in the real cosmic context as a real part of it ; but it is never ' over against ' the world as a whole." [2]

Again he writes : God " is not the highest and absolute person but the absolutely impersonal being." [3] " The moral being is not the Absolute nor the State nor anything else in the world but, singly and alone, man, the primal carrier of moral values and disvalues." [4]

The weakness of this argument is the supposition that in man we have an example of a rounded and complete personality. That is by no means the case. Man is divided within himself, so that he is always *striving after* a full and harmonious personality. And he is not complete within himself. In him we have only the adumbration of that which we believe finds its actuality in God alone.

There are two features of personality which are found only in a very imperfect state in men, but which, we believe, are found in their completeness in God. (1) *Self-consciousness.*—In man this is incomplete. (a) Memory is not full nor accurate ; where it fails there is discontinuity with the past of the self. (b) There are vast tracts of the unconscious which belong to the self but cannot be brought

---

[1] *Ethics*, translated by Stanton Coit (Allen & Unwin, 1932).
[2] *Ibid.* i. p. 333.   [3] *Ibid.* i. p. 342.
[4] *Ibid.* i. p. 343.

always within its purview. (*c*) The self is not wholly unitary. It is always, in greater or less degree, divided within, and in cases of dual or multiple personality, its unity may be very radically disturbed. (2) *Self-determination.*— Severe limits are imposed on man's freedom. (*a*) Some are imposed from without by the physical world. (*b*) Others are due to the conflicting wills of his fellow-men. (*c*) A large number are the product of internal disharmony, past failures and sins having inhibited or enfeebled the will.

In God the imperfections of personality have no place. He is infinite Reason. He can be no secret to Himself. Nothing of the past lies in His memory ; nothing of the future is seen only in purpose and tendency. " In Eternity there is no distinction of Tenses . . . for to His Eternity, which is indivisible and all together, the last Trump is already sounded, the reprobates in the flame, and the blessed in Abraham's bosom." [1] Moreover, God is the complete Good, infinitely free, determined only from within, wholly self-sufficing. Man does not really possess personality ; but only its rudiments. When it is argued that personality implies limitation (and therefore cannot be ascribed to an Absolute) the answer is that personality is that which transcends limitations. It is our conception of complete and harmonious self-consciousness together with perfect spiritual freedom. [2] There is therefore nothing here to prevent us thinking of God as the personal Creator of the world.

2. Later on, Hartmann disallows the claim that God is the sustainer and source of moral values. " It is inherent in the essence of moral values, that they have convincing power in themselves—and are self-evident and are applicable to men, only as an imperturbable Ought, in so far as their content itself, as such, bears the characteristics alleged to be derived from outside authority ; hence no

---

[1] Sir Thomas Browne, *Religio Medici*, Everyman ed. p. 13.

[2] See Lotze, *Microcosmos* ; George Galloway, *The Philosophy of Religion*, chap. xiii. ; W. R. Matthews, *Studies in Christian Philosophy*, Lecture V. ; and C. C. J. Webb's Gifford Lectures.

one could make them self-evident in their claim—even by the most powerful *fiat*—unless he were already supported therein by their own power or self-evidence. But in this case all commending of them by any person would be superfluous. Accordingly to values, which apart from Him have strength of validity, God might lend a prestige among men by His power and authority; but He could not prescribe values as a lawgiver. For if He dictated what did not harmonise with self-existent values, His dictation could be carried out only as a commandment but could never be sensed as a value." [1]

Here we have the familiar old problem, Does God command a thing because it is good? Or is it good because God commands it? The first question cannot be answered in the affirmative, since there can be nothing good which does not coincide with the divine purpose for the universe. If it is good, it is already God's command. Nor can the second question be answered affirmatively, since nothing could be " good," in this sense, for men unless it coincided with that which was their own free choice. The fulness of right moral conduct requires not only that men shall do God's will but that they shall do it wittingly, freely, intelligently.

But the alternative is not rightly expressed. You cannot separate the good from God's command as if the two were concepts that might be contrasted in time or in their own content. God's nature being love, He continuously wills the achievement of His purpose of love. There is a service which is perfect freedom. Man can see that certain duties are God's commands, and yet freely perform them; obeying, not because this or that is the commandment of God but because of the impetus of love. When we do a thing because we love someone, we do not do it because that someone commands us; still less is this the case if we do it because that someone loves us. Quite certainly, love makes the thing that which we ourselves most desire to do.

Hartmann is particularly vulnerable when he comes to

[1] *Ethics*, iii. p. 266.

speak of the critique of values. How are we to construct a scale of values ? It follows with overpowering certainty, he writes, " that there can be no derivation of any kind for the scale of values. That in it a supreme unifying principle may prevail is not to be denied, but we may deny that it can be known as such, and that it can be known before the discernment of specific values. Yet this would be required for every kind of derivation from a principle." [1] " If all positive morality rests upon genuine discernment, and if all discernment of values is itself an aprioristic perception of valuational essences, the historical relativity of morals cannot rest upon that of values, but only upon that of discernment. . . . Striving must have unity, otherwise it disintegrates and destroys itself. A man cannot walk in two directions at the same time. No one can serve two masters. . . . Where no unifying principle presents itself, current morality forces such a principle upon the diversity of discerned values. It seizes hold of one single, clearly discerned value and sets it up above the rest, and subordinates them to it. . . . The transitoriness of every current morality is not so much a consequence of a restricted view of values, as of arbitrariness in regard to a unifying principle." [2]

The impersonal ethic of values faces here its chief difficulty. Where there is a scale of values there must be a law of order, but this law is not itself a value. A thing is good or evil, not because it represents a value—that might make it only desirable or undesirable—but because it is *willed within an order of values*. The Good is determined not by a value but by the choice of the higher value according to the principle of the elevation of the value.[3]

If it is true that a moral ideal can exist only in a mind, it is also true that an absolute moral ideal can exist only in a Mind which is the source and sustainer of all reality. Such a moral ideal the Christian believes to be set before him in the New Testament concept of love. He has know-

---

[1] *Ethics*, ii. p. 63.   [2] *Ibid.* ii. pp. 65–66.
[3] Compare Brunner, *The Divine Imperative*, pp. 43, 582, 626.

ledge of it not by discernment but by revelation.[1] It is
wrong to speak of love as if it were only one among a
number of other values. Its place is unique. Professor
L. A. Reid has recently emphasised the point in this very
connection.[2] " If duty is in a privileged position, having
moral authority, love, which, when it can be given scope in
personal relationships, embodies duty in the fullest sense,
possesses also uniqueness among the values. . . . The
fulfilment of love is dependent upon real differences between
other values and other dis-values. But unlike duty, love
does not *merely* prescribe what is best to be done in any
given circumstances ; love is not the mere form of a
distinguishable content ; it is a creative power in its
very self. . . . Bestowing goods upon the poor, or
giving the body to be burned, may be itself a ' duty,'
but to do these things from duty and to do them from
love is not the same thing. . . . Love *confers* upon the
other values a meaning which apart from it they do not
possess."

The personality of God is also a critical point in another
recent book, M. Bergson's *The Two Sources of Morality and
Religion*.[3] In his chapter on " Dynamic Religion " he uses
the word " religion " in a frankly mystical sense. " God is
love, and the object of love : herein lies the whole contribution of mysticism. About this twofold love the
mystic will never have done enthusing. His description is
interminable, because what he wants to describe is ineffable.
But what he does state clearly is that divine love is not a
thing of God : it is God Himself. It is upon this point
that the philosopher must fasten who holds God to be a
person, and yet wishes to avoid anything like a gross
assimilation with man." [4] The author then suggests as an
analogy the experience of men who are fired by some
great enthusiasm, which consumes everything and fills the

[1] " In every experience of true love there lies hidden an absolute, or
rather the assent to the sphere of the absolute, a secret *credo in Deum*."
Karl Adam, *Two Essays* (Sheed & Ward, 1930), p. 65.
    [2] *Creative Morality*, p. 144.   [3] E.T., Macmillan, 1935.
    [4] *Op. cit.* p. 216.

whole soul. The individual becomes one with the emotion; and yet he was never so thoroughly *himself*.

We must see how this mystical conception is related to morality. M. Bergson distinguishes two sources of morality, "social pressure" and the "impetus of love." They are ultimately two complementary manifestations of life, the first intent on preserving the social form which was characteristic of mankind from the beginning; the second capable of transfiguring that form by a creative movement.[1]

This stimulating discussion is developed along the following lines: Commands laid upon men by society have a way of appearing like laws of nature. (We are, of course, aware of the fundamental difference; society is made up of free persons. Nevertheless, command and law are constantly confused. We imagine that the laws of nature existed in heaven from all eternity as divine commands, and on the other hand obedience to society's commands becomes habitual and unreflecting. Law borrows from command the appearance of compulsion: command borrows from law the appearance of inevitability. The habit (of obeying authority) brings command nearer to a law of nature, and religion finally bridges the gap. The divine command must be obeyed, or penalty follows.) Thus we find that the criminal's remorse is not due simply to fear of punishment, but also to the sense of estrangement from society. Society speaks to the man as he *was*, not to him. If he confesses, he will be punished, but society will then speak to *him*. His attempt to conceal all traces of the crime is largely motived by the desire to wipe out, not the evidence, but the crime. If no one knows about it, it is practically non-existent. It seems therefore that Kant and his followers were wrong in making so much of the sense of duty. That resistance of which we are conscious in making a moral choice appears only when we *disobey*. Disobedience is followed, not preceded, by the sense of duty. That sense is, in fact, a resistance against resistance.[2]

M. Bergson is surely guilty here of lapsing into doubtful

[1] P. 79.   [2] P. 11.

psychology. The sense of duty is not this doubly negative thing. According to his own view, there is a good self and a bad self, a self that is socially obedient and a self that is defiant and rebellious. The first has the placid way : the second causes resistance. According to the Kantian view, there is a good will and a bad will : the first has the feeling of tension, because inclination draws it the other way. We might picture it this way : According to Bergson, man is climbing up a staircase. He finds it easy, because the stair itself is moving. He is forced up by the pressure of society. Then he decides to come down. At once resistance is felt. According to the Kantian view, Man is climbing up a ladder, with all the weight of inclination hanging to his ankles. (Or shall we call it original sin ?) Resistance is felt from the very beginning. It may be granted that Kant did not allow enough place to the possibility of delight in obeying,[1] but that perhaps comes only at a late stage ; it belongs to a higher level of habitual obedience. Bergson puts the resistance in the social organism ; it is exercised as soon as we try to disobey. Kant (and St. Paul) put it in the individual self ; it comes into play when we try to do right. And, if we think it out, we find that M. Bergson is less satisfactory. He may have the appearance of truth in superficial cases of mere conformity to the outward requirements of society ; but quite early there arises the sense of obligation which demands inner purity, about which society has nothing to say.

M. Bergson then proceeds to give his own account of obligation. It is the form taken by necessity when it enters the sphere of choice and liberty. Obligation to society means only obligation to a " closed society," such as the family, the nation ; not to mankind. (Respect for property, for example, does not extend to the property

---

[1] We recall Schiller's epigram. A perplexed inquirer brings his difficulty before the Kantian philosopher :

" Willingly serve I my friends, but I do it, alas ! with affection.
 Hence I am plagued with the doubt, virtue I have not attained."
He receives the reply :
" This is your only resource, you must stubbornly seek to abhor them.
 Then you may do with disgust that which the law may enjoin."

of a nation's enemies.)   Love of the family or of the state
does not lead naturally towards love of humanity.   The
latter is a different kind of obligation, not reached by
stages through family and nation, but through reason or
religion.   The first manifestation of love is protective, for
the sake of discipline within the closed society against
outside powers which threaten it ; the second manifestation is absolute morality.   The first is a command ; the
second is an appeal.[1]

There are some criticisms to be made at this point.
It is true that much of man's devotion to family or to
state may be pure expediency ; but it cannot all be.
Expediency will not create the obligation to sacrifice everything for others.   However strong the pressure of " habit,"
the sense of " I must do this that I may be strong " will
not pass into the sense of " I must do this, even though I
perish, because it is right."   The theory of expediency
would imply that the individual must, at least generally,
desire benefit from his obedience to obligation.   But surely
even in the lowest form of obedience there is the embryo
of absolute moral obligation—self-sacrifice for no benefit,
but only out of a sense of rightness.   Bergson leaves un-
touched also the sense of obligation to do right even to the
detriment of the closed society.   In the sphere of the
family, we have the example of Helen Walker, immortalised
by Sir Walter Scott as Jeanie Deans.   In the sphere of
the nation, it is sufficient to remember that the motto of
every statesman is not that of the Norfolk toast, " Our
country, right or wrong."   Many great statesmen may
take the honest line, though it means that their country
will suffer by it.   Bergson may reply that they do this
because they know that ultimately the state will be better
because it has kept its honour ; but this would be to
confuse two separate things.   The state will be " better "
only in the sense of honest rather than dishonest ;
it will not necessarily be " better " in the sense of
stronger.

To be consistent, he must claim that these are examples

[1] P. 24.

of the second type of fulfilment of duty ; must transfer every awkward exception to the other category.

To his description of this second category we now turn.

Man outwits nature (p. 44). Nature intended that he should live in and serve a closed society. But there is born from time to time the genius in will as well as the genius in intellect. Men of such genius show the way to an open society ; they replace the state by mankind as an object of devotion. Pressure and aspiration have been blended in the concept of duty. Thus the purely intellectualist theory of morals is always wrong. The two things blended by it are really and always two, not one. We yield to the *pressure* of the real society, while we are *drawn* towards the ideal society.

Bergson then indicates the manner in which this genius of will exercises its influence. A new work of art, in a new style of genius, is at first merely disconcerting. Then it creates its own admirers : it makes the taste by which alone it can be appreciated. The case is similar with a movement for reform. It could come about only in such a society as would be created by its realisation.

Finally, M. Bergson indicates the part which is played by " intelligence." " It is a faculty used naturally by the individual to meet the difficulties of life ; it will not follow the direction of a force which, on the contrary, is working for the species, and which, if it considers the individual at all, does so in the interest of the species. It will make straight for selfish decisions. But this will only be its first impulse. It cannot avoid reckoning with the force of which it feels the invisible pressure. It will therefore persuade itself into thinking that an intelligent egoism must allow all other egoisms their share." [1] In order to avoid collisions and so promote its own interests, intelligence gives way to the egoism of others, but it rationalises its partial surrender by arguing that each must meet the demands of others in order to find the happiness of all. Intelligence supplies only the hesitation in obeying the organism : it sets up a hindrance, but immediately, as it

[1] P. 75.

would appear, hinders its own hindrance, resists its own resistance.

That which is called religion, M. Bergson proceeds, may be no more than an extension of moral impulses. The imperfect justice of the city of men is replaced by the perfect justice of the City of God. Or religion may be made up largely of intellectual ideas concerning the nature of God and the world. But there is a third type, the only true form of religion, that mysticism which consists in opening the soul " to the oncoming wave." [1] Intelligence brings man only to the stage of myth-making. And the myths need not have any actuality corresponding to them. But, when we pass from this static religion to *dynamic* religion, when intuition takes the place of intelligence, we have that mysticism which can make light of the natural obstacles with which intelligence must come to terms.[2]

At the end of this summary of M. Bergson's argument, certain criticisms must be made.

1. There is a grave difficulty connected with the theory of " genius of the will " ; for the problem which it is designed to solve breaks out again in the case of the genius himself. Whence does he have his love for humanity ? It seems evident that, if he has it in a great degree, all men have it in some degree. Otherwise he could never appeal to them, and they would never " aspire." We must assume that there is that in men to which the genius can appeal ; he sees more clearly what most men see dimly, or makes explicit what has only been implicit. He shows to men— themselves. In fact, we come back to the working of the Holy Spirit in men's hearts.[3]

2. Bergson's account of intelligence is too complicated. This faculty is sent on a curious, roundabout journey in order to do very little. Undoubtedly there is such a thing as intelligent self-interest, that is, intelligence *not* rationalis-

---

[1] P. 81.   [2] Chap. iii.

[3] Bergson mentions this " dormant " theory on page 81, but does not develop it. It is the really fundamental thing. And it is more worthily accounted for by the work of the Spirit than by the difficult concept of an impersonal biological force, the *élan vital*.

ing its desires at all, but using them quite craftily and deliberately. Intelligence does not always proceed to hinder its own hindrance. But there are also cases in which intelligent self-interest is given up *deliberately* for the sake of others or of the organism, without any sophistication. Bergson appears to ignore those instances in which intelligence takes a high place, willingly and wittingly sacrificing its own interests for those of the group.

What we chiefly miss in his psychological account is the inward morality, present even in the closed society; the conviction, for example, that purity of heart is right, even though it does not strengthen or defend the organism; that honesty is right and not simply those actions which happen to coincide with those of an honest man; that righteousness exalteth a nation, even though it imperils its material prosperity. Freedom, intelligence, choice—these play a much greater part in the closed society than Bergson will admit. It may be, and often is, egoistic choice; but it may be, and often is, altruistic choice, and because of this the closed society is potentially an open society. We must leave room for the prophet of morality, but we cannot forget that the prophet owes much also to society; gathers up the best in it, and shows the society the noblest that is dormant within itself.

3. There is a new (theistic) note in the book. For example (p. 188), " In our eyes, the ultimate end of mysticism is the establishment of a contact, consequently of a partial coincidence, with the creative effort of which life is the manifestation. This effort is of God, if not God Himself." But M. Bergson's discussion does not allow to failure and sin the place which is actually occupied by them in the experience of men. Nor does it say anything of the God whom sinful and forgiven men discern, in humility and wonder, to be still in love with them.

Neither morality nor religion can deny the initiative of God. The human *Ought* is intelligible only because of the divine *Is*. We do not pass from loving men to loving God, but rather from the experience of God's love for us to the challenge that we shall love men. " In the thought of

Jesus men are to be loved not because they are equally divine, but because God loves them equally ; and they are to be forgiven (the highest form of love) because all (the self included) are equally far from God and in need of His grace." [1]   Others try to show that man *is* such and such and therefore *ought to do* such and such. The right way is to show that God has revealed Himself as this and as that, and therefore man must do this and that. The divine indicative precedes the divine imperative. The moral imperative is not based on a possibility but on an order of reality. The love of God is first known through a response within man, but it *is* a response, not an initiation. Human effort is rewarded by wider vision, but it does not create that which is seen by the vision.

In the experience of redemption, man is made capable of seeing the good and of doing it. When God declares the sinner righteous, He is not saying about him that which is not true, but is acknowledging an actual new relationship produced by the Cross of Christ. In faith, man surrenders his whole being to Christ, crucified and risen, and thereby identifies himself with Christ's attitude to God and to sin.

[1] Reinhold Niebuhr, *An Interpretation of Christian Ethics*, p. 60.

CHAPTER IV
AUTHORITY AND REASON

SUMMARY

In spiritual matters certitude belongs not to reason but to love. Yet scepticism is not always sin. Reason was given for use. But there are very definite limits to scepticism. The faith of reason in itself means faith also in the ultimate rationality of the universe. In its broader meaning, reason is that which validates conviction. It includes the ethical attitude. The universe cannot be explained by its facts apart from its values. Reason includes an element akin to personal trust. It is increasingly recognised that it is harder to understand the impersonal than the personal.

In the sphere of religious knowledge it is found (i) that only the good man can understand the goodness of God ; (ii) that certainty implies obedience and consecration.

In our attitude to reason we are not confined to the alternatives of disinheritance or apotheosis. Lévy-Bruhl argues that reason has no place in the primitive mind. He finds there only pre-logical mentality. But, though there is a vast difference between the mental processes of primitive and developed man, the difference is one only of degree, not of kind. Compare the savage mind with the mental processes of the *mob* to-day and we find that the difference is greatly reduced.

Reason and Authority. The association of primitive religion with tribal *tabus* gives colour to theories of the predominance of authority in religion. It is true that the religious rite comes before the religious dogma. Nevertheless, it is clear that the rite has a meaning, an embryonic content ; that reason is at least nascent in it.

Durkheim has made a special study of the influence of the herd, the authority of the social organism. He holds, in effect, that God is simply a symbol for the social consciousness ; that the god of the clan can be nothing more than the clan itself. The truth appears to be precisely the opposite. Society is a symbol for God, and only a very inadequate symbol.

Closely linked with the influence of the herd is the part played by tradition. The Roman Catholic theologian, Karl Adam, writes that in order to arrive at the truth in matters of belief, we must get rid of self. "Autonomous" thinking lies in delusion. It may be readily granted to him that, when the mind is humble, reverent, receptive, it is then open to the deepest convictions. Man must rid himself of pride ; of the unworthy elements both in morality and in intellect. But the self must stand secure and autonomous. To seek for heteronomy is to open the door to the very doubtful and dangerous conclusion that truth may in the end be that which is given, for example, in the unconscious. The same warning is required by that trust in the authority of the words of Scripture which, being exaggerated, leads to Bibliolatry. We must not put out a person's eye and then try to persuade him to see with some one else's eye.

It may be asserted that autonomous thinking involves the danger of losing all certainty in belief. That is an unreal and unnecessary fear. Final certitude is not to be looked for, where none is in perfect communion with God. Yet it is real. In the highest forms of experience there may still be doubt, but on one point there is certainty, namely, that doubt is not due to any failure of the divine revelation, nor to any essential incomprehensibility of the Word of God.

CHAPTER IV

Authority and Reason

In spiritual matters certitude belongs not to reason but to love. Our conviction goes only so deep as our love. We persuade others of it, not by argument, but by declaration of it and by life in accordance with it. The proofs of the being of God have made many sceptics: the declaration of the love of God has made many saints.

Yet scepticism is not always and necessarily sin. Reason was given for use. Christian faith must philosophise, since Christ is the Truth as well as the Way and the Life.

The incorrigible sceptic argues that the processes of thought and the experiences of religion may, for all we know, yield no valid knowledge of reality. But there are very definite limits to scepticism. The sceptic must found his arguments on reason. Universal scepticism is a malady which cannot be cured, but it is also a position in which reason finds it impossible for a moment to rest. Reason inevitably believes in itself. Its " faith " in itself is indestructible and inexhaustible ; " and faith in itself means faith also in the ultimate rationality of the universe." [1]

" Reason " is one of those words which are very frequent on the lips and very nebulous in the mind. " Come, now, be *reasonable*," we say. What is meant by this appeal to be amenable to reason ? We should know the standard before we try to conform to it. It may not be possible to put it into words, yet apparently the meaning is discoverable, since we think of reason as that by which man, the rational being, *is* man. " Come, come," we say, " be a man ! " But, as Chesterton observed, to a crocodile that has just devoured its tenth explorer, we do not say, " Come, come, be a crocodile ! " 'Tis his nature to.

[1] Pringle-Pattison, *Scottish Philosophy*, 4th ed. p. 72.

In the sixth book of the *Republic*, Plato puts opinion (δόξα) at the lower level, discursive reason (διάνοια) next, and pure intellect or intuitive thought (νοῦς, νόησις) a stage higher. For the Stoics, λόγος is ontological. In one of its meanings it is the law that runs through the world, but reason as a procedure of the mind is not the ultimate test of truth. Like the Epicureans, they find that in experience. Among the Neo-Platonists mysticism, though a distinctive feature of the system, does not provide the criterion of truth. An experience which is ἔκστασις cannot be explained to one who has not passed through it. The criterion is reason, and the ideal reason is intuitive thought.

Intuitive reason (νοῦς in Plato) corresponds roughly to Kant's *Vernunft*, reason in an eminent sense, which seeks to comprehend experience as a total system. Discursive reason (Plato's διάνοια) then corresponds to Kant's *Verstand*, the faculty which relates one thing to another in experience, but does not rise above experience to transcendental ideas.[1]

Looking behind the terminology, perhaps we may say in general that there are two kinds of reason. (1) In the narrower sense, the word refers to the use of syllogistic argument, working on the data of observation, and acting in accordance with (*a*) the laws of thought and (*b*) the postulate of a reliable system of cause and effect. Here we have, in fact, the method of logic and of science.

(2) In its broader meaning, reason is that which validates conviction. It is not the conviction itself, but reflection on it, and it may be important to realise that reflection on an experience may *change* an experience. It is at least possible that reason in the act of reasoning may never be able to see the experience as it actually is. Reason, like the psychological method of introspection, may be in the position of the man who switches on the electric light quickly to see what darkness looks like, or the young lady who opens her eyes rapidly in front of the mirror to find what she looks like when she is asleep.

[1] See the article " Reason " in Hastings' *Encyclopædia of Religion and Ethics*, vol. x.

I. Our first argument must aim at showing that reason in the narrow sense is not sufficient of itself for any demonstration. Working as it does by syllogistic processes, it must assume the cogency of the laws of thought. It cannot " prove " them. Again, where it is employed by science or philosophy and is therefore no longer formal but provided with a content from the real world, reason must assume the self-consistency of reality. There is no point in reasoning if our conclusions are to have no bearing whatever on the probable behaviour of the world as it is. Attempts might be made to escape from the first difficulty by declaring that the laws of thought, though apparently intuitive, are really the long-established conclusions of syllogistic reasoning. But this will not serve. Intuition cannot depend on argument, since the truth is that argument depends everywhere on intuition. The conclusion follows from the premises by a kind of necessity, but it is not a necessity which can be proved by argument. The " therefore " is an important part of the syllogism. You cannot prove by argument that argument is valid. You cannot by reason demonstrate that reason is competent to do its work. There enters into reasoning an element akin to faith.

Nor can the second difficulty be outflanked. If we look outward to the object, instead of inward to the subject, we find that there is a large measure of faith in all science. With faith in man's mind as capable of comprehending, there must go faith in the orderliness of nature. " There could be no science if we began with chaos on the part of the universe and incompetency on the part of man." [1]

II. In the second place, we find that reason, even by such perfervid rationalists as Ingersoll, is taken to include the ethical attitude. Though they can give no ground for the faith that is in them, and though they appear therefore to include moral conceptions quite illegitimately, the rationalists are nevertheless right in this. Their conclusion is sound, though their premises are wrong. They are

[1] *Humanist Sermons* (1927), edited by Curtis W. Reese (The Open Court Publishing Co., Chicago), p. 39.

aware that the universe cannot be explained by an account of its *facts*; there must also be some account of its *values*. Science and philosophy alike are seeking objectivity, escape from illusions and from the danger of allowing the wish to be father to the thought. They want to understand reality. But it will not be sufficient to discover what the facts are. We must press on to inquire why it is that just these facts are there and not others. Logical self-consistency is not enough. A totally different universe might be logically self-consistent. Why do we have *this* universe and not another? The only answer to this question appears to be that of the idealist tradition from Plato onwards. Science and philosophy want to present reality as an intelligible system. But the system is not yet intelligible if we do not know why it is this system and not another. It must be shown as a self-authenticating reality. And reality can be self-authenticating only if it is *good*. " A materialistic universe," writes Professor Hodgson, " taken by itself, may have to be accepted as brute fact, but it cannot be understood. There must be intelligence in that which is intelligible. Plato took the further step of asserting that only goodness is intrinsically intelligible, so that goodness alone is ultimately real, and all things are real only in so far as they participate in it. The criteria of reality are logical consistency (which is the criterion of fact) and self-justifying goodness (which is the criterion of value). Not one or other is required, but both at once." [1]

III. Thirdly, reason includes an element akin to personal trust. It is not to be conceived as restricted in application solely to that which can be weighed and measured, counted and analysed, that is, to the subject-matter of physics, chemistry and the like. That which is amenable to these operations is not the real world. It must not be supposed that the impersonal is something easily intelligible. It is being increasingly recognised that it is in fact far harder to understand than the personal. It might even be safe to say that, though we do not understand the personal fully, we do not understand the impersonal at all.

[1] Leonard Hodgson, *The Grace of God* (Longmans, 1936), p. 51.

IV. There is, therefore, a type of judgment which is a judgment of reason, though it is not capable of syllogistic proof.

The ideal of the metaphysician is to arrive at certainty regarding the truth. How is he to reach it ? The answer depends on the kind of certainty which he desires. There are two contrasted types : (*A*) That which belongs to mathematical theorems and logical rules ; to knowledge of present-day facts ; to the records of past history. This type of certainty rests on calculation, on observation, on logical reasoning, on the testing of reports. (*B*) The second type is that which is represented by knowledge concerning, for instance, a mother's love, a friend's loyalty. In the first, concerned with matters of fact, our will must not enter. The personal equation is to be rigidly excluded. A scientist must not look only at the facts which suit a preconceived pet theory. " Sit down before fact as a little child," T. H. Huxley wrote in a letter to Charles Kingsley. " Follow humbly and to whatever abysses Nature leads, or you shall learn nothing." Facts are here the guiding stars. Desire and will have no place.

In knowledge of the second type, on the contrary, our will must enter into the matter before we can arrive at certainty. There is required of us a specific moral attitude or decision. If a man is a " trimmer," if, in the German phrase, he hangs his coat against the wind, he can never believe, with certainty, in the existence of a man on whom he can rely absolutely, whom nothing will move from the line which he has once conscientiously adopted. He believes that every man has his price. He will undertake to capture a city if the gates are wide enough for a wagon of gold to be driven in.

The first type of knowledge distrusts everything that cannot be seen and touched, measured and proved. The second rests on *trust*. In the sphere of the second type, (1) A man must have the thing within him before he can apprehend it elsewhere ; (2) a man must trust before he can be certain. The consequences for religious knowledge are therefore two : (1) Only the good man can understand the goodness of God. Only the converted man can speak the truth about redemption ; (2) Certainty implies obedience and consecration. It is the outcome of a venture of faith.

Let us see first that certainty is not to be found in the former type of knowledge. It, in turn, may be divided into two sorts—(i) truths of reason ; (ii) truths of fact— what Leibniz called *vérités de raison* and *vérités de fait*. Under (i) we have logico-mathematical truths as, for example, " Two plus Two equals Four " ; or " The straight line is the shortest distance between two points " ; or " It is impossible that the same predicate should both belong and not belong to the same thing at the same time and in the same way." [1] These appear to be the most certain statements which can be made, but on examination we find that all of them are hypothetical and no more. Mathematical statements have nothing to say of the reality of their subject-matter. Even the law of non-contradiction goes a very little way. In the case, for example, of an accused person pleading an alibi, the law of non-contradiction establishes no facts. We cannot prove by it that it is impossible for a man to be in two places at once. The rule can say nothing about the facts which it appears to control. Yet as a law it is in the strongest of positions. In the very act of questioning this law of non-contradiction, we must assume its truth. We are told, " This law is beyond all doubt." If we reply, " I do not agree ; I am going to question it," we are saying in effect, " I deny that it is beyond all doubt," implying that both cannot be true—(i) beyond doubt and (ii) not beyond doubt.

Nevertheless, even this does not go beyond the hypothetical. What it does say is that, if thinking is rational at all, it must proceed according to this law. It cannot say that thinking *is* rational.

(ii) Questions of fact. Here the opposite is quite thinkable. It involves no inner contradiction. But here we are faced by the difficulties which beset all evidence.

[1] τὸ γὰρ αὐτὸ ἅμα ὑπάρχειν τε καὶ μὴ ὑπάρχειν ἀδύνατον τῷ αὐτῷ καὶ κατὰ τὸ αὐτό (Aristotle, *Metaphysics*, Γ. iii. 1005, b. 20).

None of these truths is immediately perceived. They depend, perhaps, on the evidence of our senses, concerning which grave doubts have often been raised. (Who would have dreamed that what we see and touch is a multitude of molecules in motion ?—if it is even that.) Or we learn of happenings from other people, and that is notoriously untrustworthy evidence. (We need only point to cases of unbiased witnesses giving independent testimony in a law-court of the same occurrence.) Or we are concerned with matters which are in the past or in the future, and therefore with a process which involves still more mediation.

The first type of knowledge appears to give certainty because of its principle of non-contradiction, but this is at the expense of all contact with the matter to which these laws of thought are applied. We have here only a formal principle of certainty. As soon as we begin to fill it with content, uncertainty creeps in. For the second type of knowledge is not immediate knowledge. There is an " ugly ditch " between fact and truth.

Now therefore we must return to the second of the two larger divisions—to judgments of trust and confidence. These are in a different category from the other two (truths of reason and matters of fact). Here we have a wholly different type of certainty. It might be said, indeed, that very frequently we are confident concerning matters of fact only because of *this* kind of confidence in persons. We accept our account of things which have happened because we trust the witnesses who tell about them. It is instructive to notice the technique of " queer stories." There is a circle within a circle. The skill of the author makes us believe in the first group of people and, having suggested their veracity, he finds it easier to carry conviction about the story retailed within this group.

Judgments of the type under discussion are, in fact, made again and again with great confidence. Men trust their friends far beyond what they can see or prove, and their confidence is reasonable. (So much so that it would be considered a dishonourable proceeding to ask for *proofs* of loyalty.) We may hear derogatory rumours about a friend of our own, and we know at once that they can be denied without the formality of an investigation. The rumour may appear substantial. Nevertheless, this confidence in the character of a friend is unshaken. This is, indeed, the nearest approach to certainty that we have in human affairs. And it comes, not by proof, nor by argument, but by the way of trust. It is a different type of certainty. Its highest form is that shown by the religious man who trusts God in spite, as we say, of appearances. " Though He slay me, yet will I trust in Him " (Job xiii. 15).[1]

It is right that we should have what justification is available for what we believe, but it does not follow that the only justification is that which can be reduced to the form of a logical demonstration. " We use tests, no doubt," the late Principal Galloway says, writing of this kind of judgment, " to correct our instinctive feelings, but these tests always fall far short of demonstration. And I venture to think that what is true here is symptomatic of a wider truth, the truth, namely, that proof in the strict sense is never complete. Our deductive procedure always breaks short ; there always comes a point when we have to accept something simply as given without being able to rationalise it. Thus the man of science is constantly confronted with unrationalised elements in the realm of nature." [2]

It is important, above all, to notice that reason must not be confined to knowledge of the impersonal. There are those, says Professor Hodgson,[3] who are still under the hypnotic influence of the nineteenth century, and count nothing real unless it can be " explained " in terms of physical necessity. We have passed beyond the time when it is possible to imagine that the impersonal is more intelligible than the personal. We are realising that the impersonal must be explained by the personal, and not *vice versa*.

This supposed necessity of restricting reason to the

---

[1] See further on this subject, Karl Heim, *Glaubensgewissheit* (Dritte Auflage), pp. 1–30.

[2] *Faith and Reason in Religion*, pp. 10–11.

[3] See *Essays in Christian Philosophy*, pp. 48–51, and *The Grace of God*, p. 153.

impersonal partly accounts for a widespread modern
tendency to suspect the rational in man and to be guided by
irrational impulses and urges. A stimulating essay by René
Fülöp-Miller is entitled " The Revolt against Reason." [1] We
see this revolt in politics. In Italy, the fascists are opposed
to all that is rational in the realm of politics, enlightened
thought, liberalism, democracy. It is not the calm reason
of an educated people which is to be in control, but irrational
forces, embodying the creative will of a nation and per-
sonalised in a Duce who has been not elected but mythically
appointed. In Germany there is added to the idea of a
Messianic Führer the concept of the sacred race. All that
is greatest and most creative is rooted in instinct, in
sensation, in the blood. The God who is really worshipped
is the idol of the nation. " In the beginning was the People,
and the People was with God, and the People was God "—
that was the text of a sermon delivered at a great gathering
of German Christians.[2] " To-day," says Alfred Rosenberg,
" a new faith has arisen ; the blood-myth, the belief that
to fight for the Blood is to fight for the divine in man ;
the belief—embodied with a vision that leaves no possibility for doubt—that the Nordic Blood presents that
mystery by which the ancient sacraments are superseded
and transcended. . . . The soul of the people, bound to one
particular race, is the measure of all our thoughts, desires,
and activities, the ultimate standard of our values. . . .
This inner voice demands to-day that the blood-myth and
the soul-myth, Race and Self, People and Personality,
Blood and Honour, these alone, these and literally nothing
else, without any kind of compromise, must penetrate,
support, and determine the whole of life. . . . The God
whom we reverence would have no existence but for our
Soul and our Blood." [3]

We turn to science. Many biologists have ceased to

---

[1] *Hibbert Journal*, January, 1936.

[2] See Professor Nygren, *The Church Controversy in Germany* (Student
Christian Movement Press, 1934), p. 89.

[3] Alfred Rosenberg, *Der Mythus des 20 Jahrhunderts*, 3rd ed. 1932,
pp. 43, 129, 682. See Karl Heim, *God Transcendent*, p. 7.

look for an explanation of life in material or mechanistic terms. Hans Driesch supports his Neo-Vitalism on minute and careful experiments in embryology. His " entelechy " is not just the discredited " vital force," but that which arranges and co-ordinates. Having divided the fertilised ovum of a sea-urchin into four parts, he discovered, for example, that each part developed into a tiny but perfect sea-urchin. In some manner incomprehensible to him on the mechanistic theory, each quarter was able to develop into a fully formed adult. Phenomena such as these cannot be explained by the action of stimuli from without, nor by chemical processes from within. There is therefore some agent at work in morphogenesis which is not of the type of any known physico-chemical agents.

In astronomy again it is being said that the starry universe is not so much like a great machine as like a great thought. And, if we turn to the infinitesimal, we find Planck suggesting that nature, once supposed never to make a leap, moves all the time by leaps. Poincaré, the astronomer, even hazarded the guess that if men had possessed eyes with the power of the microscope, the laws of nature would never have been discovered. These laws are not able, he thought, to endure too close and precise a scrutiny.

In philosophy, we have Bergson turning away from rational cognition and falling back on the vital impulse, the *élan vital* ; declaring that man's real knowledge arises not from reason, but from that immediate knowledge which we call intuition.

In psychology we have learned of unconscious, irrational impulses, racial memories, and symbols influencing, perhaps determining the conscious life.

Fülöp-Miller, though a " new psychologist," is not himself a participant in this revolt against reason. His general conclusion is " that the revolt against reason now in progress will ultimately lead to a synthesis between rationalism and irrationalism, to a middle principle of practical application. The revolt will have taught us not, as heretofore, to expect everything from reason. We shall have accustomed ourselves to give due weight to the vast reality of the irrational alike in nature and in human thought and action—to give the irrational its standing-ground in our otherwise logically fashioned system of the world. From the frank recognition of the irrational as an irreducible datum, we shall gain in the long run this much, that reason, far from being sentenced to death, will have been extricated from our present-day confusions."

It is fairly plain that his essay has quoted instances of the revolt against reason which are of very different degrees of wisdom and unwisdom, and in some at least we may detect elements which are not so much irrational as un-rationalised. It is plain also that the solution does not lie in " a synthesis between rationalism and irrationalism " but rather in a widening of our concept of reason, which hitherto has been too narrowly interpreted.[1]

In our attitude towards reason we are not bound to the alternatives of disinheritance or apotheosis. It would certainly be wrong, for instance, to ascribe a high degree of rationality to the primitive mind. Dr. R. R. Marett complains of Sir James Frazer that he makes the savage reason like an honours graduate in philosophy (without, however, indicating how high is the standard thus implied). " Pure ratiocination," he says, " seems to be credited with an effectiveness without a parallel in early culture. Almost as well say that, when man found he could not make big enough bags with the throwing-stick, he sat down and excogitated the bow-and-arrow." [2]

On the other hand, we must not fall into the opposite error. Lévy-Bruhl argues that reason has no place at all in the primitive mind. He finds there only *pre-logical mentality*. The savage mind, he thinks, is not simply un-developed : it is different in kind. " The profound differ-ence existing between primitive mentality and our own is seen even in the ordinary perception, or mere apprehension

---

[1] See also de Burgh, *Towards a Religious Philosophy* (Macdonald & Evans, 1937), chap. i. Reason is not to be limited to logical inference. Will and feeling must be included or even *the intellect* is left unsatisfied.

[2] *The Threshold of Religion* (Methuen, 1914), p. 34.

of the very simplest things. Primitive perception is funda-
mentally mystic on account of the mystic nature of the
collective representations which form an integral part of
every perception." [1] "Among the differences which
distinguish the mentality of primitive communities from
our own, there is one which has attracted the attention
of many of those who have observed such peoples under
the most favourable conditions—that is, before their ideas
have been modified by prolonged association with white
races. These observers have maintained that primitives
manifest a decided distaste for reasoning, for what logicians
call the ' discursive operations of thought ' ; at the same
time they have remarked that this distaste did not arise
out of any radical incapability or any inherent defect in
their understanding, but was rather to be accounted for
by their general methods of thought." [2] "As long as we
assume that their minds are orientated like our own, that
they react as ours do to the impressions made upon them,
we assume, by implication, that they *should* reason and
reflect as ours do with regard to the phenomena and
entities of the known world. But we agree that as a matter
of fact they neither reason nor reflect thus, and to explain
this apparent anomaly we make use of a number of different
hypotheses, such as the feebleness and torpidity of their
minds, their perplexity, childlike ignorance, stupidity, etc.,
none of which take the facts sufficiently into account." If
we rid our minds of these preconceived ideas, we shall find
that the mental activity of primitives " will appear to be
normal under the conditions in which it is employed, to
be both complex and developed in its own way." [3] The
primitive, it is maintained, has but slight perception of the
law of contradiction. His mentality is essentially mystic.
" This fundamental characteristic permeates his whole
method of thinking, feeling, and acting, and from this
circumstance arises the extreme difficulty of comprehending
and following its course. Starting from sense-impressions,

[1] *Les Fonctions Mentales dans les Sociétés Inférieures*, p. 38.
[2] *Primitive Mentality* (E.T.) (Allen & Unwin, 1923), p. 21.
[3] *Ibid*. pp. 32–33.

which are alike in primitives and ourselves, it makes an abrupt turn, and enters on paths which are unknown to us, and we soon find ourselves astray. If we try to guess why primitives do, or refrain from doing, certain things, what prejudices they obey in given cases, the reasons which compel them with regard to any special course, we are most likely to be mistaken. We may find an " explanation " which is more or less probable, but nine times out of ten it will be the wrong one." [1] " The primitive mind, like our own, is anxious to find the reasons for what happens, but it does not seek these in the same direction as we do. It moves in a world where innumerable occult powers are everywhere present, and always in action or ready to act." [2]

The substratum of truth in this theory is found perhaps in two considerations : (1) For the primitive mind, action is much more important than thought. The rites and practices of worship come before the dogmas. As Dr. Marett says, savage religion is not so much *thought* out as *danced* out. (2) As with animals, primitive man is largely ruled by the association of ideas. The farmer, driving to market, finds that his horse refuses to cross the ford. He recalls that the last time they passed that way the river was in flood, and whipping up the horse he says, " Come on, Donald, your memory is better than your judgment." Again, for the savage mind, temporal sequence means necessary connection. He does not have any place for coincidence. But too much stress must not be laid on this. There are many occasions on which all of us accept sequences which we cannot explain. We drive a car, perhaps, without knowing very much about the internal combustion engine. A familiar example is given by Professor Waterhouse [3] : When we " dial " a telephone number, most of us do not know what happens. We believe that there is a scientific explanation, but it is enough for us that, given the right movements, the connection will be duly made.

It is evident that there is a vast difference between the mental processes of primitive man and those, say, of a

[1] *Primitive Mentality*, p. 431.　　　　[2] *Ibid.* p. 437.
[3] *The Dawn of Religion* (Epworth Press, 1936), p. 73.

modern scientist or philosopher. But the difference, surely, is one not of kind but of degree. Compare the savage mind with the mental processes of *the mob* to-day and we find that the difference is greatly reduced. At root the mental mechanisms of child, savage, and developed minds are alike. " Primitive emotion and superstition is not far beneath the surface of civilisation. Scratch a Russian and you find a Tartar, scratch a civilised man and you find a savage. Civilised and savage are brothers ' under the skin.' " [1]

The weakness of this theory of pre-logical mentality is seen by a single consideration. The savage could never have survived if for practical purposes he did not make use of the logical principles of causality and of non-contradiction.[2]

We have suggested that reason will always return to its rightful place. What that is we may best determine by looking at those things with which reason is usually contrasted. And, as we are concerned primarily with the relation of reason to faith, these contrasts may be reduced to three. Reason is opposed to (1) Authority ; (2) Feeling ; (3) Revelation. The second and third will be discussed in the next chapter.

1. Consider the suggestion that reason has no place in religion because authority is paramount.

According to Heraclitus, the eyes are more trustworthy than the ears, but the soul is the best witness of all.[3] This is vague enough, but it does suggest that the ears (tradition) are less reliable than the eyes (experience), while best of all is the soul (reason). It is the opposite of this that we have to consider. The soul, it is said, has no standing against the ears. Tradition, or some other form of authority, delivers the commands which must be obeyed, and declares the faith which must be held.

---

[1] Waterhouse, *op. cit.* p. 18 ; p. 17.

[2] Cf. George Galloway, *Faith and Reason in Religion*, p. 74.

[3] ὀφθαλμοὶ τῶν ὤτων ἀκριβέστεροι μάρτυρες and κακοὶ μάρτυρες ἀνθρώποισιν ὀφθαλμοὶ καὶ ὦτα βαρβάρους ψυχὰς ἐχόντων. See Burnet, *Early Greek Philosophy*, 2nd ed. p. 147, note 2. Compare *Encyclopædia of Religion and Ethics*, vol. x. p. 593 b.

The suggestion that reason has no place may take the form of saying that in actual fact it is authority which determines men's faith. A. J. Balfour used the term "authority" in contrast with reason to stand for "that group of non-rational causes, moral, social, and educational, which produces its results by psychic processes other than reasoning."[1] Auguste Sabatier defines authority as "the right of the species over the individual."[2] Gwatkin has defined it as "all weight allowed to the beliefs of persons or the teachings of institutions beyond their reasonable value as personal testimony."[3] But discussion concerning the actual influence of authority is now tending more towards a study of the phenomena of primitive religions and the light which that may throw on the nature of developed religion. The association of primitive religion with tribal *tabus* gives colour to the theory of authority. It is true that the religious *rite* comes before the religious *dogma*. Nevertheless, it is clear that the rite has a meaning, an embryonic intellectual content ; that reason is at least nascent in it.

Admittedly, the non-rational factors play a very important part in the acquisition of belief. Man is *suggestible*. He does not believe a thing chiefly because reason shows it to be credible, even undeniable. He believes it because of influences brought to bear on him. These may be found in the home, in his training and nurture as a child ; in his adolescent or adult environment ; in tradition. Suggestion might be defined as a process resulting in the acceptance and realisation of an idea in the absence of adequate logical grounds.[4] Sir Baldwin Spencer tells how he once persuaded a native of Central Australia to hold in his hand, to be photographed, a "pointing-stick"—a stick that was reputed to kill a man, even at a distance, by projecting evil influence into him. The native, holding the stick, was

[1] *The Foundations of Belief*, 8th ed. (1901), p. 232.
[2] *The Religions of Authority and the Religion of the Spirit* (E.T. 1904), p. xxiv.
[3] *The Knowledge of God*, vol. i. p. 3.
[4] See David Yellowlees, *Psychology's Defence of the Faith* (Student Christian Movement Press, 1930), p. 19.

6

suddenly convinced that the weapon had " kicked," projecting the evil influence backwards into himself. Down
he sank, and it looked as if he might die there and then.
But the professor luckily had a very potent counter-magic
with him, which brought the patient round. It consisted
of a dose of Eno's Fruit Salts.[1]

Suggestion exercises a profound and far-reaching
influence. George Steven considers, for example, the widespread effect of public opinion. It imposes itself upon us
without our knowing. We imitate modes of thought and
behaviour. We *conform*. And even the non-conformist
does not escape. Those who defy the public opinion of
which they are conscious are, in all probability, paying
deference to another public opinion too subtle for them to
detect. " A hooligan defies the police and the settled order
of the nation, but acts for the applause of the public-house
which he knows is waiting for him. At the opposite pole
of the moral world, the martyr for civil or religious liberty
may hear with his ears the yells of a frantic mob, but with
his soul the praise of good men in other lands or other
times, or it may be the ' Well done ! ' of God Himself.
We are all encompassed with a cloud of witnesses, in whose
sight we are running our race to some goal or other. It is
our spiritual, not our material, environment that fashions
us." [2]

Occasionally we see those who are *contra*-suggestible—
the rebels, the " permanent opposition," those who set
themselves violently against the current of the day. If
they hear of a " generally accepted " opinion, that is enough
for them to denounce it. If they hear the crowd shout
" Goal ! " they immediately cry, " Off-side ! " It may be
that, just as some people are super-suggestible, so there
are others who are temperamentally contra-suggestible.
Those who are too much under the influence of suggestion
are the undeveloped ; reason has not won its right place
in their lives. But those others, who make a point of

---

[1] See Marett, *Man in the Making* (Ernest Benn, 1927), p. 22.
[2] George Steven, *The Psychology of the Christian Soul* (Hodder &
Stoughton, 1911), p. 43.

resisting every suggestion, are quite as likely to be ill-equipped. Their attitude may perhaps be traced, in many cases, to an early experience of being tyrannised over. This has resulted in a constant refusal to be influenced even by a wise and legitimate authority. The contra-suggestible are, in art and religion, the *cranks*.

One aspect of the non-rational factor in belief deserves special consideration—the influence of the herd, the authority of the tribe or other social organism.

Emile Durkheim has made a special study of this aspect. (Like most pioneers, he overestimates the importance of his own sphere of investigation.) He writes as follows : " The traditional theories which thought to find the source of religion in individual feelings, like reverential fear, which inspire us all, whether it be the play of great cosmic forces or the spectacle of certain natural phenomena like that of death, must be more than suspect. We ought to look for the source in *collective* feelings, in the experiences and sentiments of the group." [1]

This is too bald and uncompromising a statement. The religious experience will never be understood without some consideration of the attitude of the individual, his private hopes and fears, joys and sorrows, despair and blessedness. But the caution is needed. Religion cannot be accounted for by these private feelings *alone*.[2] It is neither possible nor desirable to dissociate the individual from corporate religious experience. Isolation is incompatible with development. Man is a Πολιτικὸν ζῷον. If he can live a completely solitary life, he is no longer a man, but either a beast or a god.[3] Much is possible in corporate worship which could not come to a man in the isolation of his own sanctuary. In particular, as Principal Galloway wrote, " religious belief, which represents the objective aspect of religious experience, is essentially dependent on

[1] *L'Année Sociologique*, ii. p. 24.

[2] See also C. C. J. Webb, *Group Theories of Religion and the Religion of the Individual*, and Le Bon, *The Crowd*.

[3] Aristotle, *Pol.*, I. 2, 9, 1253a 2 ; *Eth. Nic.*, I. 7, 6, 1097b 11, and VII. 1, 2, 1145a 25.

the mediation of society. From the social whole it derives stability and continuity. As far back as we can trace religion we find that, like language, it is a social heritage, and the single man does little or nothing in the way of invention or innovation." [1]

Dr. R. R. Marett approaches the subject of communal religion [2] by recalling the story from Herodotus of the experiment made by Psammetichus—the "incubator-method," as Dr. Marett calls it. [3] He asks whether this *bekos* experiment could be carried out in religion. We cannot, perhaps, isolate a baby and watch to see whether, of its own accord, it begins not merely to talk, but to *pray*. We might, however, transplant a child from savage to civilised surroundings or *vice versa*. What would be the result ? " Would a young totemist notwithstanding evolve in the one case and a young Christian in the other ? Or would not the child acquire the religion of its adopted home, of the society that rears and educates it ? Even when full allowance is made for the fact that each child reacts on its education in an individual fashion, can there be the slightest shadow of doubt that the supreme determining influence must rest with the social factor ? " [4]

Professor A. N. Whitehead has declared (without,

[1] Galloway, *The Philosophy of Religion*, p. 87. It may be felt that this is so stated as to leave little place for the prophetic contribution, but it is to be remembered also that the prophet, too, has grown up in a religious environment, and that his task may largely consist of interpreting to the group its own better, but latent, potentialities ; recalling it to an inheritance of which the richness has never been entered upon or even realised.

[2] *The Threshold of Religion*, pp. 122 ff.

[3] Herodotus II. 2. Compare Pitscottie's *Cronicles of Scotland*, edited by Æ. J. G. Mackay (Blackwood, 1899), vol. i. p. 237 (I. fol. 49b) : And also the king (James IV.) " gart tak ane dum woman and pat hir in Inchekeytht and gaif hir tua zoung bairnes in companie witht hir and gart furnische them of all necessar thingis pertening to thair nurischment that is to say, meit, drink, fyre and candell, claithis, witht all wther kynd of necessaris quhilk is requyrit to man or woman desyrand the effect heirof to come to knaw quhat langage thir bairnes wald speik quhene they come to lauchfull aige. Sum sayis they spak goode hebrew bot as to my self I knew not bot be the authoris reherse."

[4] *The Threshold of Religion*, p. 135.

perhaps, intending the words to be an attempt at strict
definition) that religion is what the individual does with
his own solitariness.[1] Probably the exact opposite is true
historically. The social element is of fundamental importance. At the early stage the individual is a tribesman
rather than a man. " It was a national not a personal
Providence," says Robertson Smith, " that was taught by
ancient religion. So much was this the case that in purely
personal concerns the ancients were very apt to turn, not
to the recognised religion of the family or of the state, but
to magical superstitions." [2]

All this may be readily granted. But it is not necessary
to take the next step, which is taken by the " sociological "
school. It is said, in effect, that God is simply a symbol
for the social consciousness. Whatever is obligatory is of
social origin. An absolute command can come only from
that which is greater than ourselves, and the only thinking
being which is greater than ourselves—so empirical science
feels bound to say—is society. The religious and the social
become synonymous. The God of the clan can be nothing
else than the clan itself.

" In a general way, it is unquestionable that a society
has all that is necessary to arouse the sensation of the
divine in minds, merely by the power that it has over
them ; for to its members it is what a god is to his wor-
shippers. In fact, a god is, first of all, a being whom men
think of as superior to themselves, and upon whom they
feel that they depend. Whether it be a conscious personality,
such as Zeus or Jahveh, or merely abstract forces such as
those in play in totemism, the worshipper, in the one case
as in the other, believes himself held to certain manners
of acting which are imposed upon him by the nature of the
sacred principle with which he feels that he is in communion. Now society also gives us the sensation of a
perpetual dependence. Since it has a nature which is
peculiar to itself and different from our individual nature,
it pursues ends which are likewise special to it ; but, as it

[1] *Religion in the Making* (Cambridge, 1926), pp. 37 and 48.
[2] *The Religion of the Semites*, pp. 263–264.

cannot attain them except through our intermediacy, it
imperiously demands our aid.   It requires that, forgetful
of our own interests, we make ourselves its servitors, and
it submits us to every sort of inconvenience, privation, and
sacrifice, without which social life would be impossible.
It is because of this that at every instant we are obliged
to submit ourselves to rules of conduct and of thought
which we have neither made nor desired, and which are
sometimes even contrary to our most fundamental inclina-
tions and instincts." [1]   The religious life is the eminent
form and, as it were, the concentrated expression of the
whole collective life.   " If religion has given birth to all
that is essential in society, it is because the idea of society
is the soul of religion." [2]

Readers of Professor John Macmurray's book,[3] will
recognise the theme.   Religion, in his estimation, is simply
the sphere of personal relations.   " The field of religion is
the field of personal experience.   The centre of this field is
the experience we have of other persons in relation to
ourselves.   In all our relations with one another we are in
the field of religion " (p. 45).   It is perhaps not surprising
that Professor Macmurray, in his final chapter, on " The
Reference of Religious Ideas," mentions God only once—
and that because the word occurs in the quotation which
he makes.   He presents religion as simply community,
mutuality of relations between persons.   But this is precisely *not* religion if the Godward reference is omitted.
Pressed to its conclusion the sociological theory would find
in religion a collective hallucination which takes the
internal structure of society and transforms it into an
objective reality.[4]

It is certainly not surprising that society should exhibit
some of the features of God, since God is love and acts in
a kingdom of love.   But, so far from its being true that

[1] Durkheim, *The Elementary Forms of the Religious Life* (E.T.) (Allen
& Unwin), pp. 206-207.

[2] *Op. cit.* p. 419.

[3] *The Structure of Religious Experience* (Faber & Faber, 1936).

[4] Cf. Pringle-Pattison, *Studies in the Philosophy of Religion* (Oxford,
1930), p. 38.

God is only a symbol for society, the very reverse would appear to be the case. Society is a symbol for God, and only a very inadequate symbol. Two facts cannot be accounted for by the sociological theory. (1) Society takes notice only of the outward conformity of an act to its own laws. But, in religion, the important things are soon recognised to be the motive of the act and the purity of the heart. " Conscience takes on an authority which can, on occasion, defy all the behests of society, for man must now obey God rather than his fellows." [1] (2) The pioneer in morality is almost always the man who breaks with conventional conduct. Progress is frequently due to the martyr, and the martyr is usually the rebel against society ; his death is met at the hands of society.

Religion at its higher levels is something very different from conformity to public opinion, and that which is a criterion of real progress cannot be a non-essential at any stage in the development of religion nor altogether negligible even in the earliest stages.

Professor D. M. Baillie has rightly questioned whether sociologists like Durkheim have made a case even for the primitive religions with which they deal.[2] And Dr. Marett remarks on the " real danger lest the anthropologist should think that a scientific view of man is to be obtained by leaving out the human nature in him. This comes from the over-anxiety of evolutionary history to arrive at general principles." Anthropology " should not disdain what might

---

[1] H. H. Farmer, *The World and God* (Nisbet, 1935), p. 57. It is true that society is not altogether regardless of motives. (1) It may inquire whether there is any adequate motive to account for the commission of a crime. But this may be dismissed, since the object of the investigation is merely to aid in the establishing of guilt or innocence. (2) In pronouncing sentence, a court of law may use clemency if it feels that a man was provoked into attacking another, or that he acted in self-defence, or was in fear of his life, or had a wife and children threatened by starvation. But even here we have no more than considerations of self-protection on the part of the state. It mitigates the penalty because the full rigour of the law is not required for deterrent purposes. All that concerns the state is its own preservation and defence.

[2] See *Faith in God and its Christian Consummation* (T. & T. Clark, 1927), p. 61.

be termed the method of the historical novel. To study
the plot without studying the characters will never make
sense of the drama of human life. It may seem a truism,
but is perhaps worth recollecting at the start, that no man
or woman lacks individuality altogether, even if it cannot
be regarded in a particular case as a high individuality. No
one is a mere item. That useful figment of the statistician
has no real existence under the sun. We need to supplement the books of abstract theory with much sympathetic
insight directed towards men and women in their concrete
selfhood." [1]

How far the notion of the herd may lead even wise
men astray is illustrated in a passage from Professor Gilbert
Murray.[2] " We are gregarious animals ; our ancestors have
been such for countless ages. We cannot help looking out
on the world as gregarious animals do ; we see it in terms
of humanity and of fellowship. Students of animals under
domestication have shown us how the habits of a gregarious
creature, taken away from his kind, are shaped in a thousand details by reference to the lost pack which is no longer
there—the pack which a dog tries to smell his way back
to all the time he is out walking, the pack he calls to for
help when danger threatens. It is a strange and touching
thing, this eternal hunger of the gregarious animal for the
herd of friends who are not there. And it may be, it may
very possibly be, that, in the matter of this Friend behind
phenomena, our own yearning and our almost ineradicable
instinctive conviction, since they are certainly not founded
on either reason or observation, are in origin the groping
of a lonely-souled gregarious animal to find its herd or its
herd leader in the great spaces between the stars."

Durkheim does not consider that religion is founded on
illusion. On the contrary, the power which is reverenced
does exist. It is society. Its symbol is the totem. Principal
Galloway once asked acutely whether the totem does not
simply represent the unity of the group which traces its

---

[1] *Anthropology* (Williams & Norgate, 1911), pp. 242–243.
[2] *The Stoic Philosophy*, p. 41 ; quoted, with approval, by M. C. Otto,
Things and Ideals, p. 231.

descent back to the totem-ancestor, and added that if Durkheim's theory is to be a general account of the origin of religious beliefs, then he is committed to the view that totemism is as universal as religion. Of this, however, there is no evidence, and the known facts make it quite improbable.[1]

Closely linked with the influence of the herd instinct is the part played by *tradition*. Psychologists of the last generation and religious teachers for many centuries have recognised the importance of the family, as a social group, in fostering religion. It is in the earlier years of childhood —certainly before adolescence—that tradition is transmitted. " Much is learned after puberty, but in childhood education is more than mere learning. There, education is the growth of the disposition, the fixing of the prejudices, to which all later experience is cumulative." [2] The authority exercised on the young mind is therefore of supreme importance in the acquisition of beliefs, and just because of this it is essential that religious teachers and the Church everywhere should avoid the illegitimate exercise and pressure of authority. There is such a thing as the wrongful arrest of the personality. It may take place in childhood, or it may consist in the capturing of the adult personality through the impression of power, ecstasy, and the like, where no regard is paid to conscience, the citadel of the free personality. Truth comes, not by overruling of the personality, the wrongful arrest of it, but by the illumination, conserving, and uplifting of it.

Professor Karl Adam, of the Roman Catholic Faculty in Tübingen, makes this plea for authority : [3] In order to arrive at the truth in matters of belief, we must get rid of self. " Autonomous " thinking lies in delusion. " The first ' autonomous ' man in the ethico-religious sense was Adam, when he took the fruit of the tree of life.[4] And so man no

---

[1] *Faith and Reason in Religion*, pp. 76–77.

[2] Lippmann, *A Preface to Morals*, p. 91.

[3] *The Spirit of Catholicism* (E.T.) (Sheed & Ward, 1934), p. 38.

[4] So Professor Adam writes, meaning " the tree of the knowledge of good and evil."

longer had any source whence he might renew his strength, except his own small self. He had abandoned the eternal source of living water and dug himself a poor cistern in his own self. And the waters of this cistern were soon exhausted. Man fell sick and died. His self was his sickness and his self was his death."

We readily agree that, when the mind is humble, reverent, receptive, it is then open to the deepest convictions. Man must rid himself of pride ; of the unworthy elements both in morality and in intellect, but the *self*, surely, must stand secure and autonomous ; not in self-will, but in spiritual freedom. To get rid of it ; to seek for heteronomy, is to open the door to the very doubtful and dangerous conclusion that truth may in the end be that which is given, let us say, in the unconscious.

The same warning is required by that trust in the authority of the words of Scripture which, being exaggerated, leads to Bibliolatry. One writer has said that " we put out a person's eye, and then try to persuade him that he ought to see with some one else's eye." [1]

On the other side, it may be asserted that autonomous thinking involves the danger of losing all certainty in belief ; the danger of falling back into pure subjectivity. That is an unreal and unnecessary fear. Final certitude, indeed, is not to be looked for, where none is in perfect communion with God. It is asymptotic. Yet it is real. In the highest forms of experience there may still be doubt, but on one point there is certitude, namely, that doubt is not due to any failure in the divine revelation, nor to any essential inapprehensibility of the Word of God.

[1] Weigel, quoted by W. R. Inge, *Faith and its Psychology* (Duckworth, 1909), p. 115.

CHAPTER V
REASON AND REVELATION

SUMMARY

THE treatment of reason in connection with religion must avoid the two extremes of disinheritance and apotheosis. Two positions are still to be considered. (1) Reason may be ousted from its place in religious experience by *feeling*. In Rudolf Otto we find a graphic treatment of the specific feeling of reverential awe directed to the *numinous*. It stands for a unique, original feeling-response, which can be itself ethically neutral. Yet, over against Otto, it is to be emphasised that, in the highest manifestations of religion, the feeling of religious dread is so transfigured as to be almost unrecognisable. It is religious dread which stands before Holy *Love*. The alteration in the understanding of the object of devotion has brought about a correspondingly profound change in the nature of the feeling. The 'numinous' is also found to be that which makes impossible communion between God and man, whereas religion begins when such communion is, incredibly, shown to be the divine endowment and boon of men. Moreover, though the sense of the mysterious and ineffable will always be present in true religion, nevertheless, religion is, by the grace of God, a mystery *revealed*. "A God perfectly comprehended would not be the God of experience, but a God who was utterly incomprehensible could not be the object of trust and love."

(2) The question arises whether reason is altogether disclaimed in favour of *revelation*. The religious mind at once rejects the idea of an autonomous human reason which is able of itself to apprehend the divine. The great value of the Theology of Crisis is that it has put this matter plainly and unequivocally. But misinterpretation may arise on three points : (i) There may be a misunderstanding connected with the nature of God. No doubt men were never encouraged by Jesus to think of God as their Father without at the same time understanding that which had been hidden from them concerning the true meaning of the word. The word was not simply to be transferred. But the familiar method of the teaching of Jesus, with its constant employment of the phrase, " How much more . . .", implies that there was here at least a point of contact. Anthropomorphism is always a real menace, but, since we are men and must think in terms belonging to man, the real choice is between worthy and unworthy anthropomorphism. (ii) There is the risk of misunderstanding in connection with the account given of man. Though man is fallen, he has not lost his humanity ; the *imago dei* is not obliterated. That which constitutes the tragedy of the sinful state is the possibility that might once have been and may yet be again. (iii) A third form of misinterpretation concerns the relation between revelation and response. Barth does not appear to take full account of man's perplexities, tragedies and sorrows ; all that may impede recognition of the Word without being either finitude or sin.

And there is a danger of so construing human nature as to make it difficult to understand how an intelligible Word of God can come to creatures who are wholly different from God ; how God can reveal Himself where there is no kinship between Himself and the recipient of His revelation. If the mind of man plays no part, then only a mechanised inspiration, magically enforced, is left to us.

It is true, however, that reason is always found pointing forward to something higher, in which alone reason can become complete. Reason without revelation is not reasonable, because it is not self-consistent. Without revelation, it would not make even its own characteristic demand for consistency and self-completion. Like faith, reason also is from without, from above, from the Wholly Other.

CHAPTER V

REASON AND REVELATION

WE have affirmed that the treatment of reason in connection with religion must avoid two extremes. It must seek neither the disinheritance of reason nor its apotheosis. In this lecture we may confine ourselves to the examination of two positions mentioned in the previous chapter and not yet considered. (1) Reason may be ousted from its place in religious experience by *feeling*. (2) It may be found that reason is preponderantly a human function and therefore has no place in *revelation*, where both initiative and consummation are wholly of God.

1. The term "feeling" has often been regarded as a miscellaneous column into which everything may be thrown which is not susceptible of satisfactory classification elsewhere. It is, indeed, the purely indeterminate element in consciousness. ("Feeling!" Hegel exclaimed, "and not cognition! Then my dog is more religious than I am!") It is apt to be the most vague and characterless of experiences.[1]

We may best, therefore, take as an example of this extreme one who tried carefully to define the nature of the feeling to which he gave a central place in the religious consciousness, namely, Rudolf Otto. Before him, Schleiermacher had sought to establish a monopoly for feeling. Pious contemplation is the immediate awareness of the universal existence of all finite things in and through the Infinite, and of all temporal things in and through the Eternal. Otto now presents as the characteristic of religion, not feeling in general, nor even the feeling of absolute

---

[1] G. W. E. Russell tells in *Collections and Recollections*, chap. xxix., of a preacher who began his sermon by saying, "I feel a feeling which I feel you all feel."

dependence, but the specific feeling of reverential awe
which is directed to the numinous, the *mysterium tremendum*.
Theistic conceptions of God, he says, designate and characterise Deity by the attributes of Spirit, Reason, Purpose,
Goodwill, Power, Unity, Selfhood, and the like. All these
attributes are clear and definite *concepts* : they can
be grasped by the intellect, analysed by thought ; they
even admit of definition. Objects which can thus be thought
conceptually may be termed *rational*. Because of them,
belief is possible in contrast to mere feeling. These are
" synthetic " attributes, predicated, that is, of a subject
which, in its deeper essence, must be otherwise apprehended.
Behind them lies the ineffable (τὸ ἄρρητον). By rationalism,
Otto does not mean that narrow type which is distinguished
chiefly by its refusal to admit the miraculous. " The
difference between Rationalism and its opposite is to be
found elsewhere. It resolves itself rather into a peculiar
difference of *quality* in the mental attitude and emotional
content of the religious life itself. All depends upon this :
in our idea of God is the non-rational overborne, even
perhaps wholly excluded, by the rational ? Or, conversely,
does the non-rational itself preponderate over the rational ? " [1]
The study of religion has been pursued in terms of concepts
and ideas, and the students have, says Otto, with a resolution and cunning which one can hardly help admiring, shut
their eyes to that which is quite unique in the religious
experience, even in its most primitive manifestations. Yet
it is precisely in religion that we have the outstanding
example of that which is unmistakably specific and unique,
peculiar to itself. Religion is not exclusively contained and
exhaustively expressed in any series of " rational" assertions.
The holy or sacred is quite a distinctive category.

Otto proceeds to enlarge on the fact that the " holy "
was not originally ethical in meaning. It stands for a
unique, original feeling-response, which can be in itself
ethically neutral, and claims consideration in its own right.
To this " extra " in the meaning of the " holy," above and

[1] Rudolf Otto, *The Idea of the Holy* (E.T., by J. W. Harvey) (Oxford,
1931), p. 3.

beyond the meaning of goodness, he gives the name *Das Numinose*.

On this several observations must be made. For Otto, the essence of religion is " the Holy," and this is an *a priori* category. Religion is the non-rational experience of the Holy. He admits that Christianity is superior to other religions because it possesses *rational* conceptions and ideas in unique clarity and abundance. This, though not the sole, or even the chief, sign of its superiority, is yet a very real sign. " This must be asserted at the outset and with the most positive emphasis." [1] Now suspicion is at once aroused when we discover that a " real sign of superiority " over other religions is to be found in the *rational* element of Christianity, namely, in that which, according to Otto, is not specifically religious at all.

Most people will readily agree that " religion is not exclusively contained and exhaustively comprised in any series of ' rational ' assertions." [2] Man cannot by searching find out God. But it is very important to observe a fact for which Otto makes insufficient allowance, namely, that this feeling of the beyondness, the transcendence, of God, in the higher levels of religion, is essentially a product of man's sense of the ethical loftiness of God and the contrasted frailty of man. It was a " numinous " feeling which prompted Isaiah to exclaim, " Woe is me ! For I am undone," and Simon Peter to cry, " Depart from me ; for I am a sinful man, O Lord."

Another point must constantly be borne in mind. The origin of a thing is not its essence. It is impossible to say precisely what hopes and fears and " shudderings " gave the first impulse to man's religious groping, but, whatever they were, they are not to be regarded as the essence of the religious consciousness. This is not difficult to prove in the case before us. It might be claimed that the feeling of "awe," " religious dread," is still present even in the highest manifestations of religion ; but we should have to add immediately that it is so transfigured as to be almost unrecognisable. It is religious dread which stands before Holy

[1] *Op. cit.* p. 1.   [2] P. 4.

Love. The alteration in the understanding of the object
of devotion has brought about a correspondingly profound
change in the nature of the feeling. Instead of being
ethically neutral, the feeling is now charged with ethical
content. Indeed, in so far as it is non-ethical dread, it is
questionable whether it should be termed religious at all,
and whether " æsthetic," for example, would not be the
more appropriate word. And that which can be dispensed
with at the highest stages of religion cannot be claimed as
the essence of religion.

From another side we see that the " numinous " cannot
be an adequate characterisation of the object of religion.
It is this which makes impossible kinship between God and
man. But religion begins when kinship and communion
are, incredibly, shown to be the divine endowment and
boon of men.[1]

It is unfortunate that the real value of Otto's studies
in this aspect of religion has been obscured by those who
have accepted uncritically all his conclusions. The most
notorious instance in recent years has been mentioned
already. In Dr. Julian Huxley's *Religion without Revelation* we have the curious spectacle of the nemesis which
overtakes an unimaginative scientist. The writer never
tires of ridiculing relapses into the primitive, yet his own
account of what he considers to be the sole remaining
possibility of religion is stated in terms of the primitive.
Taking his stand on reason alone in matters of science, he
adopts, in religion, the purest irrationalism. It is clear
that, if this *mysterium tremendum* can never be grasped by
the mind, and if it is impersonal, it is no more than ju-ju.
We have the strange phenomenon of a scientist prepared
to worship the failure of the human mind. We might
expect him to reverence man's rational achievement, even
to feel awe and wonder before the natural world into whose

[1] Attention may be directed to one of the earliest studies and criticisms
of Otto published in this country, Professor Leonard Hodgson's *The Place
of Reason in Christian Apologetic* (Blackwell, 1925), and to Professor
John Baillie's *The Interpretation of Religion* (T. & T. Clark, 1929), pp.
246–255.

secrets the mind of man is able in some degree to penetrate. He does the opposite, keeping his deepest reverence for the unknown and unknowable.

Two points may be made before we pass from this subject. (1) The feelings of awe and wonder, though essential constituents of the religious consciousness, will not alone suffice. They will not account for the *selection* of this object for worship rather than of that. You cannot remove altogether religious ideas and leave the whole field open to emotions. Religious ideas contribute to the character of the religious experience, and, in particular, as Otto was prepared to acknowledge, it is the intellectual element which governs the *progress* of religion. That which is a criterion of progress cannot be neglected in determining the essence of religion. (2) The sense of the mysterious and ineffable will always be present in true religion. " Methinks there be not impossibilities enough in Religion for an active faith ; the deepest Mysteries ours contains have not only been illustrated, but maintained, by Syllogism and the rule of Reason. I love to lose myself in a mystery, to pursue my Reason to an *O altitudo* ! " [1] " O the depth of the riches both of the wisdom and knowledge of God ! How unsearchable are his judgments, and his ways past finding out ! " [2]

Nevertheless, religion is, by the grace of God, a mystery *revealed*. So long as God is a *deus absconditus* and not yet a *deus revelatus*, religion has not begun. He is not, as Lao-tse describes Him, " something hidden, with no name to describe it, an Unfathomable, nay, the absolutely Incomprehensible." Man is called not merely to self-abasement before the altogether inscrutable, but to fellowship, trust, and service. Even the holiness of God, when it is interpreted in the light of the love and sacrifice of Jesus Christ, is not unendurable. The glory of God's presence is not strange nor altogether overwhelming to those whom He has brought to know Him. The universe is homeward-bound. Man, with all his sorrows and perplexities and sins,

[1] Sir Thomas Browne, *Religio Medici*, the First Part, *sub. init.*
[2] St. Paul : Romans xi. 33.

7

is travelling home to the house of the Father and the glory of the Lord.

The associated feeling of mystery is never absent from the religious mind at any level of culture, but this is only one side of the truth. " A God perfectly comprehended would not be the God of experience, but a God who was utterly incomprehensible could not be the object of trust and love." [1]

2. Otto's insistence on the Otherness of God brings us to the next section. We must inquire concerning the Wholly Other whether it can be made ours by discovery, whether reason is competent of itself to find its way. The religious man answers with an unhesitating " No." Knowledge of the Wholly Other comes, not by search nor discernment, but by revelation. He is aware of an Other Which is seeking men, Whose nature it is to reveal Itself—an Other, therefore, Which is personal.

The question arises whether reason is altogether disclaimed in favour of revelation. The religious mind at once rejects the idea of an autonomous human reason which is able of itself to apprehend the Divine. The great value of the Theology of Crisis is that it has put this matter plainly and unequivocally. Emil Brunner sets in a clear light the inability and impotence of man's reason. " As all natural human action reveals the sinful heart, so all philosophical speculation, when left to itself, bears witness to the obscuration in the inmost recesses of our reason. For this cause it is impossible to build up the Christian proclamation of the Gospel and its theology on the basis of a philosophical doctrine of God." [2] Karl Barth, rejecting the Cartesian method, with its proofs of God from man's certainty of himself, bases his rejection not upon another and better philosophy. " Here we are not in the least interested to know whether there is such a thing." There

[1] Galloway, *Faith and Reason in Religion*, p. 86. For a most suggestive criticism of *The Idea of the Holy* in its bearing on the Christian faith, attention should be drawn to the note on page 69 of the English Translation of Emil Brunner's *The Mediator*.

[2] *God and Man*, translation by David Cairns (Student Christian Movement Press, 1936), p. 40.

follows his own declaration of the knowability of the Word of God : " Men can know the Word of God because and so far as God wills that they should know it, because and so far as over against the will of God there is only the weakness of disobedience, and because and so far as there is a revelation of the will of God in His Word, in which this weakness of disobedience is removed." [1] Man is indeed no worse in his act of thought than in his other self-realisations. But all of them—intellect along with feeling, conscience, will—are alike to be disregarded as possible " anthropological centres " at which experience of the Word of God becomes possible. [2]

This is well said, but it is not always guarded against dangers of misinterpretation.

1. There may arise a misunderstanding connected with the nature of God. It is true that Barth has now allayed the suspicions aroused by some of his earlier writings. Continued stress on the otherness and the hiddenness of God seemed to throw open the door to doubts. Could I be sure that those tracts of the Divine Being which are unknown will never contradict those which are displayed ? He has now made it more plain that the hiddenness of God is not to be taken as involving this uncertainty. It indicates simply that God is known only as He reveals Himself to faith. But there is still, I believe, room for criticism. This is most obvious, naturally, when Barth is on ground which must always be somewhat precarious for him ; dealing, that is, with the very " human " words which Jesus used in His teaching about God. There is no doubt whatever that men could never go away from Jesus with the impression that God was being set before them as anything less than utterly holy, just and righteous, Creator and Lord of all. But the word which Jesus used was " Father," and He must have known, and intended that it should be so, that the disciples would begin to think of God in terms of this least inadequate human analogy. We know that " Father "

---

[1] *Church Dogmatics*, vol. i. : *The Doctrine of the Word of God*, translated by G. T. Thomson (T. & T. Clark, 1936), p. 224.

[2] *Op. cit.* p. 231.

was not all that Jesus said about God.   The word was
interpreted by His own life, obedience, death, and resurrection.   But we cannot help feeling that Barth errs here.
Not content with saying that God is revealed as more than
Father, he goes on to imply that not even the human
analogy of "father" is in place.   "In calling God our
Father, Scripture adopts an analogy, only to break through
it at once.   So we must not estimate by natural human
fatherhood, what is meant by God being our Father (Is.
lxiii. 16).   But from the Fatherhood of God natural human
fatherhood acquires any meaning and value inherent in it." [1]
No doubt men were never encouraged by Jesus to think
of God as their Father without at the same time understanding that which had been hidden from them concerning
the true meaning of the word.   The word was not simply
to be transferred.   But the familiar method of the teaching
of Jesus, with its constant employment of the phrase " How
much more . . .," implies that there was here at least a
point of contact.   It is not just hybris to believe that by
the grace of God the affection of a human father for his
children helps men to understand the greatness of divine
love.   It will not do to say that what " we characterise and
imagine we know as fatherhood in our human creaturely
sphere " is " figurative and not literal." [2]   We cannot
indeed fail to be aware of the fault against which Barth
is warning us.   Anthropomorphism is always a very real
menace.   But it is important once again to distinguish.
It is not a matter of choosing between a monopoly of
anthropomorphism on the one hand and its entire absence
on the other.   We are men and therefore must think in
terms belonging to man, but that does not mean that all
anthropomorphic thought is deceptive.   The real choice is
between worthy and unworthy anthropomorphism.   It is
true that anthropomorphism may result, as in Greek
religion, in achieving beauty at the expense of truth.   But
the reverse may result, as in Hinduism, in grotesque and

---

[1] *Op. cit.* p. 447.

[2] Karl Barth, *Credo*, translated by J. S. M'Nab (Hodder & Stoughton,
1936), p. 24.

revolting conceptions of deity without any gain in the direction of truth. "The Hindu gods are less beautiful than
the purely anthropomorphic gods of Greek art, because
of the effort to make them more manifestly divine." [1]
The mistake of anthropomorphism consists in interpreting
God by the worse or more defective in man.[2] Barth would
acknowledge that the Word of God, made known, not to
man in general, but concretely to this man or that, is clear,
luminous, and sufficient. It ought to follow, I take it, that,
since the nature of God is of a piece, every Word of God
"for me" is an index of the Word in general. It is com-
municable. It has intellectual content. *Idea* is in it,
though idea is not all of it. Man's reason, directed and
illuminated, not only may but must work on it. And many
perhaps would acknowledge that for them adumbrations,
suggestions, or symbols, at first sight purely human, have
proved to be the medium of the Word of God. Many are
prepared to believe that such adumbrations are given in
the loyalty of friends, the love of husband and wife, the
affection between parents and children, and that these are
no less divinely given because they are manifested in human
creatures.

2. There is risk of a second misunderstanding, in connection with the account given of man. "The Word of
God is not spoken to beasts, plants, or stones, but to men." [3]
"The Word of God is not a thing, but the living, personal,
and free God." [4] These two sentences, if their content
were expanded, would guard against the possible misunderstanding, but the condition is not fulfilled.

We have to ask why it is that man is different from
beasts, plants, or stones. The answer must be that, fallen

---

[1] G. F. Moore, *History of Religions* (T. & T. Clark, 1914), vol. i. p. 346.
[2] This applies to much that is called "religion without revelation."
Julian Huxley, as we have seen, finds the sacred in the impersonal, the
depersonalised, which, when it appears in human nature, as it does
appear, indicates the deterioration of man. *This* is not the measure of
all things! It is right to interpret the divine by the highest analogy,
even though it is a human analogy; and the highest which we know in
man is personality.
[3] Barth: *Doctrine of the Word of God*, p. 230.   [4] *Op. cit.* p. 226.

though he is, he has not lost his humanity ; the *imago dei* is not obliterated. That which constitutes the tragedy of the sinful state is in fact the possibility that might once have been and yet may be again. There is in man a capacity (no need to say " a God-given capacity," since no one would suggest that the *imago dei* with all that it involves was anything other) not to find his way to God or to achieve his own salvation, but to respond to the revelation of God and to manifest that faith which makes redemption possible for him.

3. That suggests the third misunderstanding which is not sufficiently guarded against. It concerns the relation between revelation and response.

Barth rightly indicates that, in this connection, he has expressed a Yea as emphatic and as definite as his Nay. Yet it is the Nay which echoes longer in the ear. He denies " any connection between God and man, *i.e.* any knowledge of the Word of God by man and therefore any knowability of the Word of God by man, in the sense that a capacity in man in abstraction from the Word of God is to be the condition of this connection. Of course this condition cannot be fulfilled. It is the man who really knows the Word of God who also knows that he can bring no capacity to this knowledge, but must first receive all capacity." [1]

It must be said that he has not sufficiently allowed for three factors.

(i) Man's perplexities, tragedies, and sorrows. The Word of God is not always luminous and convincing, and the cause must not be looked for solely in the obscuration of man's mind by disobedience. The disability may have another source. There is something which may impede recognition of the Word, something which it would be uncharitable to call sin and misleading to call finitude. There are times, it is true, when the real duty is to trust where we cannot see, but the readiness of faith so to trust does not absolve man from that other duty—to endeavour after understanding. Nor does the obligation to such effort in

[1] *Op. cit.* p. 224.

any way impair the divine character of revelation. " We all feel certain," says Lotze in another connection (*Logic* II. ii. 212), " in the moment in which we think any truth, that we have not created it for the first time, but merely recognised it ; it was valid before we thought about it and will continue so without regard to any existence of whatsoever kind, of things or of us."

(ii) The task of the preacher. " Once in the ministry," Barth wrote in *Das Wort Gottes und die Theologie*, " I found myself growing away from these theological habits of thought and being forced back at every point more and more upon the specific *minister's* problem, the *sermon*." " On Sunday morning, when the bells ring to call the congregation and minister to church, there is in the air an *expectancy* that something great, crucial, and even moment- ous is to *happen*." Here is a *man*, " upon whom the ex- pectation of the apparently imminent event seems to rest in a special way, not only because he has studied the technique of the event and is supposed to have mastered it, not only because he is paid and employed by the com- munity or is tolerated almost without opposition in the function evidently associated with the event, but also because freedom is displayed here as well as law : the man himself chose this profession, God knows from what under- standing or misunderstanding of it, and he has now for better or for worse wedded his short, his only, life to the expectation of the event. And now before the congregation and for the congregation he will *pray*—you note : pray—to God ! He will open the *Bible* and read from it words of infinite import, words that refer, all of them, to God. And then he will enter the pulpit and—here is daring !—*preach*." [1]

It is surprising therefore that now we have not some- thing more concerning the position of the preacher. Barth writes : [2] " As Christ became true man and also remains true man to all eternity, so real proclamation becomes an event on the level of all other human events. . . . But as

[1] English Translation by Douglas Horton (Hodder & Stoughton), pp. 100, 104, 105–106.

[2] *The Doctrine of the Word of God*, p. 105.

Christ is not only true man, it is not only the volition and
execution of the man proclaiming. It is also and it is
primarily and decisively the divine volition and execution.
For that very reason the human element need not be
omitted. The question here, apparently such a burning
one, as to the mode of the operation of the two factors, side
by side and together, is a highly irrelevant one. God and
the human element are not two factors operating side by
side and together. The human element is the thing created
by God. Only in the state of disobedience is it a factor
over against God. In the case of obedience it is the service
of God. Between God and the true service of God there
can be no rivalry. The service of God need not be
omitted in order that God Himself may come to honour
in it."

Now it would be legitimate to say that in this matter
we have a paradox which cannot be resolved. It is quite
a different thing to declare that there is no paradox. The
question must always be a burning one for the preacher.
He knows that his life is not all obedience but neither,
he hopes, is it all disobedience. It is for him a matter of
spiritual life and death to know when it is the one and
when the other. And this he will try to discover, not by
prayer alone, though by that first and most, but also by
the wrestling of thought and the concentration of study.
He will not stifle his reason unless it is disobedient, defiant,
or by sin obscured.

Moreover, there is committed to him, in addition to
the task of preaching, a *cura animarum*. As a pastor, he
knows, for example, that there are times when the word
to be spoken is the word "Lord." Again, it may be the
word "Father." And he will not wait for it to be miracul-
ously revealed to him whether the soul entrusted to his
guidance needs to be recalled to the almightiness and
holiness of God or to be assured that whosoever comes to
Him will not be cast out. God will not do for him that
which He has given him reason to do for himself. God
comes down His own secret stair into each heart. The
earliest converts to Christianity came to Christ partly

because they wished to understand history. They knew, as Jews, that God's guiding hand had been with their nation in all that they read in the Scriptures of the Old Testament. They looked also, with all their brethren, for the coming of a Messiah. Evangelism among the Jews took, therefore, the natural form of proclaiming that the Messiah had come, in Jesus. He was the fulfilment of their prophecies. Others will come because they want to understand suffering. The Cross will speak to them in the universal language—the language of pain, which all men understand. The American poet, Sidney Lanier, said that " music is love in search of a word." The Cross is the Love of God seeking that word which will speak to the universal heart of man. Some will come because they want to learn the truth about life. In the matter of their eternal welfare they must have certainty. Nothing less will satisfy them. And the pastor will have to present Jesus to them as supreme in the sphere of truth. Others are most concerned about being good, and he will be required to show them that ethics are fully intelligible only in Christ. And very often he will have to deal with the breakdown of ethics. He will have to show Jesus at the heart of divine forgiveness. Since he goes as ambassador for Christ, he knows that the result is not in his hands. But tension will always be present as it was in the life of Jesus Himself. " The life-work of Jesus," says Karl Heim, " shows everywhere the tension between two things—first, the urge to bring souls to God ; second, the reverential regard of their free, inner development. He had at His disposal many outward and inward methods of compulsion, but He refused to make use of them. There lies the reason of His life ending not in triumph, but on the Cross. In His death on the Cross this tension has its highest expression. Here the Shepherd of souls lays down His life for His friends. And we too can become shepherds of souls only as we share in His sacrifice, pledging our souls for the souls of others." [1]

(iii) There is a danger of so construing human nature

[1] Karl Heim, *Glaube und Leben* (Furche-Verlag, Berlin, 1926), Essay on " Jesus als Seelsorger," p. 545.

as to make it difficult to understand how an intelligible
Word of God can come to creatures who are wholly different
from God ; how God can reveal Himself where there is no
kinship between Himself and the recipient of His revelation. If the mind of man plays no part, then only a
mechanised inspiration, magically enforced, is left to us.
Deny the authenticity of reason's judgment and you make
it for ever impossible for man to tell when he has the
truth ; when God is speaking to him. Irrationalism is in
danger of ending in agnosticism.

The truth and error contained in theology of this type
have been aptly summarised by Dr. Temple.[1] " The error
of the Barthian school of theology—for that it contains
error when judged by the canons of either natural reason
or Christian revelation I cannot doubt—is, like every other
heresy, an exaggeration of truth. To deny the reality of
moral progress, or that moral progress is an increasing
conformity to the Divine, is wanton. To deny that revelation can, and in the long run must, on pain of becoming
manifest as superstition, vindicate its claim by satisfying
reason and conscience, is fanatical. But that revelation is
altogether other than rational inference from previous
experience is vitally important. . . . In so far as God and
man are spiritual they are of one kind ; in so far as God
and man are rational, they are of one kind. But in so far
as God creates, redeems, and sanctifies, while man is
created, redeemed, and sanctified, they are of two kinds.
God is not creature ; man is not creator. God is not
redeemed sinner ; man is not redeemer from sin. At this
point the Otherness is complete."

Christian faith must philosophise, since Christ is the
Truth as well as the Way and the Life. And writers like
Emil Brunner, as Professor Hodgson points out,[2] do not
really avoid metaphysics and take their stand wholly on
the Biblical revelation. They simply bring with them
their own particular set of metaphysical presuppositions,
none of which is found in the Bible.

[1] *Nature, Man, and God* (Macmillan, 1935), p. 396.
[2] *The Grace of God*, pp. 74 ff.

Faith must make use of reason. But it is also true that reason must take faith into account. Reason validates conviction. But, to understand how comprehensive reason is, we must consider all kinds of conviction, and religious convictions (those which are subsumed under the word " faith ") form a large and important section !

For conviction itself, as distinguished from the validation of it, reason is not enough. Alone, it is either self-contradictory or in itself insufficient. To remember this is to escape the narrower and more absurd forms of rationalism, such as that represented by Colonel Ingersoll. That shallow type of thought cannot logically make use of ethical values, yet must postulate the reality of the ethical in order to save itself from disaster.

The same consideration prevents us from reducing faith to philosophy. It has been said that where the Deists had Scripture, Hegel has only metaphysics. For him, it is the cognitive side of worship which alone matters. Man is essentially rational ; he is just at bottom reason. Therefore the bond that unites him with the divine must be rational. On the other side—the approach of God to man —the process is of the same character. God is essentially rational : He is pure reason. His approach to man is through reason. The true nature of religion is the immanent dialectic of the spirit whose aim is the true apprehension of itself. Religion is divine knowledge, the knowledge which man has of God, the knowledge of himself in God. Religion is the divine spirit's knowledge of itself through the mediation of finite spirits. As we actually see it in practice, however, religion is simply reason thinking naïvely. It gives us only imaginative symbols of reality (*Vorstellungen*) ; philosophy gives us accurate concepts (*Begriffe*). According to Croce, religion is only another name for mythology. In so far as it is true religion, it is identical with philosophy. Philosophy is the true religion.

We need not concern ourselves with the triadic system of Hegel. It seemed to work so well in certain cases that he counted on it to give fruitful results in every sphere of

thought. (He suffered the fate of the unfortunate artist
who

> " had a formula for making comic rabbits.
> The formula for making comic rabbits paid ;
> But he could never overcome the tragic habits
> That formula for making comic rabbits made.")

Nor is it necessary to decry the conceptual element in
religion. Religion could come only to a nature that is
essentially rational. But religion is not the activity of
reason alone. We must agree that religious truth is apprehended and taken possession of by an activity of the
mind ; but we must avoid the mistake of supposing that
reason, which is able to appropriate religious truth, is
therefore competent to discover it. Rationalism serves an
important end by ensuring that the religious imagination
shall be held in check from unwarranted excursions in the
realm of its own wishes. Rationalism insists that religious
affirmations shall be controlled by the principle of coherence.
But it does not escape the danger of transforming living
faith into a system of metaphysical tenets. " While philosophy," says Dr. W. P. Paterson, " has been able to weaken
a religion, it has never been able to make one ; and it seems
that it should humbly regard its best thinking about God
and divine things as secondary and second-rate in comparison with the ideas that emerged in the great periods of
the Christian religion in a context of classic religious
experience and of elemental spiritual power." [1]

In our own day the question is frequently being asked
whether that which is styled " Humanism " is not enough.
It distinguishes itself from rationalism. " Historically,"
writes Dr. Curtis W. Reese, co-founder of the movement
with Dr. John H. Dietrich, " the rationalist belongs in the
group with the intellectualist, idealist, absolutist, not with
the realist, pragmatist, behaviourist, humanist. ' Reason '
is Rationalism's God, just as ' Humanity ' is Positivism's
God. Humanism finds neither absolute ' Reason ' nor
' reason ' as a faculty of the mind. But it finds intelligence
as a function of organisms in various stages of development.

[1] *The Rule of Faith* (Hodder & Stoughton, 1912), p. 343.

To Humanism, dependence on the ' Reason ' is as fallacious as dependence on the ' Bible ' or the ' Pope.' Humanism's dependence is on intelligence enriched by the experience of the years, but it knows that intelligence is not an infallible source of either knowledge or wise conduct. Rationalism is dogmatic ; Humanism is experimental." [1]

Its forces are arrayed against authority, against feeling, against revelation. In opposition to these is put a reasoned sense of the dignity of man. It is an attempt to exalt what we have called reason in the highest and widest sense, but reason which is unreasonably determined *ab initio* to deny the possibility of the supernatural.

The humanist lays stress on the scientific interpretation of the world, as if this were the only method for ensuring rigid accuracy. But the evidence for the existence of God is at least as conclusive as the scientific evidence for the existence of that objective reality which the scientist assumes that he is investigating. The same arguments which are employed in an attempt to disprove the existence of the supernatural can easily be turned to prove the non-existence of objective reality. In theistic discussion also, it should be noticed, we are not by any means confined to the traditional arguments for the being of God—cosmological, teleological, ontological, moral. We have the most important evidence in the witness of the saints, whose testimony, in their own special sphere, is as cogent evidence as that, let us say, of the physicist or chemist in his.

Faith is not reason, but faith is reasonable. And, on the other hand, every form of rationalism, every dreamed-of religion without revelation, is confronted with the insoluble problem of the unsatisfied demands of reason itself.

  1. Reason is unable to achieve what nevertheless it recognises as necessary. As we see in the dependence of syllogistic argument, as of science and philosophy, on assumptions that are themselves not amenable to rational demonstration, yet are self-authenticating, reason is from without, the gift or creation of a real Whole which is seeking to disclose itself. Dr. Dietrich makes the point that all

[1] *Humanist Sermons* (Open Court, Chicago, 1927), p. vii.

religious thoughts must pass through the mind of man.
He admits that they may come from God, but himself
prefers the hypothesis that they are purely human.[1] This
type of subjective idealism proves too much. The same
kind of statement applies to all knowledge. Yet we may
not say that nothing exists except the states of our own
mind. (The philosopher may adopt that position but the
humanist cannot, or all his belief in an external reality
with its ideals of justice, love, mercy, will disappear.) The
humanist makes much of the achievements of the scientist,
but these will count for very little if they have no more
significance than the revolving of thought within the
scientist's mind. If the scientist's knowledge amounts to
no more than this, we cannot by any stretch of the imagination describe it as *truth*. In fact, of course, the scientific
method so warmly eulogised in this connection is quite
incapable of doing the work allotted to it. Ethics is fundamental to humanism, and ethical inquiry demands not
physical but metaphysical methods.

Thus reason is always found pointing forward to something higher, in which alone reason can become complete.
Its own bafflements demand faith. It can make the
demand—indeed it makes it inevitably—but it is unable
to satisfy the demand which it cannot refrain from making.
Like faith, reason also is from without, from above, from
the Wholly Other.

2. The same is seen to be true when we turn from the
intellectual demands of reason to the emotional and ethical.
Poets and artists may recognise that their work is not their
own. (William Blake, in his dying words, cried, " It is
not mine ! It is not mine ! ") They are the instruments.
The reality which they are trying to interpret is one that
is seeking to reveal itself through them. The humanist
will not be prepared to admit those perplexities of reason
which are, for many of us, the most serious, namely, the
inability of man to repair the ethical system when it is
violated, to bring about the forgiveness of sin and the
overruling of evil for good. For an *argumentum ad hominem*,

[1] *Humanist Sermons*, pp. 95 ff.

therefore, we must go to his own conception of morals. In his essay on " The Faith of Humanism," [1] Dr. Reese writes : " Man achieves his spiritual values because he feels the need of them." It is a dangerous statement for a humanist to make, when his whole case against religion is that it is a wish-fulfilment, and yet it is a statement which he is bound to make in one form or another if he wishes to preserve his belief in morality. The idea is dangerous to the humanist's position because it proves too much, and undermines his whole attitude to theism. If man achieves his spiritual values because he feels the need for them, it will follow that he achieves belief in God because he needed God. (That is not, of course, how the religious man would express it.) For the humanist it follows that belief in God is at least as reliable as belief in moral values. You cannot remove the one without removing the reasonable grounds for accepting the other. The humanist may reply that morality is evolving, the less worthy continually being replaced by the more worthy, and similarly the idea of a personal and transcendent God must give place to the (nobler) idea of an impersonal and immanent God. The fallacy lies within the brackets. Who shall say that the impersonal idea is nobler ? That is certainly not the verdict of the saint—the religious expert. If it is claimed that it is the verdict of the intellectual, the reply is that the intellectual, as such, is not competent to judge either in morals or in religion. We stand by the verdict of those persons whose specific genius is in conduct and in faith. We look, not simply to the saint, but to Christ. Of His verdict there is no doubt.

The book entitled *Things and Ideals* is one of the few writings in which a humanist of to-day has seriously faced the profound perplexities which Humanism leaves unresolved. At the end of that book Professor M. C. Otto has a poignant chapter on " The Hunger for Cosmic Support." He advocates the renunciation of every attempt to find a Friend behind phenomena ; every quest for companionship with a Being beyond the fleeting aspect

[1] *Humanist Sermons*, p. 46.

of nature.   We acknowledge ourselves to be " adrift in
infinite space on our little earth, the sole custodians of our
ideals."   We are psychically alone.   Men, who are comrades
in doom and agents of each other's weal or woe, must not
go down the years estranged from the one friend they have
—each other.

Men have been afraid to face the truth, he says.[1]   And
the nature of their fear shows that religion is only a wish-
fulfilment.   They desire a purposive universe, and psychic
kinship with a transcendent Being.   But their fear, when
anyone threatens to remove these objects of longing, is not
a fear of intellectual confusion.   On the contrary, what
gives the demand its vitality is the fear of *emotional*
confusion.

Obviously, Professor Otto's initial mistake is to suppose
that the two types of disquietude can be separated.   It is
foolish to assume that the effect of removing the idea of
God can be confined to the intellectual field.   Suppose any
instance of the violent uprooting of a belief firmly held.
Suppose that I were to look into my shaving-mirror one
morning and find that it was no longer my own face that
the mirror reflected.   Professor Otto would say, This is
merely a strange phenomenon which we must investigate
calmly and dispassionately ;   there is no call to be upset or
alarmed.   I *should* be upset.   I demand the right to be
alarmed !

Reason is not enough.   It is true that religion must
not be *sub-rational*.   The task of reason is to make impossible
all religions save the best.   But religion must always be
supra-rational, as it were rational *plus*.   The emotional
confusion arising from the removal of the idea of God is a
proof of the firmness with which the conviction of His
being is held.   Emotional and intellectual confusion may
not always be rigidly separated.   It did not need modern
psychology to prove that emotional confusion, so far from
indicating a trifling disturbance, may arise from the denial
of truth in the inward parts.   The disappearance of the
thought of God may be due, as we well know, to apathy,

[1] P. 230.

forgetfulness, disobedience. Our peace and patience, grounded in the idea of God, are not created by any feeling of personal satisfaction, but by the *truth* which we both feel and know.

John Campbell Shairp, Professor of Humanity and later Principal of the University of St. Andrews, expressed the thoughts of many devout souls when he wrote the familiar words

> " Let me no more my comfort draw
> From my frail hold of Thee,
> In this alone rejoice with awe—
> Thy mighty grasp of me."

Christian assurance does not mean, " I am aware of my sure sense of blessedness." It *does* mean, " God's love in Christ is sufficient for me."

CHAPTER VI

THE WORD OF GOD AND THE CHURCH OF CHRIST

SUMMARY

THERE is no external and final authority, either in Church or in Scripture, which will give us the infallibility which many desire. It is our mistake that we are incurably rational, demanding proofs which in the nature of the case are not available. Better than having proofs of God is—having God. In the experience of faith there is something creative and inexplicable which carries its own conviction with it. Quite certainly mysticism is inadmissible if (i) it ignores the barrier between Saviour and sinful, Creator and creature, or if (ii) it places the initiative in the believer. But there are three types of mysticism which deserve closer consideration. (1) The *metaphysical*, which lays all the emphasis on the immediate communion of the soul with God and rules out history as irrelevant. But metaphysics cannot be allowed to settle the matter unless it can show why there should be history at all. God is One Who acts as well as speaks. We can dispense with the mediation of Jesus only by doing without the revelation which came by Him. (2) *Emotional mysticism*. This claims that the relation of man to God is purely one of feeling; that it involves no responsibilities to the world. But it is impossible for the religious man to maintain for long that duty is irrelevant. Even when perfect holiness is attained, the relation of man to man will still be important. Nevertheless, although the mystic is here presenting an exaggerated truth, it is a *truth* which he exaggerates. Creed and conduct do not exhaust religion. There is union with God in feeling. (3) *Individualistic mysticism*. Religion is regarded as a matter of ecstatic experience and therefore incommunicable. The Christian society is not given any vital place. Against this type of mysticism, which is intent on the flight of the alone to the Alone, we have to set the concept of a divine society. The religious community plays an essential part in revelation. It also has an important bearing on the religious life. We need co-operation of Christian people to combat that society of co-operative guilt which the New Testament calls " the world."

The Authority of Scripture. By one section of Christendom the divine guarantee of truth has been sought in the Bible. Over against the misuse of tradition, the Reformers set the Word of God. But they did not fall into the error of " verbal inspiration." They pointed to the moral and religious substance of Scripture, which are matters of faith : they left on one side the letter and the outward form, which are matters for history. The Christian consciousness, they taught, is absolutely sure of itself and cannot be subject to any authority other than the inner testimony of the Holy Spirit. If it is said that the conception of *testimonium spiritus sancti internum* is liable to the dangers of subjectivity, it is enough to reply that, if morality does not suffer from the subjective character of its principles, still less does the Christian religion, which forms with morality an ideal unity.

The Authority of the Church. Others have felt the need of a guaranteed interpreter to expound the meaning of the guaranteed truth. The best Roman Catholic theologians stress the fact that authority comes, not from the community, but from Christ, but they err in supposing that an institution is to be regarded as the Church of Christ because it has authority. The truth is that a Church has authority only in so far as it becomes the Church of Christ. The real test lies in the nature of the steps taken to purge the Church of its acknowledged offences and to make of its authority that which alone is appropriate for a Church which is itself under judgment. The credential of the prophet and of the Church is not tradition, but spiritual reliability.

CHAPTER VI

The Word of God and the Church of Christ

" Authority has a wax nose : it can be twisted in different directions." [1] Therefore some have agreed to abandon altogether the attempt to find an external authority, and to depend entirely on intuition, immediacy, the direct knowledge which the soul has of God. In one sense they are wholly justified. There is no external and final authority, either in Church or in Scripture, which will give us the infallibility which many desire. And that is precisely what we might expect. If God is the Ultimate, there can be no criterion of Himself outside Himself. We cannot prove our own existence, since personal experience is the presupposition of all proof ; still less, therefore, can we seek to establish certitude concerning God from anything other than God. He is the basis of all knowledge, and not the end of a chain of reasoning. It is our mistake that we are incurably rational, demanding proofs which in the nature of the case are not available. Better than having proofs of God is having—God. Here we are beyond the sphere of authority ; the conflict between autonomy and heteronomy has given place to theonomy. And the way to religious certitude is the way, not of proofs, but of worship, communion, obedience. " Faith knows nothing of external guarantees, that is, of course, faith as an original experience of the life of the spirit. It is only in the secondary exoteric sphere of the religious life that we find guarantees and a general attempt to compel faith. To demand guarantees and proofs of faith is to fail to understand its very nature by denying the free heroic act which it inspires. In really authentic

[1] *Auctoritas cereum habet nasum ; id est, in diversum potest flecti sensum* (Alanus of Lille).

and original religious experience, to the existence of which the history of the human spirit bears abundant witness, faith springs up without the aid of guarantees and compelling proofs, without any external coercion or the use of authority." [1]

It is quite true that certitude comes along this way. In the experience of faith there is something creative and inexplicable which carries its own conviction within it. Victor Hugo has a simile of a bird singing on the branch of a tree. The tree sways and bends under the violence of the storm. At last, suddenly, the bough breaks. But the bird is not harmed. It has *wings*.

It is not that faith is something magical, a substitute for other methods of knowing. For we have a helpful analogy in the realm of human friendship. When we *know* that we can trust a friend, it is not because someone has told us that we can, or that we have summed up the arguments on both sides and, by a process of reasoning, have *proved* him to be trustworthy. We trust because we cannot help it. The intuition is so sure that we should be prepared to doubt everything else before doubting this. We must, however, be on our guard against misapplication of the analogy.

A contemporary novelist has said that there are two great discoveries made by the child very early in life, the first when he says, " I am I " ; the second when he says, " I am God." Now, whether in the child or in the adult mystic, this, as an expression of religious consciousness, is either one-sided or morbid. Quite certainly there is one type of mysticism which cannot be harmonised with the higher manifestations of religion. Where the barrier between Saviour and sinful, Creator and creature, is, even momentarily, thrown down, redemptive religion has vanished away.

Again, Christianity has no place for that type of mysticism which puts the initiative in the believer. Man cannot by searching find out God. " The revelation of God bestows on him what no wish nor longing, nor act of will,

---

[1] Nicolas Berdyaev, *Freedom and the Spirit* (Bles, 1935), p. 105.

however honest, to experience God, can produce by its own effect." [1]

But there are three kinds of mysticism which deserve closer consideration. They might be called the metaphysical, the emotional, and the individualistic.

1. Metaphysical, or speculative, mysticism lays all the emphasis on the immediate communion of the individual soul with God. History it rules out as irrelevant. Neither past nor future can matter where we have the eternal present. Historical revelation cannot, it says, be the norm of religious faith. I reach communion with God through my experience here and now, and that is sufficient.

But metaphysics cannot be allowed to settle the matter, unless it is prepared also to explain why there should be history at all. If the eternal present is everything, why should there be the farce of life and time? It may be said that the Absolute has no seasons, but all at once bears its leaves, fruit, and blossoms. " The Absolute has no history of its own, though it contains histories without number." [2] But we wish to know the relation between the Timeless and its manifestations in Time. And, as a matter of fact, the speculative mystic himself would not attain his idea of God without the aid of those revelations in history and in man which he claims to renounce or despise. He kicks away the ladder by which he has climbed. True, he may say that the vital fact is not the Revealer but the truth revealed, but at least he must be prepared to give some explanation of the fact that history occurs. What, we may ask him, is the relation of God to history? If communion with the Divine as experienced in the mystic's way should indicate that God has no contact with life in time, then we have in history a surd, that which is ultimately inexplicable. But, if the answer is that God is found to be concerned with history, the consequence is that we must acknowledge Him as *Lord* of all history. He is a God Who *acts* as well as a God Who speaks, and therefore our know-

[1] Häring, *The Christian Faith*, vol. i. p. 229.
[2] F. H. Bradley, *Appearance and Reality* (Allen & Unwin, 1920), chap. xxvi. p. 499.

ledge of Him is very far from being complete if it takes no account of His acts.

Moreover, the evidence from our own inner experience alone must always be ambiguous ; at its best it cannot meet the charge of self-deception. It is in historical revelation that we have that testimony which is at once normative and self-authenticating. For the Christian, communion with the Divine Spirit, or the Soul of the World, is communion with God, the Father of Jesus Christ, and our conception of the God with Whom we are in communion determines the nature of that communion. Communion with God, the Father of Jesus Christ, is inevitably an experience different from all others. We can dispense with the mediation of Jesus only by doing without the revelation of God which came by Him. If mysticism claims to be Christian it cannot be indifferent to history.

2. Emotional mysticism claims that the relation of man to God is purely one of feeling ; that it involves no responsibilities to the world. It does not value moral action as something intrinsically good, as the realisation of values in personal life. It looks on it only as a means of deadening the senses. Moral action is only a preliminary stage on the way to absorption and knowledge. Since it conceives morality only as preparatory, mysticism feels that " the religious man struggling to gain the highest must leave the kingdom of moral ideals behind him ; he must discard the will directed towards concrete tasks and values, as well as instinctive tendencies ; he must abandon the holy works of self-discipline and the love of his neighbour as well as all his daily duties." The perfected soul is beyond good and evil. According to Plotinus " the soul must not have either good or evil traits in order that as an ' alone ' it may receive the Alone." [1]

But it is impossible for the religious man to maintain for long that duty is irrelevant ; that the whole vocation

---

[1] See Friedrich Heiler, *Prayer* (*Das Gebet*, translated by S. M'Comb (Oxford, 1932)), p. 158. Cf. the same author's *Der Katholizismus : Seine Idee und Seine Erscheinung* (Reinhardt, Munich, 1923), pp. 539 ff. " Der Einfluss der Mystik auf die katholische Frömmigkeit."

of man is self-culture of the highest type—to put *himself* right with God. For it is he who loseth his life who finds it. God is a God of love. To love Him is to love your neighbour as yourself. A man's attitude to his neighbour is not to be regarded as solely a means to his own self-development or even as a preparation for his approach to God. When perfect holiness is attained, the relation of man to man will still be important.[1]

At the same time we might observe that, although the mystic is here presenting an exaggerated truth, it is nevertheless a truth which he exaggerates. There must be union with God in feeling. Intellect is not enough. Religion is not merely the θεωρητικὸς βίος. And morality is not enough. It *is* possible to emphasise " service " to the exclusion of " salvation." It was said by someone of two of Moody's campaigns that the first, where he preached " salvation," was followed by great results, but the second, where the theme was " service," was a comparative failure.

Nevertheless, morality must have its right place. It might seem that Protestantism is precisely that system which cannot leave room for " service." In emphasising the doctrine of justification by faith, did not Luther consign us to pure passivity ? The answer is that Luther's conviction—and it works out in practice—is precisely the opposite. He held that belief in the possibility of justifying ourselves is the very thing that stands in the way of effective service. As Karl Heim, the Lutheran, has put it, " Attempting to justify ourselves by works cramps our spontaneity, and leads to self-seeking. Only belief in the unmerited forgiveness of God, as testified in the Scriptures, really frees us for activity, and delivers us from all hampering reflection on ourselves and our own accomplishments. Only faith leads to an unselfish and self-forgetful service of others. Only the believer is ' the servant of all things and subject to all men.' Belief in the Word alone is, as Luther says, ' a living, creative, active, mighty thing, so that it becomes impossible for the believer not to want to

[1] Cf. Adams Brown, *Christian Theology in Outline*, p. 194.

do good without ceasing. . . . So that it is really quite impossible to separate faith from works, just as impossible as to separate the burning and the light from the fire.' " [1]

3. Individualistic mysticism, regarding religion also as purely a matter of ecstatic experience, holds that it cannot be communicated by the way of ideas from man to man. Hence it has no place for a Christian society, or church. For it, institutions have no value, organisations have no sacredness.

It is true that, in many cases, the exaltation of the ecstatic experience above the experience of the lucid mind leads in the opposite direction. To decry the intellect may bring about its self-surrender into the hands of " authority." The understanding takes a secondary place. A higher court claims the right to interdict the whole intellectual process, and the capacity for discerning the truth submits to the judgment of that court. [2] It is true also, as Heiler points out, [3] that mysticism, while insisting on the relativity of every form of corporate faith, even the most perfect, and believing that all intellectual formulas and all rites of worship are altogether inadequate to express the inexpressible secret of the Divine ; and while not feeling obliged therefore to fight for the maintenance of any particular form, nevertheless can welcome external forms as means to its own end, the approach of the soul to God.

There are, however, other mystics, richly endowed in their own particular sphere, who feel themselves beyond the Church, independent of all dogma and all cultus. Some have stood outside every religious communion, intent on the flight of the alone to the Alone (φυγὴ μόνου πρὸς μόνου).

They desire to know only God and their own souls, these two things and no third whatever. Against this type of mysticism we have to set the concept of a divine society.

---

[1] Karl Heim, *The Church of Christ and the Problems of the Day* (Nisbet, 1936), p. 63.

[2] See Karl Heim, *Das Wesen des evangelischen Christentums,* chap. vi. (English Translation, *Spirit and Truth* (Lutterworth Press, 1935), pp. 107 ff.).

[3] *Der Katholizismus,* pp. 518 ff.

Apart from the value of corporate worship, to which the mystic may be blind, we need to emphasise the necessity of a society of Christians because of the restraint which it exercises on moral and intellectual idiosyncrasies. A secret faith which is not nourished in the currents of Christian life, if in time it does not die altogether, as a flame will go out for lack of air—will tend to become one-sided, extravagant, and misleading. The nemesis of unwholesome mysticism is eccentricity. Just as lonely, unsociable people become " queer," so the doctrines of those who live apart from the strongly-flowing life of the Church become abnormal, even pathological. The voice of the Church is the voice of God. It is clear from the Gospel of St. John that this was soon recognised in early Christianity, recognised already when the Gospel was written. For there, as Dr. E. F. Scott has indicated, we frequently find the author beginning with the words of Jesus and passing imperceptibly into the words of the tiny Church of the first Christians.[1]

The religious community plays an essential part in revelation. It also has an important bearing on the religious life. Mutual support is necessary to make the right life possible in society. We need co-operation of Christian people to combat that society of co-operative guilt which the New Testament calls " the world." [2] The divine society " calls for self-sacrifice and devoted labour in a cause which is higher than private interest. It demands discipline and co-operation, through which alone great things can be done on the field of history. It holds out a prospect of really influencing the course of events." [3]

But again we need not lose the truth concealed in this type of mysticism, the fact that no institution can embody the whole Christian faith. There will always be a discrepancy between the actual church and the ideal ; and the mystic is right in protesting against the identification

---

[1] E. F. Scott, *The Fourth Gospel* (T. & T. Clark, 1923), 2nd ed. p. 69.
[2] W. R. Inge, *Personal Religion and the Life of Devotion* (Longmans, 1924), p. 85.
[3] W. R. Inge, *Outspoken Essays*, First Series, p. 236.

of the Church of God, holy and universal, with any particular institution.

.   .   .   .

A former lecturer under this foundation and for many years the honoured Clerk to the Kerr Lectureship Committee, Dr. J. H. Leckie, has written these words on the problem of authority : " On the one hand, we know that the old imperial facts of faith remain, that the Scriptures contain a veritable word of God, that the testimony of the Church is worthy of veneration, that Jesus is Master and Lord. But, on the other hand, we find it hard to construct a rational basis on which to establish our witness. . . . We find ourselves, thus, in a strange and anomalous plight —very strong in faith, but somewhat weak in theory ; very sure of the facts of the Gospel, but greatly in doubt how best we may prove and enforce them ; rich in religious possession, but wanting in means of attesting our wealth to those who may doubt it." [1]

We are to speak now of the two outstanding claims to authoritative position in the Christian faith, one made for the Church and the other for Scripture. Because each is unable to secure a monopoly for itself, we find each falling back on the authority of Christ to justify its claim. The Roman Church points to the words of Jesus addressed to Simon Peter : " Thou art Peter and upon this rock I will build my Church." There, it is said by some, we have the authority of Jesus explicitly delegated by Himself to His Church.

But we observe that the argument is circular. This Church will not allow the sole claim of authority to the Bible, holding that the tradition of the Church is the sole interpreter of Scripture. Hence we have the claim that the Church is authorised by the words of Jesus, and the words of Jesus are authenticated by the Church. It might be argued, it is true, that the words of Jesus are not given alone in Scripture ; that the existence of the Church goes back to Jesus Himself ; that there is nothing inconceivable in the claim that the Roman Church is

[1] *Authority in Religion* (T. & T. Clark, 1909), pp. 51–52.

historically in direct continuity with Christ and His Gospel, and enjoys His delegated authority, including the right to interpret Scripture, which is a deposit of the Church's life. But, while escaping the circle, such an argument is merely transformed into a dogmatic statement.

Certain sections of Protestantism have claimed the sole supremacy for the Bible. At various points where criticism has attacked the traditional interpretation of the Bible, this school steps in to claim the authority of Jesus on matters of history and authorship. It quotes His recorded utterances about Noah, Jonah, Isaiah, Daniel. It points to His apparent recognition of the Davidic authorship of the psalms as settling the critical questions which arise in the study of the psalter.[1] The words about the law of Moses are frequently quoted as a divine guarantee of the inerrancy of the Old Testament.[2] The argument is that, since Jesus was Divine, He must have been omniscient in these matters ; that doubt here implies disbelief in His divine knowledge and nature.

Again we have a circular argument. The words of Jesus are quoted as the ultimate authority ; but when we ask, How do I know that these words were actually spoken by Him ? the only answer is, Because they are in the Bible. But the reliability of the Bible record is the point at issue.

This school of thought misinterprets the authority of Jesus. We do not think of Him as inerrant in all matters under the sun. We do not think of Him, for example, as familiar with all the discoveries of modern astronomy, physics, or medicine. If Jesus was truly man, then His knowledge was limited. It grew as life went on, in the same fashion as that in which every man's knowledge must grow. An omniscient child would not be a human child. Yet, if Jesus was not omniscient in His cradle, at what point did He become omniscient ? [3] His authority is not magical.

---

[1] Mark xii. 36.

[2] " One jot or one tittle shall in no wise pass from the law " (Matt. v. 18).

[3] Edward Grubb, *Authority in Religion* (Swarthmore Press, 1924), p. 74.

It is confined to those matters about which He was con-cerned—God, sinful man, redemption. When Jesus spoke of these, He spoke with authority. This was His subject. Here He spoke what He *knew*.

Not even the authority of Jesus is an *imposed* authority. Nevertheless, mankind is always longing for precisely this kind of authority ; some guarantee of truth irrespective of the need for effort and obedience. By one section of Chris-tendom the divine guarantee was found in the actual text of the Bible, literally understood. " Because they accept the Bible as the Word of God, they regard themselves as pledged to believe and to teach that the world was created out of nothing in a week, or that strange astronomical occurrences took place in connection with the battle of Bethhoron ; and whenever it appears that there is some way of showing that what is asserted really may have occurred, it is supposed that faith has received a new support." Another section felt the need of a guaranteed interpreter to expound the meaning of the guaranteed truth. " By this road men are forced back from the in-fallible Book to the infallible Church and to the infallible Spokesman of that Church." [1]

The Authority of Scripture. Over against the misuse of tradition, the Reformers set the Word of God. But they did not fall into the error of " verbal inspiration." They pointed to the moral and religious substance of Scripture, which were matters for faith ; they left on one side the letter and the outward form, which are matters for historical study. They did not hold that the Word of God was identical with the books contained in the Canon. Luther, for example, frankly criticises and compares the different books of the New Testament. " Christ is the Master, the Scriptures are the servants. Here is the true touchstone for testing all the books ; we must see whether they work the works of Christ or not. The book which does not teach Christ is not apostolic, were St. Peter or St. Paul its writer. On the other hand, the book which preaches

[1] See William Temple, Essay in *Revelation* : a Symposium edited by John Baillie and Hugh Martin (Faber & Faber, 1937), p. 102.

Christ is apostolic, were its author Judas, Pilate, or Herod." [1] When allowance is made for the touch of exaggeration, the statement is true.

The Reformers did not contemplate the setting up of another external authority, working in the same manner as the authority of the Church, and robbing the individual of his liberty. The Roman Catholic may agree in advance to accept all that the Church teaches, even though it should declare to be black what he sees to be white. He puts his religious and his moral convictions in subordination to the teaching of the Church. There may be Protestants who take up this attitude to the Bible. If so, they are, in their methods, so far Roman, not Protestant. The Christian consciousness—so the Reformers taught—is absolutely sure of itself and cannot be subject to any authority other than the inner testimony of the Holy Spirit, witnessing to an objective Word of God. What Jesus promised was His Spirit, not a new book. The Christian religion is not true because it is in the Bible : it is in the Bible because it is true.

All forms of revelation lead up to the Person of Christ —nature, history, Scripture, the Gospel-stories, the words of Jesus, the historical account of His death and resurrection. But the reverse also is true. Jesus points back to nature, history, the Scriptures, the experience of the Church. Even the Gospel-stories, the words of Jesus, the account of His death and resurrection, are to be understood only by those who already know Him. Is this a circular process ? It may appear to be, but it is a circle which is familiar to us in the realm of friendship. We have to learn facts about our friend before we can know the friend ; but, likewise, the personality of the friend re-interprets the facts which led us to his heart. Neither is fully intelligible apart from the other.

We might compare the phenomena of conversion, or, more generally, the many cases in which that which has been subconscious rises to the conscious level. We might compare the scientific discovery. The facts are known to

---

[1] Erlangen edition, vol. lxii. p. 128.

many ; what is still required is the hypothesis that will explain them all. " It is a matter of history," says Dr. A. S. Russell, " that for the formulation of such hypotheses something like genius is necessary." [1] Through a maze of facts we come to the leap of intuition by which all the facts are polarised. The facts have led us there ; without them we could not have arrived ; but the facts are not the intuition. Now, when the intuition has come, all the facts fall into their place, and *now*, for the first time, are rightly interpreted. So with our ascent to the knowledge of Christ. We know *about* Him, ever more and more. But the ascent is not gradual to the end. There is the vertical leap ; no new fact is added, but all facts are suddenly polarised. This is the meeting of the soul with Christ.

One writer [2] has described the way in which many people have felt that their faith was shaken when the idea of plenary inspiration of the Bible was withdrawn from them. " I am comparing," said Lord Restormel, " in my own mind religion made thus familiar to us to a fire-lit cottage at night, enclosing a sailor's child. The blinds are down, the darkness is shut out, the flickerings of the hearth give a friendliness even to the shadows in the farthest corner. The child sees everything intelligibly adjusted to its needs. If it is hungry, there is food for it in the great mysterious cupboards ; and when it is tired, it knows that there is a room above, where a pillow of rest awaits it, to be reached by a narrow stair. We are like such a child, who, having taken its cottage for the world, suddenly opens the door, and finds itself in a night like this confronted by all the stars, and by all the thunderings of the sea. Will these realities of the Universe provide us with a new home which, compared with the cottage of Christian miracles, will be a palace ? Or will they leave us roofless, with no home at all ? That's our question in general terms, isn't it ? "

This venture of faith has justified itself. Historical criticism of the Bible, so far from emptying it of its content,

---

[1] Essay in *Adventure* (Macmillan, 1927), p. 18.

[2] Mallock, W. H., *The Veil of the Temple*, p. 214.

has enriched the understanding of it, and has given a new and nobler idea of God. He is no longer bound by the letter of Scripture, confined to a static revelation. We obtain a worthier conception of Him when we discover that He is not adequately represented by the magic of a book.

Unnecessary difficulty is sometimes introduced into the conception of the *testimonium spiritus sancti internum*. To depart from the notion of external authority in Scripture, it is said, and to fall back on that of self-authenticating truth mediated by the Holy Spirit is to bring ourselves into the morass of subjectivity. But that is a word of which we are too much afraid. Auguste Sabatier has put it in this way : We cannot think with another's brain, or reason with another's reason. Personal and living faith is simply the individual appropriation of the truth. " How then shall faith be other than subjective ? And can Christian assurance be found outside of the jurisdiction of one's own consciousness ? " Consider the parallel case of morality. " Do you admit that there is anything sounder than the sense of duty? Can an exterior authority in morals ever attain to that profound and sweet security enjoyed by a conscience that clearly sees its duty and performs it ?

" If morality does not suffer from the subjective character of its principle, why should religion, especially the Christian religion, which in the last analysis is identified with the highest morality, and forms with it an ideal unity ? " [1]

Modern methods of interpreting Scripture do not set aside its authority ; on the contrary they recognise its true nature. They see in the Bible the greatest external authority because it gives the record of the most profound religious experiences, leading up to and culminating in Jesus Christ. The power of the Scriptures depends " on none of the things at present in debate, but on the record it contains of the authentic Revelation of God in Prophets and Saints and in the consciousness of Jesus Christ." [2]

We see therefore that the actual writing of the New Testament documents added no authority for the Christian

[1] *The Religions of Authority and the Religion of the Spirit*, pp. 261 ff.
[2] J. H. Leckie, *op. cit.* p. 228.

9

mind which had not been there already in the Person of Christ and His Gospel. The Scriptures must be read with understanding. Otherwise they will not be revelation at all. Unbelief is possible even in face of them. And this understanding is not a man's own contribution ; it comes from God also. It is the Holy Spirit, not even the Church, which interprets for the reader.

This means that God not only speaks but acts. That is true of all revelation, which means the self-communication of God through His own activity. God does not simply put the Bible in our hands and go away. It becomes revelation for me because it speaks to my situation. It is God Who turns the pages and speaks each word afresh to me. It is He Who unseals the sacred book. It is quite true, says Karl Barth,[1] that a man must open the door to Him (Rev. iii. 20), but even that is the work of the Christ Who stands outside. " So that the other thing also remains unreservedly true, that the risen Christ passes through closed doors (John xx. 19 f.)." The religious man does not think of his understanding of Scripture as his own accomplishment. He has been apprehended by it. The work of faith and the work of the Spirit are identified. Just as we are unable to create the revelation which is in the Bible, so we are unable to apprehend it. The faith which enables us to make response is equally the work of the grace of God.

The Authority of the Church. An infallible *living* authority is too patent an absurdity to command wide homage. " Its blunders," writes Dr. W. R. Inge,[2] " cannot be embellished by historians ; it entangles itself in conflicts where the right is obviously not all on one side. And so those who crave for a final court of appeal in religious matters generally seek for it in the past."

Psychologically it is true to say that the grounds of certitude are largely communal. We give full weight to the part played by heredity, tradition, home, training, society, the Church. Yet the " certitude " thus achieved may be deceptive. The fact that a truth is held by others, or

---

[1] *The Doctrine of the Word of God*, p. 283.
[2] *Truth and Falsehood in Religion* (John Murray, 1906), p. 50.

transmitted to us by a strong and weighty tradition, confirms our belief in it ; but the confirmation may be unreal. Truths are frequently apprehended by the rebel, the eccentric, those who are outside tradition and, perhaps, alienated from their surroundings. The best Roman Catholic theologians therefore stress the fact that authority comes, not from the community, but from Christ. Thus Karl Adam writes : [1] " The whole constitution of the Church is completely aristocratic and not democratic, her authority coming from above, from Christ, and not from below, from the community." Tertullian stressed this fact in a pregnant sentence, " The Church is from the apostles, the apostles from Christ, Christ from God." [2]

The difficulty to be surmounted is the fact that the community certainly played its part in determining who should be entrusted with the authority. The Roman Catholic theologian, concerned to show that the power was nevertheless exclusively in the hands of the bishops, who derived from the apostles, is forced to reduce the part played by the community to that of an automaton merely registering the choice of God. Surely, he will say, God *does* guide the community when it seeks His guidance in prayer. And it is true that God does so ; but you cannot be sure, on these principles, *when* the community has prayed sincerely enough to receive the guidance, nor can the Roman Catholic believer rid himself of the fear that the guidance may after all be with Protestantism. The original mistake which lies at the back of all these errors is that of supposing that an institution is to be regarded as the Church of Christ because it has authority. The truth is that a Church has authority only in so far as it becomes the Church of Christ. It is the community, not the individual, says Professor Adam, which is the bearer of the Spirit of Christ.[3] But, even if that assertion were fully established, there would still remain the difficulty of decid-

---

[1] *Spirit of Catholicism* (Sheed & Ward, 1934), p. 23.
[2] *Ecclesia ab apostolis, apostoli a Christo, Christus a deo.—De Praescriptione* 37.
[3] *Op. cit.* pp. 40–42.

ing *which* is the true community.   Another criterion is
needed, and it can only be the criterion of spiritual power,
obedience, and insight.

At the close of this book, *The Spirit of Catholicism*, the
author writes : " The Church has from God the guarantee
that she will not fall into error regarding faith or morals ;
but she has no guarantee whatever that every act and
decision of ecclesiastical authority will be excellent and
perfect. . . . An immoral laity, bad priests, bishops, and
popes—these are the saddest wounds of the Body of the
mystical Christ." [1]   This frank chapter compels us to ask
how, if this Church is really the supernatural organisation
which it is claimed to be, these abuses and offences are
conceivable.   Appearing in any part, they may be present
in all parts.   The real test is in the nature of the steps
taken to purge the Church of these offences and to make
of its authority that which alone is appropriate for a Church
which is itself under judgment.   Yet this Church " as the
authorised preacher of the truth " will never cease " to
give her authoritative witness to it and to oblige all con-
sciences to accept it." [2]   An example of this method is seen
in the anti-modernist oath demanded of theologians in
1910, in which Roman Catholic theologians in Europe felt
once again " the cold hand from over the mountains."
" The Church," says Professor Adam, " does not supplicate,
or discuss terms with conscience ;   she makes a direct
demand upon it and requires that it surrender itself to the
word of God "—that might be intelligible, but the sentence
is not yet finished—" to the word of God as proclaimed
by her " (p. 229).

We must further inquire whether there may not be
such a thing as a pragmatic justification of such authority.
This must, in fact, be what is in the minds of many besides
the Jesuits who submit their own opinions and convictions
to the judgment of the Church—many of those, for example,
who took the anti-modernist oath in 1910, surrendering
their liberty of inquiry into historical and critical questions.
For many of them the submission was tragic and painful,

---

[1] Pp. 242–250.   [2] *Op. cit.* p. 228.

but they went under the Caudine yoke because of their conviction that there were more important considerations than their own personal liberty of inquiry.

As soldiers in an army we submit to authority, and feel that it is right to do so, because, in our own opinion, there are things more valuable than our own opinion—for example, unity, order, victory. This type of authority is necessary in an army. Even if a command is wrong, it must be obeyed because of the greater thing, discipline. Why may we not have the same thing in religion ? The answer is that a Church may invent whatever discipline it may please, but must always remember that it has nothing whatever to do with *truth*.

The authority of a Church depends on her spiritual purity and not *vice versa*. Rome argues that she must be the holy Church because she has the authority. That is just the reverse of the truth concerning spiritual operations. Nothing can be revealed to an irreligious mind. Revelation goes hand in hand with readiness, and worthiness, to receive. Look for the Church which is pure, and you find the Church which has authority. The credential of the prophet and of the Church is not tradition, but spiritual reliability.

Tradition, as interpreted by the Roman Church, cannot give a satisfactory answer to the pregnant question, *If* authority, *why* controversy ? " We are shut up to the dilemma that either there was no organ in the Church which was in possession of authoritative traditions . . . or that it was guilty of a grave dereliction of duty in so long withholding the assured knowledge, and thus became a sharer in the guilt of will-worship and error." [1] The grounds for believing in the Roman doctrine of authority are not the legitimate grounds of faith. They are, for example, the desire for objectivity at any cost ; the longing for assurance rather than for the truth ; the desire for mystical ecstasy ; the love of " style " ; a universalism which is not the true type of universalism foreshadowed by original Christianity. It might be said that Protestantism also

[1] Dr. W. P. Paterson, *The Rule of Faith* (Hodder & Stoughton, 1912), chap. i. p. 35.

frequently bases its beliefs on inadequate, unworthy grounds. But Protestantism retains the principle of continual correction by the record of the classical period of Gospel faith and the working of the Spirit. Roman Catholicism does not. There is such a thing as an inadequate objectivity (the *Church* is certainly not the absolute which we seek in order to escape from relativity) ; there is a spurious mysticism ; a dangerous love of " style " ; a weak universalism. " The visible Church," says Father Tyrrell, in *A Much Abused Letter*, " is but a means, a way, a creature, to be used where it helps, to be left where it hinders."

Having seen that the claims of one particular Church to be the sole trustee of revelation have broken down, we must then consider the possibility that, nevertheless, such a Church was envisaged when the revelation was given. May it not be, someone asks, that God considered it essential, for the preservation of the Gospel in its purity, to found and to maintain an institution which should safeguard it supernaturally ? And indeed we must assume that, as all was done that had to be done in providing salvation through Christ, so all was done that had to be done in preserving the essentials of salvation for men and women of the future. God must have "taken the precautions" that were necessary to prevent the life and death of Jesus being forgotten or altogether misunderstood. In matters of salvation certainty is to be found. Thus it is at least a plausible theory that a supernatural and inerrant Church has somewhere been divinely established and maintained by God.

We must remember, however, that it is at least an equally likely assumption that this supernatural safeguard was invested in the individual and that it consists of the natural appeal of truth to the pure mind and conscience, led and enlightened by the Spirit. And we have seen reason to believe that the real Church is the Spirit immanent in humanity. The theory of one particular corporation being chosen as sole trustee makes the mistake of substituting the Church for the Spirit. Truth is not supernaturally but *spiritually* safeguarded. It is clear that the doctrine of the infallibility of the Church is held, more or less explicitly, by every living and believing Church. Each believes that there has been committed to it truth which is eternal and unchangeable, and it trusts the promise of Christ that the Spirit will guide men into all truth. " It may be," writes Dr. W. P. Paterson,[1] " that the Churches of Christendom, coming together in humility and in charity, as well as in dependence on divine help, would be assured of the needed guidance, while yet it may be an utterly incredible hypothesis that God has bestowed the office of infallible teacher upon a particular fragment which maintains the Roman attitude of uncharitable and hostile isolation in the family of Christendom."

The claim made by the Roman Church is not a Christian claim : it sets in opposition to the absoluteness of Christ the absoluteness of an earthly, fallible, and temporal institution. The Church also is under judgment. Even in her proclamation of the Gospel she knows that her responsibility implies temptation and the possibility of failure. She must live in confession and obedience, by prayer and the grace of God.

The visible Church is not the kingdom of God, and in its very hiddenness, as well as in its disunity, we have signs of its being under judgment.[2] According to the Orthodox conception, the Church is prior, in its mystical reality, to the individual. Man is not alone in his contact with Christ ; he is one with the whole Christian world, with all who are in Christ whether living or departed. Nicolas Berdyaev can even say that " It is in the Church that the grass grows and the flowers blossom, for the Church is nothing less than the cosmos Christianised." [3] The distinction between " ideal " and " empirical " is thought of as between " virtual " and " actual." The historic Church does not exhaust the fulness of the virtual, mystical Church. Thomas Aquinas, drawing on Aristotle, identified virtuality, or potentiality, with imperfection. True being is perfect and is that which is wholly in action. So Thomist and

---

[1] *The Rule of Faith*, p. 42.
[2] Cf. Karl Barth, *Credo*, chap. xiv.
[3] *Freedom and the Spirit*, p. 331.

Catholic thought has been forced to look on the historic Church as though it were in its true being. But there is another conception of potentiality, found, for example, in Böhme and in Schelling. Virtuality is always richer than its actual manifestation. The virtual Church is infinitely greater than the actual Church.

Outside the visible Church, says the Westminster Confession of Faith, " there is no ordinary possibility of salvation." Two things are implied. First, that the Church, as a divinely instituted means of grace, is not to be regarded as in any way of only moderate significance. Ordinarily, God does not work outside its sphere ; and beyond that salvation would not be found were it not that with God all things are possible. Second, membership of any Church does not guarantee salvation. Profession of the true religion may be very far from the actual presence of true religious principles. There are those who belong to no visible communion on earth who yet will be numbered among the members of the Church in Heaven ; and there are others who call Jesus " Lord " in the corporate adoration of their religious community who nevertheless are excluded from the true Church. Only God knoweth the heart. Nevertheless, of the particular embodiment of the Church in the world it may be said that it makes an important contribution to the revelation of God and the experience of forgiveness.[1] It is in the Church that Christian forgiveness is seen in practice. " Praised be my Lord," says St. Francis in the Canticle of the Sun, " for all those who pardon one another for His love's sake ! " And, on the other side, since the ungraciousness and dispeace of men may hide from men the grace and peace of God, it may be only through the channel of the Church, where sincere Christian friendship is practised, that forgiveness ceases to be a mere empty word and becomes the personal witness of those who are forgiven and forgiving.

[1] See H. R. Mackintosh, *The Christian Experience of Forgiveness*, chap. xii.

CHAPTER VII

REVELATION AND HISTORY. I. The Historic Jesus and the Present Christ

SUMMARY

THE Greek mind was dominated by the idea of cyclic change. The idea of culmination, consummation, is from the Jews. The peculiar feature of their religion was that its eyes were turned to the future. History is the workshop of God.

A faith which rests only on history will not stand against the facts of history. The only thing that can overcome the world is that which cannot be explained in terms of the world. Christianity rests on history, but it cannot be explained in terms of history alone. Tyrrell prophesied that Christianity would one day be reduced to "mysticism and charity," having broken free from the shackles of historical happenings. And it is true that Christianity is the faith which is most profoundly affected by the problem of the inter-relation of revelation and history. Three aspects of this question are to be noticed: (1) In the *Old Testament* it possessed a sacred book, which presented certain historical events and institutions, and claimed for them a unique value in the divine revelation. (2) God communicates His will through *historical personalities* (the prophets) and entrusts His revelation to a *historical community*. (3) This religion is marked out from all others by the *deification of its historical Founder*, the apotheosis of an earthly life within the confines of monotheism. The first two elements are transformed in their significance by consideration of the third. Scripture becomes something quite different when seen from its culmination in Jesus. The history of Israel is seen in true perspective only from the point in which it is fulfilled. History, in itself relative, is found to have absolute significance by its reference to the Person of Christ. All history, we believe, is under the control of God. He can turn even rebellion to His purpose. But in the religion of Israel and in the Person of Christ we see that portion of the historic process which has fulfilled the divine plan. Revelation was consummated, not in a perfect doctrine or guide to salvation, but in a Person.

It has seemed to some that the anchorage in history has now become a stumbling-block, a perplexing problem of Christian apologetics. Troeltsch argued that it is only a piece of foolishness to hope that we may find the Absolute in history at one single point. But he tends to confuse the absolute appearance with man's capability of apprehending it. The truth is that the historian cannot have the deciding word about the Jesus of past history unless he has also the requisite evidence concerning the Jesus of present experience, and this he cannot have without faith. Troeltsch, in his final formulation, declared that the claim of Christianity to absoluteness did not preclude the possibility of other racial groups making a similar claim. But, again confusing the final apprehension of truth with the truth itself, he failed to show why the absolute should be "the future of history" and not the historical appearance occurring at one point in the stream of history. Some religions have their centre in an *imperative*—commandments, fastings, prayers. Others present an *optative*, as in the Messianic hope. Christianity is founded on an *indicative*. Pure facts placed the world in a new situation. Mystical religion is not so independent of history as might appear to be the case. The Christian is bound to preserve both aspects—the historical in the mystical and the mystical in the historical. The Historic Jesus is also the Present Christ, the contemporary of us all. He is the Lord, determining the destiny of men and calling men to decision.

CHAPTER VII

REVELATION AND HISTORY

I. THE HISTORIC JESUS AND THE PRESENT CHRIST

THE Greek mind was dominated by the idea of cyclic change. Perfection is not in the future. History has no end or goal. Every cycle may leave things almost exactly as they were before. For Plato the real world is changeless and eternal ; it has nothing to do with time. The perfect world is already complete.

The idea of culmination, of consummation, is from the Jews. The Hebrews had the notion of God's promise or covenant. Thus the peculiar feature of their religion was that its eyes were turned to the future. History is the workshop of God. " A place of honour is due those great figures of religion who have put their soul into the task of serving and seeing the will of God *in history*." [1]

A faith which rests *only* on history will not stand against the *facts* of history. The only thing that can overcome the world is that which cannot be explained in terms of the world. Christianity rests on history, but it cannot be explained in terms of history alone.

A curious remark is made by Ernst Troeltsch (in his article " Historiography " in Hastings' *Encyclopædia of Religion and Ethics*). He affirms that Christianity revived the mythological representation of history. " The early Christian conception of mankind, alike as regards time and as regards space, was narrow in the extreme. . . . The history of the human race . . . was saturated with mythology ; in the middle stood the miracle of the Incarnation and the rise of the Church. Interest was once more concentrated upon the inexplicable."

[1] Söderblom, *The Nature of Revelation* (Oxford, 1933), p. 168.

There are two strange misunderstandings in that passage. The first is to suppose that there can be any narrowness in the conception of mankind as the object of divine holy love. The greater part of the New Testament was written, not by theologians, but by missionaries. Of one of these at least it was true that his parish was the world. There could be for them no narrow conception of mankind. They were not retired theologians with time on their hands, but " ardent missionaries who had taken their *lives* in their hands." [1]

The second curious misconception is to suppose that history can disregard the inexplicable. The Gospel accounts of the birth and life and death of Jesus are " anchors in the actual." But what if that actual should prove to be precisely that which can overcome the world, because it is inexplicable in terms of the world ? History cannot really be indifferent to that question.

Tyrrell prophesied that Christianity would one day be reduced to " mysticism and charity," having broken free from the shackles of historical happenings. And it may always be difficult to reconcile timeless truth with the historical medium by which it is conveyed. The limit of time is what Lessing called it, an "ugly ditch." "Accidental truths of history," he thought, " can never be evidence for necessary truths of reason." Herrmann expressed it : [2] It is a fatal drawback that " no historical judgment, however certain it may appear, ever attains anything more than probability. . . . It is impossible to attach religious conviction to a mere historical decision." It is fatal error to attempt to establish the basis of faith by means of historical investigation. The basis of our faith must be something fixed : the results of historical study are continually changing.

Naturally, Christianity is the faith which is most profoundly affected by this problem. It is everywhere rooted in history. Three particular forms of this dependence are to be noticed.

    1. *The Old Testament.* Christianity at the outset

---

[1] W. R. Maltby, *Christ and His Cross*, p. 23.
[2] *Communion with God* (E.T.) (Williams & Norgate), pp. 60 ff.

possessed a sacred book which it accepted as inspired, and as revealing the nature of the God Who was worshipped. This book presents certain historical events, personalities, and institutions, and the claim is made that these have, not a relative, but a unique value in connection with the divine revelation. In this book there are promises and warnings, laws, ritual, and psalms of praise, but everything is set in the framework of one people's history. Moreover, this history is set forth as the history of all mankind ; Jahveh is the God, not of Israel only, but of the race. With its fulfilment in the New Testament, we have the conception of a unified process, beginning with creation, passing through the fall in Adam, and moving on to redemption by Christ, and the final return of the Redeemer to judgment.[1] It is plain, therefore, that historical criticism, as it has developed in our own time, presents a very difficult problem. A revolution in Christian thought was occasioned by the entrance of Copernican astronomy ; another by the advances in biology, leading to the doctrines of evolution. But, in the application to the Biblical writings of the methods employed in criticism of secular literature, we see the greatest of all revolutions. " The application to these of principles accepted everywhere else as applicable to the study of ancient literature has brought about . . . a revolution, than which Christianity has probably known none more complete—though others have been more spectacular, because accompanied by greater changes in ecclesiastical organisation and in the external forms of worship and piety—since the Church was compelled to abandon the expectation of her Master's return in the lifetime of the generation which had seen Him in the flesh." [2]

[1] Cf. C. C. J. Webb, *The Historical Element in Religion* (Allen & Unwin, 1935), pp. 37 ff., 80 ff., and Christopher Dawson, *Progress and Religion* (Sheed & Ward, 1936), p. 156: " Thus the Jewish affirmation of the significance and value of history found a yet wider development in Christianity. The world process was conceived not as an unchanging order governed by the fatal law of necessity, but as a divine drama whose successive acts were the Creation and Fall of Man, his Redemption, and his glorious restoration."

[2] Webb, *op. cit.* p. 81.

2. A second form of the dependence of Christianity on history is seen in the way in which the divine revelation is mediated. God communicates His will through historical personalities (the prophets) and entrusts His revelation to a historical community. Of first-rate importance to the Christian is the record of the past of that community to which he belongs. It is true that God has not left Himself anywhere without a witness, but, for the Christian, His revelation through the prophets and through the religious community of Israel is unique. In other communities, there is not to be observed the same steady and consistent advance ; " isolated spots of light appear, but surrounded by impenetrable darkness." [1]

3. The third respect in which Christianity is dependent on history is that which marks out this religion from all others, namely, its recognition of the divine in the earthly life of its historical Founder—and this *within the confines of monotheism*. [2]

Let us first of all make this point, that the two historical elements already referred to (the Old Testament as a sacred book, and the prophets and community as medium of revelation) are quite transformed in their significance by consideration of this third feature. Scripture becomes something quite different when seen from its culmination in Jesus. (To take an obvious example, crude doctrines of verbal inspiration drop away when once we have the spirit by which the words are to be interpreted.) Again, the history of Israel is seen in true perspective only from the point in which it culminates. Its interpretation lies in its fulfilment. It is easy, perhaps, to argue that no historical fact recorded in the Old Testament can be of more than relative significance ; that we might, in some newly-discovered histories of forgotten peoples, find a better

---

[1] H. R. Mackintosh, *The Christian Apprehension of God*, chap. iii.

[2] " To hold that the founder of one's religion is *a* god is of course common enough. But in Christianity the historical Founder is regarded not as *a* god but as God in the strict sense which the word bears to a monotheist, nay, to a Jewish monotheist, the first article of whose faith is ' Thy God is One ' and the first commandment of his code the precept to have no gods beside that One " (C. C. J. Webb, *op. cit.* p. 44).

account of God's dealings with the world; but the plausibility of this argument vanishes when we reach the peak of this historical revelation—in Jesus. Everything falls into place. If God is what we see Him to be in Jesus, then it is His nature to reveal the absolute truth about Himself by historical means.

Secondly, concerning the personalities of the prophets and the entrusting of the divine revelation to a particular community. These factors are seen in their right significance only from the culminating point in Jesus. We recall the striking words at the end of Otto's *The Idea of the Holy*, words which, in their effect, seem to contradict in large measure the rest of the book: " We can look, beyond the prophet, to one in whom is found the Spirit in all its plenitude, and who at the same time, in his person and in his performance, is become most completely the object of divination, in whom Holiness is recognised apparent.

"Such a one is more than Prophet. He is the Son."

Now it is at least conceivable that only through prophets and through communal revelation can men understand the Son when He comes in the fulness of time. And the Christian contention is that it is not merely conceivable but that this is the actual way of God's working. It might seem easy to say that the prophets and the community have only relative value; that others have been found or may yet be found of equal significance; but the Christian claim is that the force of this argument fails when we look on prophets and community from the culmination in Jesus. History, in itself relative, is found to have absolute significance by its reference to the Person of Christ.

All history, we must believe, is under the control of God. It is true that we must also find room for the reality of the moral struggle, but there is more than " a fighting chance " of safety, of history going in the direction of God's will. He can turn even rebellion to His purpose. In the prophets we have always the chance that they may prove unfaithful to their vocation. Probably many did prove unfaithful. There were lying prophets as well as genuine ones. But this does not disturb the final plans of God.

As He can turn even rebellion to His purpose, so He can teach His lessons, by contrast, even through the lying spirits by which the unfaithful prophets are informed. In truth, it is in the religion of Israel and in the Person of Christ that we see that portion of the historic process which *has fulfilled* the divine plan. It is this which makes it absolute in significance.

All comes down, therefore, in the end, to this third way in which the Christian religion is dependent on the historical. " A thing, unheard-of in the history of religion, took place, creating the paradox of Christianity, namely, the fact that the religion of revelation was consummated, not in a perfect doctrine or guide to salvation, but in a person. ' No other foundation can be laid.' In this person the human and divine, the objective and the subjective, are one, so that at one and the same time he is, in the words of Fredrik Fehr, ' the consummation of divine love and of human loyalty' and is the mediator between his own and God." [1]

The teaching and the life of Jesus cannot be taken as only exemplifications of a truth which is timeless. If, says Professor Webb, a Christian should say, " It matters not who taught this—I thought it was Jesus, but I may be mistaken about that—it is the teaching itself that matters," then he is not a Christian in the only legitimate sense of that term. Similarly, if he declares, " Perhaps Jesus did not live thus, but this is the kind of life that I see it is best to live," again he is not true to the most characteristic feature of Christianity.[2] " The death and resurrection of this person and the life which was the prelude thereto become thus not mere exemplifications of timeless realities (though it must not be forgotten that even in the New Testament there are instances of their being thus interpreted, as when we read of the Lamb slain from the foundation of the world—Rev. xiii. 3) but the actual vehicles of the divine presence and certificates to Christians of their power to recognise it and to count upon it." [3]

[1] Söderblom, *The Living God* (Oxford, 1933), p. 316.

[2] Cf. Webb, *op. cit.* pp. 77-78.

[3] *Op. cit.* p. 48.

It was this very feature of Christianity which gave it the decisive advantage over Mithraism. That rival faith could offer only a divine hero who belonged to mythical antiquity, and could even be identified with the Sun in the heavens. Biographies rightly weigh more with men than romances.[1] Yet it would appear that the anchorage in history which gave to Christianity one feature of its superiority over its rivals, has now become a disadvantage, a stumbling-block, a perplexing problem of Christian apologetics.

The Gospel is intimately bound up with fact. " The passion and exaltation of Christ is neither symbol nor allegory, but a story of what *has been done* for man by a real man, who was also something more than a real man, the story of a real *transaction* at once divine and human." [2]

What we may call the first position of Troeltsch in this matter [3] may be summarised from some of his own essays published after his death.[4] He first discounts the naïve claim to validity which is made by all religions, simply because their view is confined to their own horizon. Next, he rejects the attempts to establish the supreme claim of any religion by evidence of the miraculous, including under this term not simply those " nature-miracles " which involve an infringement of natural law, but also the " miracles of interior conversion and the attainment of a higher quality of life through communion with Jesus and His community." [5] Thirdly, Troeltsch rejects no less summarily what he calls the concept of evolution, according to which, as in Hegel's view, Christianity is simply the perfected expression of religion as such. This view must be set aside. Christianity is a particular, independent historical principle.

Troeltsch considered that he had found a solution.

[1] H. G. Wood, *Christianity and the Nature of History*, p. xxvii.

[2] A. E. Taylor, *The Faith of a Moralist*, vol. ii. p. 117.

[3] *Die Absolutheit des Christentums und die Religionsgeschichte*, 1909.

[4] *Christian Thought : its History and Application*, 1923 (University of London Press).

[5] *Christian Thought*, p. 9.

10

The validity which is claimed for Christianity rests on the fine point of personal conviction. But we require a broader foundation in actual objective facts. He believed that he had discovered such a foundation in the very nature of the claim to validity. It does not depend in any way upon human reflection or a laborious process of reasoning, but upon an overwhelming manifestation of God in the persons and lives of the great prophets.

He felt that he had thus escaped the antithesis of relativism and absolutism.[1] What he envisaged was the steady pursuit of an absolute goal in and through the relative. Absolute value lies, not in history, but in the future of history. There *might* be a higher revelation than that given in Jesus, but the personal conviction of Christian people declares that a new, higher religion is utterly impossible. That, he says, is as far as we have any right to go. To wish to have the Absolute in history, in an absolute form at one single point, is a piece of foolishness.

If these last words mean simply that in Jesus we see, not God, but God incarnate, we should agree. But the words mean much more than that. They mean that the Absolute has appeared only in such a limited way as is possible at the contemporary stage of man's advance. They make the absolute appearance dependent on man's capability of apprehending. This is quite unwarranted. It is not surprising that, in his last writings, Troeltsch was forced to go much further. In these last essays he is much more radical. He was right in insisting that Christianity cannot give up its historical anchorage, or interpret the Person of Jesus as merely a symbol, but what he did not realise was this, that in these realms history *may* be faced by the inexplicable ; that the spectator-attitude is not adequate in dealing with these facts. The historian cannot have the deciding word about the Jesus of past history unless he has also the requisite evidence concerning the Jesus of present experience, and this he cannot have without faith. " The truth is," says Professor D. M. Baillie, " that

[1] See A. C. Bouquet, *Is Christianity the Final Religion ?* p. 202.

without faith no man can be a good historian of religious matters." [1]

This consideration seems always to have escaped the attention of Troeltsch, and hence he passed to his later position. Undoubtedly, he says, it is the profound inner experience which is the criterion of our faith's validity, but, be it noted, only of its validity *for us*. " It is God's countenance as revealed to us ; it is the way in which, being what we are, we receive, and react to, the revelation of God." This does not preclude the possibility of other racial groups making a similar claim. " Who will presume to make a really final pronouncement here ? Only God Himself, who has determined these differences, can do that." [2]

Von Hügel, commenting on this passage, refers to the curious conception of a chameleon-like truth which, though polymorphous, is nevertheless taken by Troeltsch to be Truth and Life in very deed.[3] " Midas," he says, " died of hunger from his fatal gift of turning all he touched into gold ; so also Troeltsch, *qua* vehement individualist, finds himself incapable of deriving spiritual force and food from those entrancing historical perspectives which everywhere arise under his magical touch." [4]

For our purpose the important point is this : Troeltsch dismisses *a priori* the possibility of the Absolute appearing in history. This dismissal is quite indefensible. He himself declares that there is no proof of continual progress. But, if that is true, the Absolute need not be " the future of history " ; there is no reason whatever for saying that it cannot appear at one point in the stream of history. Development, certainly, there may be, but development in man's apprehension of what was given once for all. We can imagine nothing greater than divine holy love as revealed in the life and death and resurrection of Jesus.

[1] *Faith in God and its Christian Consummation* (T. & T. Clark, 1927), p. 226. Cf. also Söderblom, *The Nature of Revelation*, p. 168 : " I purposely use the order, *serve and see*. For in the kingdom of God no one can see so long as he remains merely a spectator. Those only who serve the will of God freely and sacrificially can see the will of God."

[2] *Christian Thought*, p. 27.

[3] *Ibid.* p. xx.　　　　　　　　　　　　　　[4] *Ibid.* p. xxxiii.

Troeltsch confuses the final apprehension of the truth that is given in Jesus with that truth itself. There is nothing to indicate that this absolute truth cannot be given at one single point—even though the understanding and apprehension of it may not yet be achieved.

Johannes Wendland [1] rightly says, " Faith has therefore good grounds for continuing to believe that a higher than the Christian Gospel cannot be conceived, and that it is the goal of all history, so that all nations will come at length to recognise Jesus as the Lord and Mediator of their faith." " Even the ancient civilised peoples of Asia will have not merely to complete those things in their equipment which seem resemblances to Christianity, but also in addition to the approximations and syncretisms which will probably not be wanting, consciously accept the Person of Jesus as the full expression of those elements of truth which were already in their midst." They need not merely education and uplifting, but also conversion to Christ.

It is clear that, in spite of the comprehensive and illuminating studies made by Troeltsch, the whole question stands to-day in need of re-examination.

.   .   .   .

Other religions have their centre in an *imperative*. They say, Exercise yourself in the Buddhist meditation, and you will attain to Nirvana. Or they say, Fast and pray and obey the commandments, and you will help to bring in the kingdom of God. [2] Or it may be that a faith presents an *optative*, an εἴθε γένοιτο as in the Messianic hope. But Christianity is founded on an *indicative*, and a perfect indicative. Pure facts, quite independent of that which man may do or say or hope or think, placed the world in a new situation.

Let us see how those fare who dispense with the indicative. There is no inevitability of progress, they say. History may be retrograde. It is well, therefore, to sever

[1] *Zeitschrift für Theologie und Kirche*, 1914, quoted Bouquet, *op. cit.* p. 252.
[2] See Karl Heim, *Glaube und Leben* (Furche-Verlag, Berlin, 1926), p. 432.

religion completely from history, to cut it off "with a hatchet." They do not find God at all in the process of history ; its vacillations offer to them no secure foundation for faith. On the one side, they are deeply conscious of the difficulty involved in determining precisely what happened at any period in the past ; and, on the other, they see no guarantee that the true and the righteous will be perpetuated by the course of history, or the false and the evil overcome. *Facts*, they say, cannot be certainly ascertained, and *values* are not inevitably preserved. They feel no confidence in the house of the historical. But they have an inner citadel into which they can retreat, and there be safe. The mystical experience is something which is wholly unaffected by the flux of time. Here, they feel, is timeless truth. It is an eternal possession which the vicissitudes of history cannot alter.

There are, however, certain difficulties which this position cannot meet. (1) If it is *Christian* mysticism, then it *must* take history seriously. The God with Whom the mystic is in touch is God the Father of Jesus ; the God fully and finally revealed in the Jesus of history. The Christian communion is not with an ideal Christ, but with Christ incarnate, crucified, risen. (2) If it is *non-Christian* mysticism, it can escape from the necessity of taking into account the anchorage of faith in a historic happening. It can take refuge in denying the ultimate reality of that which "takes place." It may pretend not to take history seriously. But, as a matter of fact, history will not be dismissed even here. There are two sides to the experience of communion. It is quite possible to claim that one of these two sides, the divine, is timeless and out of history. But that claim cannot be made for the other side. The experience is possible only in a *centre* of experience. The nature of this centre, this ego, is historically determined. It is an " I " which has had such and such a history ; an " I " also which is what it is because of its share in the life of a certain community. The mystic's experience would be different if his own history had been different. And the influence of his community would be different if *its* past had been different. In fact, the form of the experience is determined by the whole past course of human history. The man who tries to offer a faith which has no dependence on history is attempting the impossible. He must begin with experiences such as this, and all of them must be historically conditioned. All the evidence that is available for him is evidence shot through and through with history.

He may reply, it is true, " Origins do not matter ; I am concerned solely with the timeless experience, which is very real to me, indeed the only real." But he cannot escape, nevertheless, from giving some account of what he understands the historical root of the experience to signify. His own past history and his own present circumstances are given to him in time. How are they determined ? Is it by Fate, by pure Casualty, or by God ? This question he cannot ignore. The answer must take history seriously. The reply which he gives affects his estimate of the experience, and since it determines his conception of the God with Whom he is in contact, it must therefore affect the experience itself.

Moreover, the method of dealing with the evidence is historically conditioned. We may say, " I cut myself off from history : I deal with the evidence on its face value." But this cannot be. Past history has determined, in part, in what manner I shall deal with the evidence. I can never reach the position of the timeless spectator who *sees* only, without experiencing. Even if I could, I should not be dealing with the same evidence ; I should have lost that part of it which is most vital—the part which comes only to the centre of experience.

Von Hügel quotes [1] three opinions which emphasise the difficulties raised by linking religion closely with history. The first is from a letter of Kant (1774) : " If a religion comes to be so placed that the critical knowledge of ancient languages—philological and antiquarian learning—constitutes the basis upon which it must remain built up, throughout all ages and all races ; then the man who is

[1] *Essays and Addresses*, second series, p. 27.

most at home in Greek and Hebrew and the like will drag all the orthodox believers, in spite of all their wry faces— as though they were so many children—whithersoever he may choose." The second is that passage already quoted —from a letter of Lessing to Schumann (1777) : " Contingent truths of history can never become the proof for necessary truths of reason." And the third from Paul de Lagarde (1873) : " The entire Christian Church has accepted the Jewish principle of considering as the object of religious emotion a something that has occurred once for all, instead of something which is evermore happening anew—the past instead of the present. . . . Yet the spirit of man, essentially eternal, cannot be satisfied with what happens just once for all. It is not religion, it is sheer sentimentality, to absorb one's self in what has come and gone. We require, not the mere past of God and of the divine, but their very presence, here and now."

Von Hügel meets these difficulties by a reminder of the difference between the science of nature and the science of history. The first is concerned with the universal, with that which can be brought under general laws ; the second is concerned with the particular. It is true that general laws may also be formulated here, but it is important to observe that precisely those features which escape the general laws of history are those which possess the greatest significance. " All our ultimate interests and standards, all our valuations of life and of men, ever and intrinsically, suppose and refer to the particular and the unique. ' Precisely in this uniqueness, this incomparableness of the objects,' says Professor Rickert, ' reside all our feelings and standards as to the ultimate worth of anything and of all things. And even the totality of the historic process derives its worth for us from its unrepeatableness ; indeed, it was this principle of Uniqueness—a unique Fall, a unique Redemption, a unique life's Trial here, and a unique Judgment hereafter—which decided the victory in favour of the Christian philosophy, in its patristic stage and form, as against Hellenism with its ever-increasing insistence upon the Universal and upon indefinite Repetition or, at least, repeatableness.' " [1]

We might compare with this a point made by Karl Heim.[2] Our own age, in spite of its secularism, is better able to reach an understanding of primitive Christianity than anyone who lived half a century ago. Ours is an age in which emphasis is laid, not on ideas and principles, but on *leaders*. Mankind is organised in fields of force, each of which is under the power of the magnetic attraction of a leader, like Lenin, Gandhi, Hitler, Mussolini. The age in which ideas were king was further removed than ours from a comprehension of the original Christian movement.[3] They made Christ into a Christian idea or a Christian principle. But the essence of Christianity does not lie in a philosophy or a system of doctrine, nor in an ethic, but in a Person.[4]

There is even more than this to be said. The mystic's religion is never so independent of history as he makes out. Even the language employed would frequently be unintelligible apart from the historic process by which his religion came to him. The Christian is bound to preserve both— the historical in the mystical and the mystical in the historical. (i) The Christ with Whom the mystic can describe himself as being in communion is that One Who was the Jesus of Nazareth. (ii) The Jesus of history, *rightly understood*, is the Jesus Who cannot but be the living and eternal Christ.

The Historic Jesus is also the Present Christ, the contemporary of us all.

Of this central thought there is a valuable philosophical treatment in Karl Heim's *Jesus der Herr*. The first Christians believed that they had living fellowship with one who was no longer on the earth. At one time that belief might have been set aside as the delusion of people who did not understand the limits of personal intercourse. But, says Heim, the modern philosophy of the " I " and the " Thou " has

[1] Pp. 30–31.
[2] *The Church of Christ and the Problems of the Day*, chap. v.
[3] P. 109.   [4] P. 99.

removed any *metaphysical* objection. We now know that the essence of the I-Thou relation need not exclude that of persons who are not historically contemporary. We see the mistake of reducing the Thou-relation to the level of an It-relation. Metaphysically, the conception of intercourse or estrangement, near or far, between persons, between a you and a me, has nothing necessarily to do with proximity or separation in space or in time.[1] Luther and Goethe were better understood by posterity than by their historical contemporaries. In this new " Dimension " we must be prepared for altogether new possibilities, and of these the most pregnant is that which we discover to be actual fact : there is one " Thou " which is different from all others, implying a new and hitherto unknown dimension ; because He is Lord, determining the destiny of men, calling men to decision.

Dr. H. G. Wood calls attention to a passage in Professor A. E. Taylor's Gifford Lectures : " In the world of intelligent human action, the remembered past seems to be able to mould the future directly and immediately, striking, so to say, out of its remote pastness, even though there has been no continuous persistence of itself or its effects through the interval," and he adds that we cannot confine the influence of the creative events recorded in the New Testament to the channels in which we can trace the continuous persistence of such influence. Nothing can prevent St. Paul speaking directly to kindred spirits through the generations, however embarrassing may be the response of Marcion, or Augustine, or Luther, or John Wesley, or Karl Barth.[2] In one important sense Croce is right in saying that all history is contemporary.

This is in line with the verdict of the religious consciousness. Our indicative is not simply a past, " Jesus was born, lived, died, rose again," but also a present, " God speaks through Him to me now, and deals with my life in such and such a way."

[1] *Jesus der Herr* (Furche-Verlag, Berlin, 1935), pp. 214 ff.
[2] H. G. Wood, *Christianity and the Nature of History*, pp. 25–26.

" It is found," says H. R. Mackintosh,[1] " that Jesus is only past while we refuse to think of Him. Let the supreme issues be taken up in moral earnest and at once He steps forward from the page of history, a tremendous and exacting reality."

[1] *Some Aspects of Christian Belief*, p. 12.

CHAPTER VIII

REVELATION AND HISTORY. II. THE HISTORIES OF SOULS

SUMMARY

THREE points must be kept in view if the relation of Christianity to history is not to be obscured. (1) Christianity began with an indicative; not a belief in messianism, but a Messiah. (2) The indicative took this particular form : " God was in Christ reconciling the world unto Himself." (3) This historical figure is also the contemporary of all generations. The Hegelian dialectic is out of place. We cannot hold to belief in the inevitability of human progress. There is in civilisation no inherent upward tendency. And the dialectic of Kierkegaard is inadequate. Revelation, according to the Theology of Crisis, is the disruption of the process of history. But the notion of *Urgeschichte* (primal history) does not help greatly in describing the manner in which the eternal world breaks through into the temporal process. If we find *Urgeschichte* at every crisis of history, we must find it also at every stage through which the crisis was prepared ; in every right choice made by men, in every sincere prophet, in every beginning of an upward tendency, however infinitesimal. God is always and everywhere at work in history, though man does not always and everywhere recognise or accept Him. The evolution of history may be the evolution of sin, but it is also the story of redemption. The determining question is not whether Jesus belongs to history or to primal history, but Who this is Who has appeared on earth. The positive emphasis of St. Paul is the wiser emphasis. God chooses the weak things of the world to confound the mighty. History is a domain in which God is bringing reality to pass. God is at the helm, though very secretly.

The difficulties suggested by Form-Criticism are very real. (i) It seems that we cannot know, with certainty, what kind of person Jesus was. Any individual story in the record may not be the account of an actual occurrence, but a symbolic representation of that which the community saw in Him. (ii) We cannot say precisely what was the content of His teaching. Much may be community interpretation rather than verbatim report. Yet we must realise that the impression made by Jesus on those who knew Him is exceedingly important for determining what manner of man He was. The early Church may have ante-dated many discoveries about Him. But, with a life which does not end with any *date*, ante-dating is not a serious mistake. The form-critic may declare that this or that is not evidence for what Jesus did or said in Galilee. Nevertheless, it may be valuable evidence for the nature of Him Who lived and spoke in Galilee. Where Form-Criticism questions the evidence, we discover that it is evidence concerning that in which we are not primarily interested. The unique cosmical significance of Jesus is not established by induction from the recorded events of His life. In a very real sense, the value authenticates the fact. The value is a revelation of God, but, since God is also Lord of the historical process, it appears to follow that the history must substantiate the revelation. The spiritually-minded man insists on the historicity of certain facts, because the denial of them would mean the surrendering of a more or less adequate conception of God.

Christian people are in possession of a line of evidence which is not weakened but strengthened by the movement of Form-Criticism. It is the testimony, not of historians, but of the histories of souls. The real presence of the Jesus of history is established by the experience of the Christian community, the Church down the ages and the Church to-day ; by the communion of men known to us with the living Christ.

CHAPTER VIII

REVELATION AND HISTORY.

II. THE HISTORIES OF SOULS

THERE are thus three points which must be kept in view if the relation of Christianity to history is not to be obscured.

1. Christianity begins with an indicative—not a doctrine of monotheism, but a new act or word of the one living God ; not a belief in messianism, but an actual Messiah ; not a Pharisaic doctrine of resurrection but a risen Person.[1] (It is not without significance that the indicative is absent from the later essay of Troeltsch. Its title is *The Place of Christianity among the World-Religions* (*Die Stellung des Christentums unter den Weltreligionen*), but in the whole course of the lecture the name of Jesus is not mentioned.)

2. It is not even with *an* indicative that we are concerned, but with this particular indicative : " God was in Christ reconciling the world unto Himself." [2]

3. This historical figure is also the contemporary of all generations.

It is clear that the Hegelian dialectic is out of place here. It does not provide for the new creation which takes place in history. The course of history is not simply the natural unfolding of what is implicit in man from the outset. " To affirm, as Hegel did, that the whole wealth of historic development is potential in the beginnings of mind, is a statement which it would be impossible to justify historically. The lesson of history is rather that at certain times men of genius initiate new movements which, though related to the past, are not explained by it." [3] There is much more than the development of that which was

[1] Cf. H. G. Wood, *Christianity and the Nature of History*, p. 66.
[2] 2 Cor. v. 19.
[3] Galloway, *The Philosophy of Religion*, p. 446.

implicit from the outset. There are crises, creative moments, the results of which cannot be foretold, nor, when they are determined, explained by what has preceded them. Nor can we any longer hold to that belief in the *inevitability* of progress which satisfied many minds in last century. There is no system of human evolution which will, without fail, produce generations of mankind in an ever-ascending series of melioration. Many are content with the superficial confidence that there *is* such a law at work ; the humanist will have it that civilisation tends inevitably upwards. Turgenieff declared, " I believe in civilisation and I require no further creed." That faith should have received a mortal blow from the events of August, 1914, and subsequent years. There is in civilisation no inherent upward tendency. Its gains have to be preserved by endless vigilance and strife, or, as the religious man prefers to put it, they are given by the grace of God where faithfulness and obedience make it possible to receive them.

The Hegelian dialectic is out of place. It is equally clear that the dialectic of Kierkegaard is inadequate. History, Barth would say, reveals God's abrupt No to man's affirmation. To Christianity, history is a very different thing from history as it appears to any other religion or philosophy. Barth writes : [1] " The Word of God in the highest sense makes history"; and again [2] " By the thing it calls revelation the Bible always means a unique event, one occurring in that place and at that time. Thus, for all its ' errors ' in such and such a variety of cases—and in this respect it is simply quite unconcerned—in its statements about place and time, according to the canons of present-day historical science, the important thing is not the more or less ' correct ' content of these statements, but the fact of them. This fact, that the Bible of the Old Testament and New Testament repeatedly and with extraordinary emphasis makes chronological and topographical statements, that therefore it means every time to ascribe to the revelation of God of which it tells a

[1] *The Doctrine of the Word of God*, (E.T.), p. 163.
[2] *Op. cit.* p. 374.

temporally and spatially circumscribed place, that it includes the events narrated by it, in which revelation is imparted to men, in the framework of other events which happened at that time and place, that ancient Egypt, Assyria, and Babylon come into view as the horizon of the experiences of the nation Israel, that Cyrenius, the governor in Syria, cannot be left out of the story of Christmas, and that Pontius Pilate genuinely belongs to the Creed—all that asserts the Bible's claim, in its account of revelation, to relate history, *i.e.* however, a claim to recount not a relationship between God and man existing generally, always and everywhere, or discoverable in process, but an event that took place there and only there, then and only then, between God and certain perfectly definite men. The divine self-unveiling of which it tells, together with the holiness it ascribes to God in this act of His, is imparted not simply to man, but to such and such men in a perfectly definite situation." The factor which determines our hearing or not hearing of the Bible story is not therefore the question of its *general* historicity, but the question of its *special* historicity. The historical event is not simply an exponent of a general occurrence, a special case under a rule, or the realisation of a general possibility. History is not to be looked on as the frame within which revelation can take place. If it were that, then we should have to reject the concept of historicity. On the contrary, revelation takes place vertically from heaven.[1]

In the ordinary sense of the word, Brunner writes:[2] Christianity " is not concerned with history at all. It is what it is through its relation to a unique event, which, although it is a fact of history, does not gain its unique character from its historical connection. It is this which determines the peculiar relation of the Christian faith to history in general. To the Christian faith, revelation does not mean a reverent process of tracing the ways of God in history. Indeed, history as such is not a divine revelation ; it merely represents humanity as a whole

[1] *Op. cit.* pp. 378–379.
[2] *The Mediator*, p. 153.

in its need of redemption." Revelation is the breaking-in of God—as it were, the disruption of the process of history.

This descent of God "straight down from above" (*senkrecht von oben*) is a conception with which all may agree. The divine coming is not an *evolutio* but an *ingressio*. Yet it is necessary further to examine the manner in which it takes place. Does God's descent take account of the situation as it is ? Or does it involve an abrupt cleavage, complete discontinuity between the new and the old ?

The answer of the Theology of Crisis has been given in the word *Urgeschichte*. Barth, in the second edition of his *Dogmatik*, has dropped the word, but the idea is still retained.[1] *Urgeschichte* is described as the germ of all history ; what the historian relates to us as " history " is its manifestation in space and time.[2] " Biblical *history* in the Old and New Testaments is not really history at all, but seen from above is a series of free divine acts and seen from below a series of fruitless attempts to undertake something in itself impossible."[3] When God enters, history ceases to be ; something wholly different and new begins—a history with its own distinct grounds, possibilities, and hypotheses. God breaks through from the eternal world into " this dim spot which men call earth."[4]

I question whether much is gained by the conception of *Urgeschichte*. " The Kingdom of God," it is said,[5] " is not the goal of historical evolution, not the emergence of divine forces latent in the process of history. It is the new world of God, and must come, in and through the action of God Himself. The revelation event which betokens this is not therefore an historical but a super-historical, an

---

[1] See English Translation, pp. 164 ff. and 373 ff.

[2] Cf. Brunner, *The Philosophy of Religion* (E.T.), pp. 123, 160. The term is taken from Franz Overbeck and has been translated "pre-history" (Birch Hoyle), "super-history" (Camfield), "revelation history" (M'Connachie), "primal history" (Hoskyns, Dickie), "primordial history" (Farrer, Woolf).

[3] Barth, *Das Wort Gottes und die Theologie* (E.T., *The Word of God and the Word of Man*), p. 72.

[4] Cf. Brunner, *God and Man*, pp. 51 ff.

[5] F. W. Camfield, *Revelation and the Holy Spirit* (Eliot Stock, 1933), p. 218.

urgeschichtlich event." An historical movement has no value nor promise in itself. " Apart from the infusion into it of critical and creative power from without and from above, it deteriorates, hardens, turns to evil. This can be seen in all the great and beneficent movements of history. They have in spite of all their value a nisus towards evil. They cannot be allowed to run on, through their own momentum, evolve through their own innate life and power. The evolution of history is *per se* the evolution of sin." [1]

It may be questioned whether this amounts to more than what will readily be granted, namely, that what is good in the process of the world's development is of God, from above.

> " And every virtue we possess,
> And every victory won,
> And every thought of holiness,
> Are His alone."

It does not offer any help in investigating the manner in which God breaks through, the relation between the eternal world and the temporal process.

It is plain that the arriving of the divine movement in the world does not involve discontinuity. God is in control of the historical process at every point. When He intervenes it is not a new situation that is created, but the old one transfigured. The unity and the character of God are enough by themselves to justify Christians in finding revelation in history. God is found " in the confirmation afforded by history to the maxim that ' righteousness exalteth a nation.' " [2]

If we find *Urgeschichte* at every *crisis* of history (the point at which a movement coming down from God arrives) then we must find it also at every stage through which the crisis was prepared ; in every right choice made by men, in every sincere prophet, in every beginning of an upward tendency, however infinitesimal. In fact, God is always and everywhere at work in history. Only—man does not

---

[1] *Revelation and the Holy Spirit*, p. 220.
[2] H. R. Mackintosh, *The Christian Apprehension of God*, end of chap. iii.

always and everywhere recognise or accept Him. Divine
forces *are* latent in history. Had it not been so, history
would have had a much more sorry tale to tell ; would
perhaps have ended long ago. The evolution of history
may be the evolution of sin, but it is also the story of
redemption.

Certainly the unfolding of history has been characterised
by wrong choices, wrong actions, wrong aims ; and revelation cannot come (directly) through these (though it may
come *out* of them by way of warning, or through the
overruling of evil for good) ; but it does not greatly
help to use the terms " historical " and " super-historical "
when that which is signified is simply bad and good.
In these simple terms there are problems enough to be
tackled.[1]

Every crisis has its antecedents. The Barthian is
chiefly concerned with the divine side ; history has to be
acted on creatively by God. And, in this connection,
Urgeschichte means little more than this, that there are
degrees of revelation ; that revelation is progressive, and
that it is dependent on the responsiveness of the human
spirit. God does not give the next lesson till the last has
been learned. *Geschichte* is God in history unseen or
defied. *Urgeschichte* is God in history recognised and
accepted. The determining question for Christianity is not,
Is Jesus *Geschichte* or *Urgeschichte* ? The question is, Who

[1] Admittedly, says the Dean of St. Paul's (W. R. Matthews, *The
Purpose of God* (Nisbet, 1935), p. 151), history presents us with " a wavering line and not with a rational curve, still less with a straight, upward
path. What is the cause of that wavering ? Not, I suggest, that the
waverings as such are part of the divine plan, but rather that the possibility of wavering was an element in the design. The set-backs and
disasters, the catastrophes which intervene and bring high promise to
nothing, the more deadly slow decay of once vigorous civilisations, are
partly due to that irrational element in human life which we may describe
as ' chance.' But they are also due in part to the failure of persons and
societies to respond to their vocation. . . . The course of history
is studded with occasions when the future depended on whether
a few individuals had the insight to see what might be done and
the courage to do it, and with other occasions when the few who perceived the signs of the times could not make their vision effective in
social action."

is this Who has appeared on earth, has lived and taught, was crucified and is risen ? The term *Urgeschichte* is perhaps only a name to conceal our ignorance. The conception of history and super-history does not really meet the recurrent problem, the reconciliation of timeless truth with the historical medium by which it is conveyed. Dr. H. G. Wood suggests that the positive emphasis of St. Paul is the wiser emphasis. God chooses the weak things of this world to confound the mighty.[1] History is a domain in which God is bringing reality to pass. " God was at the helm," Augustine said, " though very secretly." [2] " History is such that salvation may come by way of it." [3] In a fine phrase of Professor Farmer there is a divine purpose " which is fashioning men in time for that which time cannot contain." [4]

We have seen that the Christian is bound to preserve both sides of his faith—the historical in the mystical and the mystical in the historical. In the first place, the Christ of our day-by-day communion is that One Who was the Jesus of Nazareth. In the second place, the Jesus of history, rightly understood, is the Jesus Who cannot but be the living and eternal Christ.

Here we must meet that important challenge which comes to-day from the school of Form-Criticism. Much that was hitherto accepted as the authentic record of the acts performed by Jesus and the words spoken by Him may be the product of the early Christian community. Nor is it easy to set a limit to the amount of transference of material from one category to the other which may yet be demanded. As the community is in some sense the author of the story, may it not also be the hero ? [5]

There are indeed several weighty considerations which serve to minimise the importance of the results announced already by *Formgeschichte*. Its contention is that a very

---

[1] Cf. *Christianity and the Nature of History*, p. 189.

[2] *Confessions*, iv. 14.

[3] H. R. Mackintosh, *Some Aspects of Christian Belief*, p. 16.

[4] H. H. Farmer, *The World and God* (Nisbet, 1935), p. 301.

[5] Cf. H. G. Wood, *op. cit.* pp. 40 and 70.

large proportion of the Gospel records must be ascribed to creation by the community and a very small proportion to selection by it ; whereas the truth is probably the reverse. Bultmann, for example, admits that a community-saying is not a pure invention out of the void, but a construction which would not, and could not, have been made without the movement created by Jesus Himself. Indeed, the record which grows out of the community is the best testimony for the teaching of Jesus.[1]

Nevertheless, the difficulty raised is a very real one. (i) It appears that we cannot know, with certainty, what kind of *person* Jesus was. Any individual story in the record of His life may not be the account of an actual occurrence but simply a symbolic representation of that which the community saw in Him. (ii) We cannot say precisely what was the content of His *teaching*. Much of our record is community-interpretation rather than actual verbatim report. Montefiore has put it in this way : " We cannot get beyond the Jesus—' *des ältesten Gemeinde-glaubens* '—the Jesus as the faith of the earliest community conceived Him. Old history and new faith are fused together ; the picture of Jesus which the Synoptics show has not only many painful gaps, but is throughout covered with a varnish which here and there does not allow anything of the original to shine through. Just where we most want to know, we must always be content to conjecture." [2]

To meet this perplexity we must consider afresh the nature of the evidence available. The school of Form-Criticism lays emphasis on the historical method of arriving at the truth about Christianity. Therefore, a very important question is, Where is *good* history to be found ? Now, in answering this question, we find one essential class of evidence in the experience of the early Christian Church. That possesses communal memory. Recollections about

---

[1] *Jesus* (Deutsche Bibliothek, Berlin), p. 72.
[2] *Synoptic Gospels* (Macmillan, 1909), p. lxvii. The passage is partly based on Jülicher, *Neue Linien in der Kritik der evangelischen Überlieferung*.

Jesus are pooled : each contributes his share to the common stock of memories. And the contribution of each is checked by the fact that others have also been witnesses. There was little possibility of emotional inventiveness getting the upper hand in dealing with material which was to become canonical. If we had the option of citing any dozen witnesses it is here that we should seek for them. Moreover, *if* the truth is the twofold truth which Christians believe it to be, namely, that Jesus lived once on earth *and* that He is now alive and in communion with the Christian, then the *sole* direct evidence for this twofold truth is precisely the evidence of the Christian community in the days immediately following His death and resurrection. Neglect this evidence and you cut yourself off from the possibility of finding this truth. *Formgeschichte* can lessen the evidence available for knowing what the historical Jesus was like (showing, perhaps, that this and that were not actual incidents), but at the same time it adds to the evidence for the interpretation of the Person of Jesus by His early followers. That which is taken away from one category is transferred to the other. " Thereby losing its value," the critic might interpolate. But this is not necessarily so. The impression made by Jesus upon those who knew Him or were members of the early Church is exceedingly important for determining what manner of man He was. Even false anecdotes may be good history. But there is much more here, for we admit the single-mindedness of the " myth-makers " ; they were *honest* witnesses. Yes, the critic may reply, honest but *mistaken* : we can prove it by showing the mistake appearing ; can film it, as it were, and demonstrate how, in all innocence, it arose. To this we may reply that the " mistaken witness " cannot have altered in any essential particular the truth about the Person of Jesus. Just as some of the miracles may not be historically authentic and yet may give essential information about the kind of person Jesus was, so that without the account of these miracles we should lose something of our evidence for estimating His Person, so " mistaken witness " may be valuable, even indispensable, evidence, especially when we remember again that the *honesty* of the witnesses is not impugned.

Next, concerning the witness of to-day. It is evident that the nature of the Person of Jesus has been more fully revealed with the passing of the centuries of the Christian Church. Wherever there has been obedience and loyalty, there has been given a new insight into the mind of Christ. Where the Church has been faithful, she has both learned and taught new things about her Lord. Her deeds are *His* deeds. The Gospels are still being written.

The form-critic may enter this caution : That which is discovered to-day about the nature of Christ is not admissible as evidence for what He did in His lifetime on the earth. And we should at once agree. But the life of Jesus did not end with His life on earth. The early Church may have ante-dated many discoveries about Him. They were made only through the fuller experience of an obedient community, but they believed—or, perhaps, *came* to believe—that these discoveries had been made in His earthly life, from deeds which He performed or words which He spoke. But, with a life which does not end with any *date*, ante-dating is not a serious mistake. In fact, that which Form-Criticism casts doubt upon is the " historic Jesus "—meaning by that the picture of Jesus as He lived between birth and death (or between birth and resurrection) ; but this is not all that Christians are concerned with. Christian believers to-day, like the Christians of the early Church, are concerned with the *eternal* Jesus. To-day we believe in Him still living, still acting, still responding to prayer. Professor Paul Tillich writes : [1] " The foundation of Christian belief is not the historical Jesus, but the Biblical picture of Christ. The criterion of human thought and action is not the constantly changing and artificial product of historical research, but the picture of Christ as it is rooted in ecclesiastical belief and human experience." At the earliest period of Gospel-writing

---

[1] *The Interpretation of History* (Scribners, 1936), p. 34.

(or Gospel-preaching) men believed in Him as God incarnate and therefore as Someone more than a human being whose life is bounded by birth and death. The witness with which we have to deal is witness about *this* Jesus.[1]

The form-critic may declare that this or that is not evidence for what Jesus did or said in Galilee. Nevertheless, it may be evidence for the nature of Him Who lived and spoke in Galilee. And it will still be necessary to show how this witness arose. *We* say that it came out of a fuller experience of Christ. Where *Formgeschichte* questions the evidence, we discover that it is evidence concerning that in which we are not *primarily* interested. The unique cosmical significance of Jesus cannot be proved by induction from the recorded events of His life. " That the Word has been ' made flesh,' and made flesh in just the specific person whom a Christian calls Lord, is a proposition which admits of no establishment by the empirical appeal to certified fact." [2] What chiefly weighed with the earliest believers was, first, the direct impression made by their Master of the presence in Him of something " numinous," not to be understood in terms of ordinary human life ; and, next, the confirmation of this impression by the transcendent events of the resurrection on the third day and the wonderful manifestations of the Day of Pentecost.[3] " One may intelligibly hold that the belief in the real continued

---

[1] Cf. Brunner, *The Mediator*, p. 159, note : " Hence, from the theological point of view, the preference for the Synoptic Gospels evinced by theologians (not by historians) is always a sign of bondage to the historical point of view. In faith we are not concerned with the Jesus of History, as historical science sees Him, but with the Jesus Christ of personal testimony, who is the real Christ, and Whom John shows us just as plainly . . . as the Synoptists." And, again, p. 172 : " If once the conviction is regained that the Christian faith does not arise out of the picture of the historical Jesus, but out of the testimony to Christ as such—this includes the witness of the prophets as well as that of the Apostles—and that it is based upon this testimony, then inevitably the preference for the Synoptic Gospels and for the actual words of Jesus, which was the usual position of the last generation, will disappear."

[2] A. E. Taylor, *The Faith of a Moralist*, ii. p. 126.

[3] *Ibid.* p. 129.

personal activity and the supremacy of Christ, and in the reality of the contacts between the still living Christ and His disciples, out of which Christianity arose, is what is essential in the historical *credendum*, and everything else matter for criticism and speculation, not affecting the true substance of the Christian faith." [1]

Before considering the challenge of Form-Criticism in its extreme form, we should look for a moment at the conception of " communal memory " to which a central place must be given in the method we have here followed. Quite plainly, its importance is not confined to the period in which the Gospels were being composed. We are dependent on it in every age. Knowledge of Christ is mediated to every Christian not alone by the Gospels and Epistles but by the family to which he belongs, the society of which he is a part, the Church of which he is a member. Family, society, Church—all are handing on a tradition which runs back to the beginning of Christianity, which, moreover, has received *enrichment* in every period when faithfulness, loyalty, and obedience resulted in a more profound understanding of the mind of Christ. There is no need to postulate an infallible institution, to which tradition has been entrusted. What must be affirmed, however, is the legitimacy of trusting the " communal memory " where the community has been faithful ; and this is no more than affirming faith in the Holy Spirit as guiding aright the thoughts of *good* people concerning their Master, and bringing to those who themselves have something of the mind of Christ new understanding of His life and will. When we speak of the immediate experience of the soul with Christ to-day, we are not, therefore, indicating an experience which begins and ends with the individual soul, but something which is the outcome also of the Spirit's work, uninterrupted, down nineteen centuries.

Finally, we must take the extreme case. Suppose that Form-Criticism should be able to apply its methods to prove that Jesus had never lived. There are those who say that their theology is such that nothing in it would require

[1] *The Faith of a Moralist*, ii. p. 140.

to be changed if it should be proved to-morrow that the figure of Christ was non-historical.[1]

Would our Christianity be unchanged in such circumstances ? Should we even feel that the tradition carried the same message ? It is surely clear that it would involve a fundamental change to realise that we had, so to speak, been deceived. Having been led to faith in this highest conception of God as One Who is self-imparting in this noblest of all conceivable ways, to find that God had *not* so revealed Himself in Jesus—that would be to discover that He was less in goodness and love than He might have been.

In a very real sense, the value authenticates the fact. The value is a revelation of God, but, God being also the God of historical fact, it seems to follow that the history must substantiate the revelation. " The disjunction between ' value ' and ' fact ' is not absolute, the supreme ' value,' God, being also the ultimate source of the whole course of historical ' fact.' . . . What leads the spiritually minded man to insist on the ' historicity ' of a certain event really is a perception that denial of the fact would involve surrendering a more or less adequate conception of God." [2]

Fortunately, it is not necessary to invoke any ontological argument to prove that Jesus lived. Drews' book on the Christ-myths, said H. R. Mackintosh, is " more interesting as a symptom than as a contribution." [3] It would be impossible to *prove* that Napoleon ever lived. We should readily doubt his existence if we determined to doubt the authenticity of all records and all traditions. But this would be to make history impossible ; to deny continuity in experience and to fall back simply on timeless idea as the sole truth, and even on the *momentary* idea —since all ideas have a history too, and it determines their nature and their significance.

[1] Bultmann, for example, in *Jesus*, pp. 16–17, holds that we cannot say how far the portrait of Jesus has been objectively preserved, but this is not of great importance in the study of that complex of thoughts presented by the earliest traditions, since if it were discovered that Jesus had never lived, the tradition would still be unaffected.

[2] A. E. Taylor, *op. cit.* ii. p. 147.

[3] *Some Aspects of Christian Belief*, p. 9.

An earlier example of the claim that history could make no alteration in his faith was P. W. Schmiedel. " My most intimate religious life would not be harmed," he declared, " even if to-day I were forced to acknowledge that Jesus never existed. . . . I would still know that I could not lose the degree of piety which I attained long ago, simply because I could no longer trace it back to Him." [1] Brunner considers, on the contrary, that *everything* would be lost. Christianity might still be a very brilliant idea, but it would not be a religion. That is not strictly true. There would still remain more than the *idea* of such a God as the Father sending His Son into the world ; there would be the possibility, indeed the unquenchable, confident faith, that He would one day reveal Himself as we believed He had done already in Jesus. It would still be open to us to put forward this new kind of ontological argument. Descartes maintained [2] that the idea of God, who is infinite and perfect, cannot be formed in man by any finite object, and must therefore be caused by God Himself. So, we might say, it cannot be denied that the *idea* of God Incarnate as we understand it in the Gospels was present to the minds of the first century. In the intellectual and religious *entourage* of that time, moreover, there is nothing to account for the rise of such an idea. It must therefore have come from God Himself, and God cannot prove less in goodness and love than the noblest idea of God.

Happily, there is no danger of Christianity being reduced to the form of a Messianic hope not yet fulfilled. Our religion, our creed, *would* be different, should it be proved that Jesus never lived. But, if that should be proved, the demonstration would at the same time invalidate all history and all science.

Faith knows, for reasons which are not accessible to the historian as such, that the inquiry concerning the historical fact of Christ's appearance in the world " cannot yield a negative result." [3] We are in possession of a line of proof which is not weakened but strengthened by the

---

[1] Quoted in *The Mediator*, p. 155, note.   [2] *Meditation*, iii.
[3] Brunner, *The Mediator*, p. 166.

movement of Form-Criticism. It is the testimony, not of historians, but of the histories of souls. The real presence of the Jesus of history is established by the experience of the Christian community, the Church down the ages and the Church to-day ; by the communion of men known to us with the living Christ ; and, not least for us, by that which He has said to *us* and done for *us* ; is saying and doing.

Man, in Time, cannot form any valid conception of Eternity or of the end of History. Jesus left these in darkness. It is perhaps part of the holy command of God that we should remain all our earthly life in a kind of trembling uncertainty. Jesus has not drawn back the veil ; we must submit to the necessity of bowing our heads in darkness. But, here as everywhere, we go forward trusting to His guidance, believing where we cannot see.[1] Nevertheless, we know that the nature of God will always be what it is shown in Jesus to be ; that God's method will always and everywhere be the same, that of divine holy love.

> "With this ambiguous earth
> His dealings have been told us. These abide :
>   The signal to a maid, the human birth,
> The lesson, and the young Man crucified.
>
>   But not a star of all
> The innumerable host of stars has heard
>   How He administered this terrestrial ball.
> Our race have kept their Lord's entrusted Word.
>
>   But in the eternities,
> Doubtless we shall compare together, hear
>   A million alien Gospels, in what guise
> He trod the Pleiades, the Lyre, the Bear.
>
>   Oh, be prepared, my soul !
> To read the inconceivable, to scan
>   The million forms of God those stars unroll
> When, in our turn, we show to them a Man."[2]

[1] Cf. Karl Heim, *Jesus der Weltvollender* (Furche-Verlag, Berlin, 1937), p. 228.
[2] Alice Meynell, *Christ in the Universe* (Oates & Washbourne, 1924).

CHAPTER IX

RELIGIOUS CERTAINTY. I. Theology of Crisis

SUMMARY

THOSE whose life-work it is to preach the Gospel ; to comfort or to convince where faith is imperilled, are aware of their need of some sheet-anchor, some sure word of God, some certainty. It is not simply psychological certitude that is sought—that degree of assurance which overcomes all doubt in the individual mind or even prevents it entering. This may be no more than "habitual conviction" or "readiness to act on a belief."

We come nearer to our requirement when we speak of "logical certainty." In this connection, certainty is contrasted with mere probability. But here we must notice that there is also such a thing as non-logical conviction. Instances may be found in judgments of a friend's character, loyalty, and trustworthiness. Morality and religion have their own particular type of certainty, determined by the nature of their subject-matter. If the term "subjective" is employed here, it does not mean that there is any element of arbitrariness or bias.

The difficulty of the Calvinist attitude is that the immutable divine decree as the ultimate ground of certainty is equally external with the Roman Catholic doctrine of special revelation. That which we are seeking is the divinely-given security of present forgiveness and adoption. We have to return to the Pauline treatment of the theme, which is in large measure also that of Luther. The Spirit itself beareth witness with our spirit, that we are the children of God. It would be wrong to identify this religious certainty, as is sometimes done, with personal assurance of salvation. The eyes of the believer are not fixed on his own blessedness but on the wonder of God's love.

In matters of *æsthetic appreciation*, certainty may be felt, but it appears to build on a flimsy foundation. If it is challenged, it finds it hard to give a reasoned defence of itself. The *metaphysician* may base his epistemology on the axiom that truth can never be self-contradictory, deducing from this the positive criterion that truth is proved to be true by showing itself at once comprehensive and systematic. But here we are faced with the difficulty of setting the mind to criticise itself ; making it both the subject and the organ of criticism. At the very least, the ultimatum of metaphysics is no more sure than the ultimatum of religion, namely, that the Reality which we are endeavouring to apprehend is personal, and is seeking to reveal itself to us. Oswald Spengler, looking for a General Theory of Relativity in *ethical* matters, claims to have brought about a Copernican revolution ; to have removed the centre-point of ethical orientation. All ethical systems are declared to be relative ; they will decline when their day is done.

The Theology of Crisis meets the challenge of the relativist with the declaration that revelation gives a fixed point, an absolute. Between time and eternity there is an infinite qualitative difference. In the Word of God eternity breaks into time. It is true that there are times when Barth, for example, appears to be speaking of a transcendent God of Whom man can never know anything. But, behind the occasional over-emphasis, is the fundamental truth that revelation, if it is truly revelation, is something absolute and ultimate and therefore not open to testing by anything else whatsoever except revelation.

CHAPTER IX

Religious Certainty

I. THEOLOGY OF CRISIS

" Man with his burning soul
Has but an hour of breath
To build a ship of truth
In which his soul may sail—
Sail on the sea of death,
For death takes toll
Of beauty, courage, youth,
Of all but truth." [1]

THOSE whose life-work it is to preach the Gospel, to comfort or to convince where faith is imperilled, whether through weakness within or through attack from without, are aware of their need of some sheet-anchor, some sure word of God, some *certainty*. It is their aim, Sunday by Sunday, to send their hearers out again " into a world transformed." How is it to be accomplished ? Not by eloquence. We appreciate Verlaine's recipe for poetry, " Take eloquence and wring its neck ! " The most moving appeal to the imagination may leave no more permanent impression than " the wind blowing in a horse's ear." If, from the scholar, we expect first erudition, and from the artist, vision, from the preacher we expect certainty. Without that, his sermons at their best are likely to share with Hood's " Song of the Shirt " the reputation of having " great success and no results."

Note that it is not simply *psychological certitude* that is sought—that degree of assurance which overcomes all doubt in the individual mind or even prevents it entering. This may be no more than " habitual conviction " or " readiness to act on a belief." [2]   Recent investigations appear to

---

[1] John Masefield, " Truth " (in *Philip the King*).
[2] See Bosanquet, *Logic*, vol. i. chap. ix. p. 377.

show that men are naturally inclined to believe *more* rather than *less*. Scepticism is relatively rare. There may be wide differences of opinion on religious matters. Many people are completely certain in one direction, and others completely certain in the very opposite direction. But relatively few people have *no* convictions at all. We might expect, finding a vast difference in people's opinions, to find also a great many who have no belief at all ; who are pure sceptics. They have discovered that doctors differ. We might expect them to reserve their judgment, implying that truth is not for them. But this is precisely what psychological investigation appears *not* to disclose. Men are prepared to say, " I have not the training to say whether this or that is the truth about wireless telephony ; or about the cure of rheumatism ; or about theories of social credit ; and therefore I have no beliefs whatever in these matters." But men are not prepared to adopt the same attitude towards religion. Here we find a strong " tendency to certainty," and a curious feature, according to Dr. R. H. Thouless, who has conducted many interesting investigations on this point,[1] is that this tendency is quite as strong among unbelievers as among the pious. Scepticism is rare, and it is not any commoner among the more intelligent than among the less intelligent. It seems to follow that the real opponent of religion to-day is not scepticism but positive disbelief. The " will to believe " appears to have its counterpart in the will to disbelieve.

We come nearer to our requirement when we speak of " logical certainty," which indicates that the evidence in favour of some judgment is so conclusive as to place the judgment beyond doubt. In this connection certainty is contrasted with mere probability. The Greeks said that it belonged to knowledge as compared with opinion.

But here we must notice that there is such a thing as non-logical conviction. This is not to be confused with the irresponsible advocacy of the will to believe, as if merely emotional pressure is to be allowed to override the reason.

---

[1] " The Tendency to Certainty in Religious Belief ": *British Journal of Psychology*, vol. xxvi. part 1. July 1935.

It is rather the type of conviction which *might* be rationalised if sufficient knowledge were attained. Newman took up consideration of it in *Oxford University Sermons* and in *The Grammar of Assent*. He speaks of the distinction between Implicit Reason and Explicit Reason, between the actual grounds of a belief and the reflective analysis of these grounds. As an example he points to the empirical weather-lore of the peasant with his confident prediction of fair or foul weather. Better instances might perhaps be found in judgments of a friend's character, loyalty, and trustworthiness, to which we have already drawn attention.

This brings us to the heart of the matter. It is found in the fact that morality and religion have their own particular type of certainty, determined by the nature of their subject-matter. It has been said that real scepticism lies in the attempt " to make morality and religion subsist on a borrowed certainty." The term " subjective " has frequently been used to describe the more personal and intimate certainties of faith as contrasted with an impersonal scientific knowledge, but this does not for a moment imply " that moral or religious certitude is unevidenced and groundless, or that there is any element of arbitrariness, bias, or fancifulness in it." [1]

Calvin built up his doctrine of the certitude of salvation on the eternal nature of God. The certainty of election is not to be found in ourselves but in God. Thus it is said in *The Westminster Confession*,[2] " True believers may have the assurance of their salvation divers ways shaken, diminished, and intermitted ; as, by negligence in preserving of it ; by falling into some special sin, which woundeth the conscience and grieveth the Spirit ; by some sudden or vehement temptation ; by God's withdrawing the light of His countenance, and suffering even such as fear Him to walk in darkness, and to have no light ; yet are they never utterly destitute of that seed of God, and life of faith, that love of Christ and the brethren, that sincerity

---

[1] Henry Barker in Hastings' *Encyclopædia of Religion and Ethics*, vol. iii. 324 b.
[2] Chap. xviii. section IV.

12

of heart and conscience of duty, out of which, by the operation of the Spirit, this assurance may in due time be revived, and by the which, in the meantime, they are supported from utter despair."

The difficulty is that the immutable divine decree as the ultimate ground of certainty is equally external with the Roman Catholic doctrine of special revelation. According to the Council of Trent no one can know, with a certainty of faith, which cannot be subject to illusion, that he has obtained the grace of God. No one can know whom God has chosen for Himself except by special revelation.[1] Assurance is given in the authoritative voice of the father-confessor, but it can be only for the moment of absolution. It may well be that the first mortal sin committed thereafter may remove the sinner from his standing in God's grace. So, in the Calvinistic doctrine of double predestination, where the decree of God is separated from the thought of God's fatherly love for all men, there may be complete confidence that the elect of God are safe, but there can be no conviction on my part that God's grace is for me. That which we are seeking is the divinely-given security of present forgiveness and adoption.

We have to return to the Pauline treatment of the theme (which is in large measure also that of Luther). Religious certainty means the conviction that God is gracious and that He is Lord of all even in spite of the tragic phenomena of human sin. And this assurance, coming from God Himself through His Son, is not presumptuous. " When we look believingly at God in Christ, where is the presumption in being quite sure of His compassion to the sinful ? Can we be too sure of it, too trustful in claiming it for our own deep need ? "[2] The relevant passages in St. Paul's epistles are Romans viii. 15 ff. and Galatians iv. 6. It is the Spirit Who produces in the believer the conviction of his sonship. " Ye have not received the spirit of bondage again to fear ; but ye have received the Spirit of adoption, whereby we cry, Abba,

---

[1] Session vi. 12.
[2] H. R. Mackintosh, *The Christian Experience of Forgiveness*, p. 249.

Father. The Spirit itself beareth witness with our spirit,
that we are the children of God." " Because ye are sons,
God hath sent forth the Spirit of His Son into your hearts,
crying, Abba, Father." We have not only the status, but
the heart of sons, says Denney, commenting on the passage
in Romans. " Our own spirit tells us we are God's children,
but the voice with which it speaks is, as we know, prompted
and inspired by the Divine Spirit itself." [1]

It would be wrong to identify this religious certainty,
as is sometimes done, with personal assurance of salvation.
The eyes of the believer are not fixed on his own blessedness
but on the wonder of God's love. Moses felt that he was
ready, if his people should perish, to perish with them.[2]
St. Paul, in the next chapter of his letter to the Romans,
is prepared to go even a step further, and to perish *for* them,
if that were possible.[3] Whatever happens, God can be
trusted, utterly and to the end and in all things. " He that
spared not His own Son, but delivered him up for us all,
how shall He not with him also freely give us all things ? " [4]
The assurance of faith is not limited, since it is grounded in
the illimitable love of God in Christ Jesus.

To-day, many are concerned because the certainties are
shaken. They confess themselves, not finders, but seekers.
They are aware of the tentativeness of their beliefs. This
is the crisis of religion. For a religion cannot be tentative.[5]
And attempts are being made to find certainty elsewhere.

Is certainty attainable outside religion ?

1. *In Æsthetics ?* When we repeat the words :

> " At my back I alwaies hear
> Time's wingèd chariot hurrying near,"

we are *sure* that there is beauty there. When we read,
" Intreat me not to leave thee, or to return from following
after thee . . .," once again we are *certain*. And yet our

[1] *The Expositor's Greek Testament*, ad. loc.
[2] Ex. xxxii. 32, " Yet now, if Thou wilt forgive their sin— ; and if
not, blot me, I pray Thee, out of Thy book which Thou hast written."
[3] Rom. ix. 3, " I could wish that myself were accursed from Christ
for my brethren, my kinsmen according to the flesh."
[4] Rom. viii. 32.   [5] Cf. Pauck, *Karl Barth*, p. 6.

certainty seems to build on a flimsy foundation. Were it challenged, it could give no reasoned defence of itself. So precarious is æsthetic criticism that a distinguished professor of English Literature can say only guardedly, " If I were shown a new poem as great as Keats' last sonnet, I *think* that I should recognise its merit. I am not sure."

2. *In Metaphysics?* What is truth? asks the doubting philosopher, and he appears to give innumerable answers—all mutually destructive. (*a*) Perhaps he says that truth is the correspondence of thought with the real world. But consider the implications. To attain certainty, then, you are required to know three things—the contents of your thought, the nature of reality, and the degree of correspondence between the first and the second. Even then, who shall say that our minds are capable of pronouncing on this correspondence or lack of it? (*b*) Perhaps the philosopher says that truth is that which works; successful action is the criterion of truth. Here the difficulty is that problems may be solved, with apparent satisfaction, by falsehood or illusion, and this is the obstacle which Pragmatism has not surmounted. (In Herman Melville's *Moby Dick*, Queequeg, on first seeing a wheel-barrow, puts his sea-chest on it; lashes it fast, and then shoulders the barrow and marches up the wharf. As a pragmatist, he has proved the truth about wheel-barrows, because his theory has worked. He has brought his sea-chest safely home.)

If the emphasis is laid on feeling instead of action, the case is no better. A thought is not necessarily true because it satisfies my feelings or meets my desires. " Needs and desires of themselves give us no standard of value. It will not do to alter the multiplication-table because we are getting into debt." [1] We cannot decree, as one state is reputed to have done, that for the future, in the interests of convenient calculation, the symbol π shall have the value of exactly 3.

(*c*) Again, it may be that the metaphysician takes some simple, axiomatic principle, and builds on it an inverted

[1] Ritchie, *Philosophical Studies*, p. 69, quoted Inge, *Truth and Falsehood in Religion*, p. 107, note 2.

pyramid of truth. It may be the Cartesian principle *Cogito, ergo sum.* Or he may proclaim himself a solipsist, believing that nothing exists except himself and the states of his own mind. (" I am so glad to hear," wrote a dear old lady to a philosopher, " that you are a Solipsist. There should be more of us.") Perhaps, like Kant, he begins with the fact that pure mathematics is possible, and proceeds to build up a monumental pyramid in the shape of a Critique of Pure Reason. Or he bases his epistemology on the axiom that truth can never be self-contradictory, deducing from that the positive criterion that truth is proved to be true by showing itself at once comprehensive and systematic. Here he feels himself unassailable. This criterion of reality is shown to be infallible by the surest of tests. The truth of it has to be assumed in the very process of calling it in question. (The only way in which to prove that the criterion is a false one is by showing that it is self-contra-dictory—thereby accepting the criterion.)

This last appears to be a very satisfying theory. Yet even here a difficulty remains. Who is to decide whether a theory of reality is self-contradictory ? Who is to weigh the evidence and give the verdict ? *Quis custodiet ipsum custodem ?* How are we to criticise the mind, which is itself the organ of criticism ? And, unless such criticism is possible, how are we to arrive at certainty ?

In a word, the *ultimatum* of metaphysics is, at the very least, no more sure than the *ultimatum* of religion, namely, that the Reality which we are endeavouring to apprehend is personal, and is seeking to reveal itself to us.

3. Can we have certainty *in Ethics* ? The age in which we live is facing the perplexing problem of the relativity of knowledge. Oswald Spengler, searching for a General Theory of Relativity in ethical matters, claims to have brought about a Copernican revolution ; to have removed the centre-point of ethical orientation. The sense of " duty," which has hitherto been regarded as absolute, and universal in all men, is, he would say, quite as naive a piece of self-deception as any to which the geocentric astronomers were prone. To-day men are prepared to die for that

which they consider right. But rightness can be determined only by an omniscient spectator of all time and all experience. Not being that, we have no guarantee that our view of the ethical obligation is anything more than a parochial prejudice. The man of the future may feel it his duty to die for the very opposite of that for which men to-day are ready to die. " Both, logic and ethics alike, are systems of absolute and eternal truths for the intellect, and correspondingly untruths for history. However completely the inner eye may triumph over the outer in the domain of thought, in the realm of facts the belief in eternal truths is a petty and absurd stage-play that exists only in the heads of individuals." [1] " Systematic philosophy, then, lies immensely far behind us, and ethical has been wound up. *But a third possibility, corresponding to the Classical Scepticism, still remains to the soul-world of the present-day West. . . .* Whereas the Sceptic philosophy arose within Hellenism as the negation of philosophy— declaring philosophy to be purposeless — we, on the contrary, regard the *history of philosophy* as, in the last resort, philosophy's gravest theme. This *is* ' skepsis,' in the true sense, for whereas the Greek is led to renounce absolute standpoints by contempt for the intellectual past, we are led to do so by comprehension of that past as an organism." [2] " The secret of the world appears successively as a knowledge problem, a valuation problem and a form problem. Kant saw Ethics as an object of knowledge, the nineteenth century saw it as an object of valuation. The Sceptic would deal with *both* simply as the historical expression of a Culture." [3]

It sounds alarming. In all our thinking we must have some fixed point, whether it be axiom or value. If Spengler takes this away, we have lost all. Nor is it sufficient to answer that, if you take away every ideal that sheds its light on reality, then life loses all meaning. For his reply is that we are returning to the Ptolemaic standpoint. To

---

[1] Oswald Spengler, *The Decline of the West* (E.T.) (Allen & Unwin, 1926 and 1928), vol. ii. p. 144.
[2] *Op. cit.* vol. i. p. 45.   [3] *Op. cit.* vol. i. p. 374.

declare that life has a meaning may itself be only a parochial prejudice.

According to Spengler, therefore, all ethical systems are relative. They will decline when their day is done. None is better than another. (And we might as well add, None is worse than another.) Value, in fact, disappears from the world.

It seems that certitude may readily be challenged in æsthetics, or in metaphysics, or in ethics, if these stand by themselves. In the last of these we might confidently have expected to find some bridge leading over into the country of certain knowledge which we believe to be ours in religion. But the bridge is mined.

Here is the challenge with which Christianity is faced in our day. Let us consider two ways of answering it, that of the Theology of Crisis, and that of Karl Heim, of Tübingen.[1]

I. The famous book of Oswald Spengler, says Brunner,[2] " has called to our attention in glaring headlines, what all of us have more or less felt, that the disintegrating tendencies of our modern world have led us to a decisive point where the issue can be only one of two things : either new life or death." The crisis which Spengler has condensed into his pessimistic vision of the decline of the West " amounts to the decay of all spiritual substance. An age which has lost its faith in an absolute has lost everything. It must perish ; it has no vitality left to pass the crisis ; its end can only be—the end." [3] We must, however, be clear on one point—Where do we expect to find an absolute ? Science, says Brunner,[4] makes only observations and time-tables. Metaphysics, unable to shake itself free from ' world-spectatorship ' [5] gives an æsthetic view of God, without passion or personal decision. But religion represents the search for truth with the whole

---

[1] The latter has made a special study of Oswald Spengler. See *Glaube und Leben*, first ed. 1926, pp. 348–403.

[2] *The Theology of Crisis*, p. 1.

[3] *Ibid.* p. 8.   [4] *Ibid.* pp. 23 ff.

[5] Aristotle's θεωρητικὸς βίος. Cf. *Ethics*, i. 2, 5, 1095a 19, etc.

soul and the whole of existence at stake. Faith is not perception ; it is decision.[1]

Barth has always been vividly conscious of the danger to theology from the familiar idea of relativism, the lack of any absolute. Troeltsch reached the conclusion that the final synthesis in philosophy and religion does not lie within the scope of human thought ; all attempts to reach it lead to contradiction. Herrmann, Barth's teacher, found that it is a fatal drawback that no historical judgment, however certain it may appear, ever attains anything more than probability. Now Spengler sees no God nor purpose at work ; blind fate rules the destinies of men. Barth challenges this pessimism with his declaration that the perilous seas of relativity may be safely voyaged on, because we have the raft of the Divine Word ; and with the declaration that Revelation gives a fixed point, an absolute.

1. *God's transcendence*. God is the " completely other," the absolute over against all relative. Because man is fallen from God, therefore he is incapable of the divine. Modernism is older than Christianity. The Stoics and the Neo-Platonists were modernists. They held to the fatal error that " man is good ; his spirit is divine." And modernism is the antithesis of Christianity. All immanence-religions break down on the fact of sin—which is more than a not-yet. In religion, God is the central theme, not man's emotions. The supreme heresy is to make man the measure of all things. Between time and eternity there is an infinite qualitative difference (Kierkegaard). God is radically different from that which we find *a priori* or *a posteriori*. He is unknown except as He reveals Himself.

2. *Human brokenness*. An unbridgeable gulf separates man from God. For man to venture a way to God is pride, Promethean titanism. To build a theology on the religious data supplied by human experience (the way of Schleier-

---

[1] Dr. Willy Bremi, in *Was ist das Gewissen ?* has a similar caution to make in the realm of ethics. Much work on this subject, he says, has been vitiated because the authors have treated conscience as *Verständnis*, when it ought to be treated as *Stellungnahme*.

macher) is *hybris*, presumption. (*a*) Religion fails. (Though
it might be fairer if we translated the German word here
as " religiosity.") It brings man no solution of his problems.
It only discovers to him his helplessness. (*b*) The Church
fails. (Again, it is fair to point out that by this term we
are to understand the Church as it is organised by fallible
men.) Like this world, the Church is under judgment. In
it, revelation is turned from the eternal into the temporal.
The lightning of Heaven is converted into a domestic
slow-combustion stove. Herein is the sin of the Church
that it attempts to bring about the kingdom of God
through the æsthetic cleverness of its worship. The Church,
like religion, is only the way of bringing home to man his
fatal sickness.[1]

3. *The Word of God.* The eternal breaks into time.
The first gleam of hope might seem to be in the ethical
consciousness of man ; in Kant's categorical imperative.
But this is an abstraction, not a Person. A command of
God is a form of speech and implies an answer. Conscience,
Brunner once said, is the boundary-fence of immanence.
Again, he has called it one of the " points of contact " in
man for the Word of God. But it is a grim feature of man's
life, both in character and in content. " The sinister thing
about conscience is precisely this, that primarily it has
nothing to do with God at all, that it attacks man like an
alien, dark, hostile power." It is " like the inarticulate
groaning of a prisoner in his dungeon, which only penetrates
into clear consciousness in a dim obscure manner. It is,
indeed, simply the man himself as he feels himself in the
centre of his existence to be disturbed, injured, affected by
the contradiction, the consciousness that ' things are not
right with him,' that they ' are out of order.' " " Conscience
is the fear of God—in the sense of the ' fear that hath
torment '—hence it drives the soul away from God, and
yet it is also the longing of the soul for God ; but it so

[1] See, in particular, Barth's commentary on *Romans* (sixth edition,
translated by the late Sir Edwyn Hoskyns) and his *Das Wort Gottes und
die Theologie* (translated by Douglas Horton, *The Word of God and the
Word of Man*).

distorts the way back to God that the soul can see nothing clearly ; the soul does not know that it is *God* of whom it is afraid and for whom it longs." [1]

Nor will Barth have it that in conscience man has apprehended God. Ethics has its place. It brings man into the deep despair and distress of finding that he is incapable of doing God's will. Nevertheless, God is not to be found in nature, in history, or in human experience of any kind, but only in Revelation as it has reached us in the Bible, and the distinctive feature of the Bible is not its ethics, nor its religion, nor its history, but the breaking through of the Divine into human life. " It is not the right human thoughts about God which form the content of the Bible, but the right divine thoughts about men. The Bible tells us not how we should talk with God but what He says to us." The *Word of God* stands in the Bible. [2] This Word of God finds its complete expression in Christ. He is the breaking through and the appearing of the world of God in the profane life. Barth affirms the paradox, the impossibility, of Christ ; the miracle of the God-man in Jesus. Time is joined with eternity, man with the Altogether Other, only by an inexplicable mystery.

Some of the earlier utterances of the dialectical theologians on *Historismus* and *Psychologismus* carried all the marks of over-emphasis. They discounted the possibility that God has so made men that they are enabled to recognise when, in history or in the states of their own souls, they are in touch with God. We may be in danger at times of making man the measure of all things, but, on the other hand, depreciation of the potentialities of the human spirit may be carried to such lengths as to end in distrust of man's Creator. We cannot argue from the Unknown to the known, but must begin from experience. This is not *hybris*, but common sense. To set up, as an absolute standard against the relativity of knowledge, God apart from man, is like jumping off our own shadow. The

---

[1] Brunner, *The Divine Imperative* (E.T.) (Lutterworth Press), pp. 156–158.

[2] See *The Word of God and the Word of Man*, p. 43.

standard must somewhere include man, or it could mean
nothing to man ; it would be an *imposed* standard, which
man could never comprehend ; to conform to which would
be submission to the magical. There is nothing sacred for
man that is not mixed with man. In speaking of a transcendent God, Barth seems sometimes to be speaking of a
God of Whom we can never know anything. The only
God Whom we can know is God as He enters into relationship with man, namely, " God in experience." It is not a
God far off Whom we know, but a God Who has drawn
near. That is one fact of which we can be certain. All the
rest is mythology. Even the phrase, " the finite is not
capable of the infinite" is ambiguous, for it puts the
" capacity " only a stage later. It does not seem to matter
greatly which is true : (1) God *made* man " capax infiniti,"
or (2) God, when He sends His revelation, *makes* man
" capax infiniti." In creation there was grace at work and
creation is a continued activity. It follows that, in spite of
the Fall of man, there is grace at work in the creative
activity of God to-day as it is exercised on finite souls.
Thus Barth himself soon became aware of the difficulty
involved in his first statements. He now lays much less
stress on the phrase *finitum non capax infiniti*. It is not
the *finiteness* of man that is the decisive impediment. It
is his *sinfulness*. Thus Barth adopts instead the phrase
homo peccator non capax verbi divini.[1] God's power to
establish intercourse with us, he writes, is assuredly called
in question by the fact that He is infinite while we are finite,
that He is Lord over life and death while we are bounded
by death, that He is the Creator while we are called
out of nothing into being and existence. But that is only
one very small part of the barrier between us and God.
The real obstacle to His intercourse with us is that we are
God's *enemies*. It is this that makes us incapable of receiving
the Word of God.

The situation is certainly better described in these
later terms. If man's disability were to be sought in his
finitude alone, it would be hard to avoid attributing the

[1] See *The Doctrine of the Word of God*, p. 466.

blame of it to God. But the same difficulty is still to sur-
mount. It does not seem to matter greatly which of two
things we say : (1) In spite of man's sin, God does not
allow him to become altogether incapable of hearing the
Word of God, or (2) in spite of man's sin God *makes* him
capable of receiving the Word ; and it would certainly be
hard to pronounce dogmatically in favour of one or the
other. In both, Grace is affirmed. (Indeed, Barth himself
appears on the next page of his *Dogmatik* to accept the first
way of expressing it. " The Word of God, the revelation of
which is attested in Scripture, tells man that he is a rebel,
who has wantonly abandoned the communion between
himself as creature and God as Creator, and has placed
himself in a situation in which this communion is impossible." [1] The Word of God speaks to man *in his rebel
state*. Therefore man, as sinner, *is* capable of receiving the
Word of God.) [2]

Both theories, it is true, allow for the possibility that a
man may place himself beyond salvation. In both, that
would mean that the *imago dei* was destroyed beyond
restoration. But it is with the other possibility that both
statements are concerned (and which of us shall say that it
ever ceases to be a possibility ?), namely, that the man is
capable of being saved. Barth would say that the yearning
for God has completely gone : only God can bring it back ;
but it is at least equally true to say that God's grace has
never permitted the yearning wholly to die out.

Secondly, it has been felt widely that, just as the
statement of divine transcendence has left the door open
for grave misunderstanding, so also has the description of

---

[1] *Op. cit.* p. 467.

[2] Brunner has recently made a similar point in a note on p. 116 of
God and Man : Barth " overlooks the possibility, that also the *personalitas*
and *humanitas* of man, that which makes us men in distinction from the
rest of creation, rests upon God's actual Word addressed to us, so that
man, even in his sin, never stands beyond reach of this Word spoken to
him by God, and therefore is never out of relationship with God. Only
because man has some kind of knowledge about God can he be a sinner."
Brunner adds that a complete denial of natural knowledge of God would
involve also the denial of sin.

" human brokenness." A doctrine is surely fallible which sees in the doing of good, and the turning from evil ; in the keeping of the pure heart, in prayer, in the public worship of God, only human Titanism and not the coming of God to man. If there is one certainty in human life it is that God is speaking in conscience. A conscience stabbed awake (*erschrockenes Gewissen*) is God's voice ; is man in touch with very God. And, because this is the Father of Jesus, the last word of the stricken conscience is not man's " Depart from me " but God's " Come unto Me."

Thirdly, and most important, a note of hesitancy or a mark of interrogation concerning Barth's exposition of the topic of the Word of God. What is the criterion by which the Word may be recognised ? " He scarcely explains," wrote the late Professor H. R. Mackintosh,[1] " why we believe one thing to be revelation rather than another ; and when he tells us, truly enough, that faith affirms paradoxes, he offers no criterion to decide why it is only some paradoxes that are affirmed. We don't believe *every* paradox : not even Mr. Chesterton does." In his *Dogmatik*, Barth seeks to evade this conclusion. He emphasises his contention that he is writing *Church* Dogmatics. Apart from the Church there would be no Bible. The New Testament is handed down by the Church. If we ask, Who determines which *is* the Word of God ? the answer is, The Holy Spirit speaking to the Church. The Church, listening to the witness of the Holy Spirit, chose the books which are to be authoritative for Christian faith. This is the *written* Word of God.

Barth's conception of the three-in-oneness of the Word is developed in the second edition of *The Doctrine of the Word of God*, page 98 and the following pages of the English translation.

1. *The Word proclaimed*. There are, he says, two *human* motives for preaching, first the existence of objective truth, second the subjective personal conviction. But these are *only* human. We cannot get away from them, just as we cannot escape from our own shadow, but this

[1] *Expository Times*, 1926, p. 283.

is the point at which we have to look for the divine
commission.

One cannot help asking here whether these are not in
fact part of the divine commission itself. If there is
objective truth to be declared it is difficult to know what is
meant by the term if it is not truth which has entered the
mind of man and become personal conviction ; and where
there is personal conviction, it cannot be separated from the
calling of God. The divine commission is not something
added on. Can we really believe that the preacher has to
wait for something else beyond his personal conviction ?
It is true that Lancelot Andrewes could say, " He that
preacheth twice on Sunday prateth once," meaning perhaps
that God commissions the preacher more rarely than the
preacher preaches. But, if that is the interpretation, the
saying is simply not true. If this is the man's vocation
and he is in earnest about his vocation, the message will be
there.

2. *The Written Word.* All that the Church can do, says
Barth, is (i) to set forth the Word to speak for itself.
Exegesis is needed not, as some have said, for the sake of
free thinking, but for the sake of a free Bible.[1] (ii) To
preserve the Word. Tradition is not sufficient. The real
apostolical succession rests on the written Word. " Everything depends for the idea of a living succession upon the
antecessor being thought of as still alive and possessed of
free power as compared with the *successor*. But if, as is
the case here, the *antecessor* is one who has long been dead,
this can only happen when his proclamation is fixed in
writing and when it is recognised that he still has life and
free power to-day over the Church in this very written Word
of His." [2]

It might be thought that it is the Church which chooses
which written words shall stand in the Canon. Barth would
not agree. It is the Canon which *imposes itself.* We have
no other measure with which to measure the Bible.[3] The
Church does not choose : it has the choice forced on it.

3. *The Word Revealed.* When Barth speaks of the

[1] P. 119.   [2] P. 117.   [3] P. 120.

" imposition " of the Canon, he is certainly employing the wrong term, but he is perhaps driven to it by the difficulty which arises when he seeks to determine the inter-relations of the three aspects of the Word. He cannot say that he is speaking of the Bible as it lies there in a man's hand, ready to be opened, and simply by the printed words to answer all a man's questions. No, he says, I mean the Bible as it becomes the Word of God, that is, as it speaks to man's heart in the moment of his own decision. " The Word of God is understood primarily as a decision or it is not understood at all." [1] The printed Bible contains only *witness*. But witness can become *revelation* when God determines that it shall be so for any man. Barth will even say that " in faith men have real experience of the Word of God, and no *finitum non capax infiniti*, and no *peccator non capax verbi divini* either, should now hinder us from taking this statement seriously with all its consequences." [2] But he hastens to add that this does not mean the entrance of any *human* capacity. " The possibility of faith as it is given to man in the reality of faith can only be regarded as one lent to man by God and lent exclusively for use."

The truth that shines through all this is that revelation, if it *is* revelation, is something absolute and ultimate and therefore not open to testing by anything else whatsoever except *revelation*.

In his last study of Barth, H. R. Mackintosh wrote of this as an attractive position, yet one with difficulties of its own. " We are led to ask how the ' once-for-allness ' of the event of revelation in Jesus Christ is to be harmonised with the contention that revelation, as complete, includes man's believing acknowledgment of its reality. Is the ' givenness ' of revelation in Christ quite real and unconditioned if after all, to be fully realised, it must be apprehended by man, even if that apprehension is wrought in us by the Spirit ? Is not God's gift of Himself in Christ fully real whether it be received or not ? " [3]

This criticism was tentative and is left undeveloped,

---

[1] P. 178.   [2] P. 272.
[3] H. R. Mackintosh, *Types of Modern Theology*, p. 281.

but its vital character will be seen when we remember man's responsibility for accepting or rejecting the revelation which is offered to him. " How shall we escape, if we neglect so great salvation ? " The peril of neglecting the Word of God is real : the responsibility for rejection may not be laid on God.

We shall require to see whether there is not to be found elsewhere a more adequate study of revelation in respect of this free response of man.

CHAPTER X

RELIGIOUS CERTAINTY. II. A New Dimension

SUMMARY

It has been said that the certainties of religious people are subjective only. But that is to make the mistake of Feuerbach ; to suppose that the evidence of the outsider is conclusive, while that of the experience itself may be disregarded. They are not *deceptive* satisfactions. Nor are they *premature* satisfactions. They arise, indeed, precisely at those points where there might appear to be reason for uncertainty. In Jesus we see One Who knew and suffered the consequences of evil as none other has ever done ; who knew also the extent, the profundity, and the seriousness of human sin as no one else could know them ; yet we find that His sureness of God did not waver.

Certitude is present as a fact to be reckoned with. But the situation may be altered when we come to speculate about its nature. To examine the experience may change the experience. Nevertheless, there are two things which theology can do, and ought to do. (1) It can remove difficulties which are unreal or non-vital. Many are profoundly troubled when they discover that others cannot see what they see. They have a natural desire, for the sake of these others, to produce evidence or argument which will appeal to them. We must recognise that this may be a profitless task. In the realm of the spirit it is necessary to have a certain character before the truth can be apprehended. Faith can offer its evidence only to those who have lived in its sunlight and eaten of its bread. (2) Theology has also the task of constructing a theory of religious knowledge. It must set itself to bring out more clearly the nature of the religious experience. Heresies are not so much false doctrines as distorted spiritual experience.

We have seen the difficulty inherent in the Barthian theology on this point. Between the All-Real and the not-real there cannot even be distance. The impression which is sometimes conveyed is that there are two Gods, first the *Deus absconditus*, and second the God Who reveals Himself. It is at this point that Karl Heim takes up the question of religious certainty. There are two ways in which the ego may approach reality. (1) The way of experience, which is immediate, and cannot be defined. (2) The way of what is called " scientific knowledge." It is to be remembered that the second way, quite as much as the first, assumes an ultimate which cannot be proved. From his discussion of intra-mundane forms of transcendence (the Dimensional theology of his book, *God Transcendent*), two things have been gained. (1) That which appears as paradox may be the truth. Truth *must* appear as paradox to those who are as yet blind to the dimension in which it lies. (2) The study of the important relation I-Thou has given a new prominence in contemporary thought to the transcendence of Space and Time involved in personal relations. This is of great importance when we come to consider the authority of Christ over the knowing and willing faculties of men in all ages. Jesus, the Lord, is the contemporary of all His followers. (We notice also the undesigned affinities with the philosophy of Nicolas Berdyaev.)

The theory of Oswald Spengler might be designated as the *horizontal hypothesis*. There is no fixed point. One man's centre is for another only the horizon. All is a level plain. All values are equally valueless. Barth's may be called the *vertical hypothesis*. God comes straight down from above. The eternal breaks through into the temporal. Heim's may then be called the *Bethel hypothesis*. There is traffic between earth and heaven. It would be wrong to ignore the possibility that in the relationship between the believer and Christ man is offered that absolute view-point which the relativist denies.

CHAPTER X

Religious Certainty

II. A NEW DIMENSION

WHEN the poet Henley was under the care of Lord Lister in Edinburgh, he wrote of Lister's " large, placid brow, the soft lines of tranquil thought, the benign face, the faculties of patience and unyielding will, and his wise, rare smile, *so sweet with certainties.*"

It might be said that certainties of religious people are subjective only. But that is to make the mistake of Feuerbach ; to suppose that the evidence of the outsider is conclusive, while that of the experience itself may be disregarded. It is not easy to see why Plato, Aristotle, Leibniz, and Kant ; why again Pheidias and Michael Angelo, Raphael and Rembrandt, Bach and Beethoven, Homer and Shakespeare are to be regarded as revealers of various kinds of truth and reality, if Amos and Isaiah, Augustine and Aquinas, Francis of Assisi and Joan of Arc are to be treated as pure illusionists in precisely what constitutes their specific greatness.[1] The certainties of religious people are not *deceptive* satisfactions.

Nor are they *premature* satisfactions. They arise, indeed, at precisely those points where there might appear to be reason for uncertainty. They come, not through turning away from difficulties and perplexities, but from facing them ; not from timid contentment with a few comforting rays of light, but from the courageous, steady look into the darkness. When we turn to consider the supreme example, we discover One Who knew and suffered the consequences of evil as none other has ever done ; Who knew also the extent, the profundity, and the serious-

---

[1] Cf. von Hügel, *Essays and Addresses*, i. p. 38.

ness of human sin as no one else could know them ; and yet, in Christ, we find One Whose sureness of God did not waver. When He spoke about God, He was speaking on His own subject. The best of men have failed to fulfil the spiritual conditions for right knowledge of God. They discern these realities only dimly and fitfully. But in Him the conditions were fulfilled. And, when He speaks of God, it is to say that man, this tiny creature, may cry, and he is heard by the God who built the atom and flung out the stars.

Religious certainty is of its own distinctive type. The organ of spiritual knowledge is spiritual. Brunner has expressed it in this way : "The thing that matters supremely is not whether man is ' aware ' of or has a ' feeling ' for ' something divine,' but whether he knows God as the One Who challenges him to decision." [1] And Karl Heim has the same in mind when he speaks of the " inward attitude " which is " entirely different from that involved in the technical recasting of Nature. In this case I am not playing the part of a cool spectator. My personality is at stake. It is all engaged in the transaction. This is the willing, believing, praying attitude." [2] These are all, indeed, interpretations of the words, " If any man will do His will, he shall know of the doctrine." The organ of this knowledge is spiritual. It will record the truth only if it is kept pure and sensitive. If we differ from the poets about poetry, we may be sure that it is *we* who are wrong. If we disagree with the saints about religion, it is probable that *we* have missed the truth ; they are seeing things which our eyes are not clear enough to behold.

This certitude, then, is *there*, a fact to be acknowledged, a certitude of its own distinctive type. But it is quite a different exercise when we come to speculate about the nature of it. To examine the experience changes the experience. Nevertheless, there are certain things which theology can do, and ought to do.

1. *It can remove difficulties which are unreal or non-*

---

[1] *The Mediator* (E.T.), p. 13.
[2] *The New Divine Order* (E.T.), p. 43.

vital. Many are profoundly troubled when they discover that others cannot see what they see. They have a natural desire, for the sake of these others, to produce evidence or argument which will appeal to them. We must recognise that this is a profitless task. Herrmann declares that it is impossible to prove to the unbeliever the things which the Christian knows. The affirmations of spiritual experience, like those of all the higher regions of thought, æsthetic, ethical, and the others, are not capable of logical demonstration.[1] Faith knows nothing of external guarantees. To demand them is to fail to understand its very nature as a free heroic act. In this it is different from other kinds of knowledge. The truths of mathematics, of the natural sciences, and of history, are convincing because they must be accepted indifferently by men who are spiritually opposed to one another. Unity is possible, in the realm of mathematical and physical truth, between those who are hostile in outlook to one another. It is not so in the realm of the spirit. There it is necessary to have a certain *character* before the truth can be apprehended.

If it can be said that " Science is the great cleanser of human thinking ; it makes impossible any religion but the highest," [2] it might be added that theology has as its aim the purification of belief ; it ensures that there shall be no rest in premature satisfaction ; that truth shall be acknowledged only when it rests on the highest type of evidence. Faith can offer its evidence only to those who have lived in its sunlight and eaten of its bread.

But theology may remove a difficulty in the minds of those who have not had the experience of religious certitude. It reminds them, not only that there may be evidence which they have not taken into account, but also that their disregard of this evidence may falsify their interpretation of those facts which they seem, by their very detachment, best fitted to explain. Science has marvellously revealed and explained the substructure of the world, the protons and electrons and waves which underlie the constitution

[1] Cf. A. Martin, *Finality of Jesus for Faith* (T. & T. Clark, 1933), p. 216.
[2] B. H. Streeter, *Reality*, p. 272.

of matter as we know it. But science cannot explain the meaning and purpose of the world. It is not the whirling electrons that explain the rose, but the rose that explains the flying electrons. Suppose a tribe of men who had eyes so penetrating that they were able to discern the electrons which constitute a flower. They would be aware of a world inexplicable and terrifying. But suppose that some scientist in the tribe discovered a way of reducing their visual powers so that the flower became visible in its beauty and freshness, they would discover a wonderful explanation of the inexplicable dance of atoms.[1] Convictions about the world, acquired in another sphere than the spiritual, may need for their explanation precisely that experience which has been left out of the reckoning.

2. Of Metaphysics, F. H. Bradley writes in his notebook, "Metaphysics is the finding of bad reasons for what we believe upon instinct, but to find these reasons is no less an instinct."[2] In the second place, therefore, the task of theology is to *construct a theory of religious knowledge*. It must set itself to bring out more clearly the nature of the religious experience ; to distinguish between experiences which are transient and those which are ultimate ; between those which have relative value and those which are absolute ; between those which are individual and eccentric and those which are general and fundamental. Nevertheless, it must always be borne in mind that the *theory* cannot have certitude. That belongs to an experience, not to a theory of it. Spiritual experience is reality—perhaps the only reality—it is not simply a state of man's soul or a religious feeling. Heresies are not false doctrines but distorted spiritual experience.

Convictions do not always remain vivid and self-authenticating ; instead of the soul in touch with God, we may have only memories, impressions, and results of that communion. It follows, therefore, that great importance must be attached also to the experience of the *com-*

---

[1] R. C. Macfie, *Science Rediscovers God* (T. & T. Clark, 1930), pp. 252 ff.

[2] *Appearance and Reality*, p. xiv.

munity. The Church is the guarantee that the individual's faith will not always fluctuate with his own private vision of God.

Certain philosophies begin with a self-authenticating experience. For example, from the postulate of thought, Hegel proceeds to show by dialectic how the Universal Thought unfolds itself in the cosmos. But the best example is Descartes. Truth is that which is *clear* and *distinct* ; clear, in that it is self-evident ; distinct, in that it depends on nothing else. Nothing in the outward world can provide such evidence, since it might be only imagination or fancy ; and since, moreover, it can be known only indirectly through our senses. Then Descartes found that which, he thought, it was impossible to doubt—his own existence as a thinking being. *Cogito, ergo sum.*

It is fairly easy to see that *cogito, ergo sum* says at once too much and too little—too much, because the act of thinking does not prove the continued existence of the ego which thinks, can say nothing indubitable of its past or of its future ; personal identity is not proved ; and too little, because it ignores the other aspect of the case ; thinking, perceiving, doubting are impossible, certainly, unless there is something that thinks, perceives, doubts ; but they are equally impossible if there is not something that is thought, perceived, doubted. This latter point is emphasised again by Husserl in passages on the *intentionality* of consciousness. (Consciousness is always consciousness *of* something. A *cogitatio* implies a *cogitatum*.) The phenomenological method discoveres the *a priori*, not, with Kant, in the mind, but in the thing itself. The necessity of the *a priori* is a necessity not of thought, but of being.[1]

It appears that *cogito, ergo sum* (I think, therefore I am) is no truer nor more fundamental than *cogito, ergo sunt* (I think, therefore things are). And this brings us to examine another conceivable postulate—*cogito, ergo es* (I think, therefore thou art). Heidegger plainly declares [2] that the

---

[1] See *Ideas : General Introduction to Pure Phenomenology*, translated by Boyce Gibson, 1931.

[2] *Sein und Zeit*, p. 113 ff.

ego can as little be given without other egos as without
the external world. But, many years before, F. H. Bradley
had written a brief, but pregnant, paragraph, which foreshadowed much of contemporary philosophy of the " I "
and the " Thou."   It occurs in his chapter on " Solipsism " [1]
" If I am asked to justify my belief that other selves,
beside my own, are in the world, the answer must be this :
I arrive at other souls by means of other bodies, and the
argument starts from the ground of my own body. My
own body is one of the groups which are formed in my
experience. And it is connected, immediately and specially,
with pleasure and pain, and again with sensations and
volitions, as no other group can be. But, since there are
other groups like my body, these must also be qualified
by similar attendants. With my feelings and my volitions
these groups cannot correspond. For they are usually
irrelevant and indifferent, and often even hostile ; and
they enter into collision with one another and with my
body. Therefore these foreign bodies have, each of them,
a foreign self of its own."

This relation is, clearly, of very great importance to
the theologian. The relation I-Thou may prove to be an
analogy of the relation I-God. *Persons* are different from
things. There is a Thou-world and there is an It-world.
Without the It, man cannot live ; yet, if he has nothing
but the It, he is not man. The It-world is ruled by causality ;
man's real world is the world of personal relations. An
expression of this attitude is the word " Love " or the word
" Spirit." These are not in the It-world ; nor are they in
the ego alone, but between the " I " and the " Thou."
Whereas the external world is ruled by causality, this
world is ruled by freedom. The tragedy is that we cannot
encounter a " Thou " without seeking to turn it into
an " It," objectifying it, destroying its freedom. But
there is, in God, an eternal Thou which can never
become an It, can never be objectified. It is not really
of God that we speak when we speak of Him in the *third*
person. Our attitude to God has been described as the

---

[1] *Appearance and Reality*, p. 255.

feeling of dependence. Against Schleiermacher and Otto, Buber shows that, while the feeling of dependence may be connected with it, it is not its essence. The one analogy is the relation of an " I " to a " Thou." What is the nature of this relation when it concerns man on the one side and God on the other ?

Barth, in his attack on idealism and subjectivism, opposes to the idealist's unity of God and man the doctrine of distance between them, qualitative difference. Christian faith, he says, is the recognition of this distance, leaving God as God and man as man. The qualitative difference between Time and Eternity provides a thesis and antithesis of which there is no synthesis—not even in faith. Barth's solution is the negation of the human side. Man is nothing ; God is all. The difficulty inherent in the Barthian theology on this point is that you cannot destroy one side without destroying the whole relation. Between the All-Real and the not-real there cannot even be distance ! The *religious* aspect of distance is concerned, not with two metaphysical qualities, but with personalities. The real form of Christian belief is this : Faith is communion with God ; distance is the result of the estrangement of sin. With Barth, sin was for long rather metaphysically than ethically conceived. For him, the sentence " All men are sinners before God " was really parallel with the sentence, " God is all ; man is nothing."

In his search for objectivity in religious knowledge, Barth was thus driven to study this attitude which is characteristic of personal relations. He accepted the position that God is always subject, never object, and he faced the problem, How can God become object of our knowledge ? His answer is that the real object of religious knowledge is not God Himself but our being known by God. (It is difficult, however, to see how we can be conscious of being known by God without at the same time having some knowledge of God.) Barth then takes up the valuable suggestion that God's Word is not simply spoken, but " addressed " (not only *Rede* but *An-Rede*). God, in revelation, is not a neutral force, but a Person. We inquire concerning the possibility of revelation, and we find that the Divine " I " must become a " Thou," in order to be known by men. God becomes incarnate in order to have fellowship with men.[1]

The impression conveyed by much of this dialectic is that there are two Gods—first, the *Deus absconditus*, God in Himself (there is a perilous affinity here with Kant's " thing-in-itself ") ; and, second, the God Who reveals Himself. The God of faith is different from the God of metaphysics, not simply, as we might say with justification, inadequately apprehended by metaphysics (because the personal relation is left out of account) but actually different. This is an inevitable result. If we do not *begin* with the personality of God, we cannot *arrive at* it.

It is at this point that Karl Heim takes up the question of religious certainty.[2] " Previous generations," he has written,[3] " in their struggle with life, were aware that they were wandering in a land that could be surveyed, in which it was possible for them in some measure to find their way by the aid of a map. *We* have the feeling of those who walk in mist. We see no more than a few steps ahead of us. This can be endured if we have a road under our feet, which will somehow lead us upwards, even though it be in wearisome curves and tortuous windings." At the least we must have someone going ahead—it may be with a wide space intervening—whom we may assume to be familiar with the direction, and to whom we can say, " The way I know not, yet—Thou knowest it well ! " If everything fails, we can indeed live on when all goes well. But as soon as we have a difficult choice to make, as soon as we find that some overwhelming stroke has frustrated all our plans, and that we are torn from our safe moorings, then our confidence collapses. All world-views have to-day collapsed ; have failed to give us this certainty which we need. From that we learn at least one thing : If there is certainty we cannot have produced it ourselves. It must have its home in the

---

[1] *Doctrine of the Word of God*, p. 438.

[2] One of his earlier books is entitled *Glaubensgewissheit*.

[3] In the first edition of *Glaube und Denken*.

beyond. (In ethics, for example, it is quite clear that no decision of *my own* could carry me to the point of sacrificing myself. Only a command which I have not laid upon myself can be obligatory for me when it threatens my existence.)

How do we become aware of this other Power which can command us ? Not in the way by which science acquires its knowledge. Science is like the doctor, who can test the heart, the pulse, the respiration, but cannot see into the soul. It is our Christian conviction that we have another mode of knowing the Power which is over us. It frequently happens, in the case of some person, that we know him first only by his appearance, his step, his movements. Suddenly, by a look in his eyes, or a word spoken, we see his soul. There springs up between us a different relation altogether, a relation of *trust* (*Vertrauen*), which abides.[1]

There are two ways in which the ego may approach reality. (1) The way of experience, which is immediate, and cannot be defined. (2) The way of what is called "scientific knowledge." It is to be remembered that the second way, quite as much as the first, assumes an ultimate which cannot be proved. It must presuppose, for example, that two things which we take to be different, are actually different. To probe into the ultimate means to analyse the form and significance of this function of differentiation. At first this is a simple matter. The book is different from the table on which it lies. (Spatial determination decides this.) This note C is different from that played a moment ago. (Temporal determination decides this.) But how are we to differentiate Space from Time ? Here we have differentiation of the second grade—differentiation between spheres of differentiation. These spheres of differentiation Heim calls *Dimensions*. The presence of a Dimension is indicated by an Either-Or ; the entrance of another Dimension by escape from the apparently decisive Either-Or. The entrance of another Dimension he calls a " dimensional cleavage." A content belonging to *n* Dimensions suddenly

[1] Cf. also Heim, *Weltanschauung der Bibel*.

stands in $n+1$ Dimensions. This involves a paradox. What is now seen to be possible can be expressed, for those who have no knowledge of this new Dimension, only in a paradox. Dimensions belong together, inseparably. They condition one another (polarity). Yet a person may be " blind " to a Dimension.

Heidegger saw that we cannot be conscious of our self without being at the same time conscious of the world, from which, as background, the self is differentiated. *Cogito, ergo sum* runs out into *cogito, ergo sunt*. The ego and the world can be thought of apart only in abstraction. Between them is a relation of polarity. It is a distinctive feature of Heim's philosophy that he identifies with this relation I-the World, a relation which at first appears altogether different, the relation Present-Past. These, says Heim, are the same from different aspects. " I " stands always for that which is present and not yet determined ; the World (It) is that which is past, decided, brought under the reign of causality ; the precipitate of the fluid present.

It may be that the relation I-Thou and the relation I-God are altogether different from the relation I-It. To think only of the I-It type may be to lose the chance of probing to the ultimate. But this is the only relation which scientific knowledge takes into account. Cartesian thought also missed the fact that the ego is related in a peculiar way to the Thou. It dealt only with the I-It relation. The discovery of the I-Thou relation is a revolution in Western thought. Here we have a new Dimension. That which is true within it can be expressed only in paradox to those who are blind to it. To them its truths will appear as impossibilities.

The paradox appears at once when we realise that here, in the Thou, we have a second perspective centre *of the same world*, claiming to be a centre from which truth is seen in its absolute nature. A seen point turns into a seeing point. Here is a contradiction of the fundamental rule of the I-It world, that there can be only one absolute stand-point. This is a sign that a new dimension has entered. This dimensional cleavage comes from the tension between

doing and suffering, action and passion. (I am aware of
the other according as his will coincides or interferes with
mine.) The Thou claims to be the perspective middle-
point. If its claim is allowed, then we can no longer hold
to our objective picture of the world. The " world " becomes
now the unity of world-aspects of possibly innumerable
subjects, each of which may confront me as a Thou. But
the " world " of scientific knowledge is an It, that which is
past, amenable to measurement and calculation. Heim
argues that the opposition of realism and idealism is not
the primary one. There is no point in discussing whether
the distinctions are in the known or in the knower, when
already we are making a distinction in speaking of " known "
and " knower." We must first of all analyse this prior
distinction. In *Jesus der Herr* (pp. 23–29) he points to
the universal *polarity* of our common knowledge. This
concept may be applied to the very forms of space and
time. The idea of Past and that of Present can be thought
of only as each is opposed to the other. And, moreover,
the distinction Past-Present cannot be thought of until
we can contrast that relation with the background of the
nunc æternum, in which there is neither Past nor Present.
Similarly with the contrast Here-There. One cannot be
known save in opposition to the other, and the spatial
correlation cannot be conceived except as in opposition to
that which is indifferent to relationship in space.[1]

We see, therefore, that in metaphysics, Heim is neither
idealist nor realist. With Heidegger, he refuses to make
the ego an absolute. It is not the ego itself which is elevated
above space, time, and individuality, but the ego which is

[1] It is doubtful, however, whether Heim succeeds in overcoming this
difficulty : All our " common knowledge " is polar. But, if so, the concept
of polarity, as it is applied to Rest-Motion, to Here-There, to Space-Time,
can also be applied to the idea Polar-Non-Polar. *A*. " Polar " can be
thought of only in distinction from " Non-Polar." *B*. The correlation
Polar-Non-Polar can be thought of only in distinction from that which
is indifferent to polarity and non-polarity. It might appear to many
that this form of argument leads to scepticism. But, though Heim does
not make this point, it is perhaps possible to escape this negative conclusion by showing that the difficulty arises through a confusion of
" thinking the non-polar " with " non-polar thinking."

" here and now."   Hence it is impossible to fall into the mistake of idealism, of identifying the ego with God. Second, the realist's thing-in-itself disappears.   Every-" thing " depends on some perspective centre.[1]

From this study of intramundane relations of transcendence, Heim turns to consider the ultimate Dimension. God is the true " Thou " of every " I " ; He is the eternal and omnipresent Thou.   He cannot be objectified, and it is only when we give up the attempt so to objectify Him that the way is open for our understanding of the relation which exists between Him and men.   But we must be careful to insist that this final Dimension is not one among many others.   It is the Dimension of Dimensions, that which includes all the others.   It is the Dimension of the " Wholly Other." [2]

Is it possible to express the transcendence of the omnipresent God in terms of an intramundane relationship ? He finds that neither the I-Thou relation nor the I-It relation is adequate.   This is made clear when we consider the two fundamental problems by which we are confronted as human beings who know and will.   There is the question propounded by our *knowing* faculty—the question of origins. We may postulate a First Cause, but this is only arbitrarily chosen.   We make a halt in our regress, and say, Here let us assume a beginning.   Alternatively, we find the origin of all in the infinite totality of the causal system.   A similar result is obtained when we consider the problem presented by our *wills*, the problem of the ultimate sanction of our actions.   Here also it is possible to halt at some arbitrarily selected member of the series, or to fall back on the infinite inter-relationship of the entire world-process.   But the characteristic feature of the divine transcendence is that God belongs to a realm which lies beyond the contrast of these two possibilities ; beyond the contrast of idolatry and pantheism.[3]

---

[1] Cf. Cullberg, *Das Du und Die Wirklichkeit* (A. B. Lundequistska Bokhandeln, Uppsala, 1933).

[2] *Glaube und Denken*, zweite Auflage (Furche-Verlag, Berlin, 1931), pp. 316–321.   [3] *Vide supra*, pp. 40–41.

In *Glaube und Denken*, in its three editions,[1] Heim faces the problem of immediacy and beyondness, of experience and authority. He maintains that they are held over against each other in a paradoxical synthesis. The difficulty is in the form of a dilemma : If we cling to immediate knowledge, we may have certainty, but it remains subjective. And if we fall back on authority, we secure objectivity, but at the expense of certainty. Heim seeks a synthesis of experience and authority through the concept of a personal meeting. Though in the third edition of *Glaube und Denken* he lays more emphasis on the side of authority and less on immediate experience, he nevertheless holds strongly throughout to the fact of a genuine human experience in which our apprehension is a real and immediate one and our decision is geniune and responsible. The Word of God is a demand for practical effort ; to hear it is a moral determination as well as an acknowledgment.[2] Known and knower come upon the same plane. God and man meet in the plane of the Holy Spirit. God does not create man, and nowhere treats man, as means only, but always as a person, a Thou, not an It.[3] He would agree with Barth in maintaining that purely human knowledge is wholly perverse and rebellious, while insisting at the same time that our actual human knowledge has always some degree of Divine help, however much we may thwart it.

From Heim's discussion of the forms of transcendence two things, I believe, have been gained. (1) We have seen that there may be different types of certitude. That which appears as paradox may be the truth : truth *must* appear as paradox to those who are as yet blind to the dimension in which it lies. Man of himself is incapable of apprehending the ultimate. It must come to him as revelation. (2) The study of the important relation *I-Thou* has given a new prominence in contemporary thought to the transcendence of Space and Time involved in personal relationships.

---

[1] The third edition is translated under the title *God Transcendent*.

[2] See *Jesus der Herr*, p. 184.

[3] See *Jesus der Herr*, pp. 170, 174, 185, and *Glaube und Denken*, second ed. pp. 407 ff.

This is of great importance when we come to consider the authority of Christ over the knowing and the willing faculties of men in all ages. Jesus, the Lord, is the contemporary of all His followers. Those who knew Him as Incarnate Son of God have, over others, an advantage which is only relative, not absolute.

Let us now see how these premises apply to our problem. Deliberately and confidently, Heim places Christ at the centre of metaphysics. Ethical systems and ethical problems are bound up with our attitude towards three entities : I, Thou, and the World. And our philosophy of these has hitherto been invalidated by spatial metaphors. Consider the relation between " I " and " Thou." They each exist in a world with which space has nothing to do. There may, therefore, be an immediate connection between them, which overleaps all spatial separation. There may be a secret unity behind the duality. Consider this as it applies to the relation of a man with Christ. In the pages of the New Testament we find that which shatters philosophy—a man who has now passed from the world, and yet is not only present, but is the master of the world's fate ! Place the reality of Christ in the midst of our other ideas of reality, and it shatters them. Logic must bow under reality. He puts it elsewhere in another way. According to Spengler, the most intense problem presented to us by life is the problem of why we should be living " here and now," instead of in any other of the innumerable ages and places. In this Spengler finds the most deadly manifestation of relativity. Both Space and Time being relative, my standpoint in Space and Time can have no absolute value in the universe. I am forced back on the conception of Fate (*Schicksal*), that is, Chance, *Moira, Heimarmene, Ananke*. My position, in this " here and now," is casual, not causal. And this, says Heim, we should have to admit, if we regarded solely *my* position. Any man's existence is relative. From his own standpoint alone he can be certain of nothing. Not even his values are absolute. But, when we set alongside his existence the existence of Christ, everything is changed. Our minds are necessarily involved in and infected by relativity. To pass beyond this and into the realm of the absolute, we have to come face to face with Christ. *He* is our *Schicksal*, our Destiny, our " Fate." [1]

The person of Christ is placed at the heart of metaphysics. Christianity is no longer an " organisation intended to lighten the work of the police, or to make the workingman comfortable. It claims to be the one true interpretation of existence in space and time ; it claims to give the genuine, eternal values of all transitory experience." [2]

From this standpoint, Heim is able to see revelation in history. The Theology of Crisis has fought against *Historismus*. History, it declares, is not merely the life-process of the Absolute. " History," says Gogarten, " is not a shadow of eternity, but a place of decisions." Heim would agree, but with this caution, that every historical situation is in the hands of God. Before he makes each decision, a man is free, and, after it is made, he acknowledges it as his own free decision. Nevertheless, the situation, both before and after, is God's. The Divine is given in God's dealings with the historical situation left by man's action. God takes the situation, *with all the complications we have introduced*, and deals with it, still in love.

It will be seen that both Barth and Heim begin from the helplessness of man. But Heim recognises in the sense of brokenness the advent of God, the beginning of the soul's communion with Him. Both make the central point the forgiveness of sins. But to Barth, the apprehension of God in " religious experience " is only the apprehension of the apparent impossibility of redemption : with Heim it is part of the redemptive process. Psychologism, like Historism, is for Heim a name for one of the ways of bringing a man face to face with his " Fate," which is Christ.

With Barth, the unit of religious knowledge is the Divine alone. When we believe savingly, he is almost compelled to say, it is Christ Who believes for us. With Heim, the unit of religious experience is *God and man.*

---

[1] See Heim, *Glaube und Leben* : Essay on " Der Schicksalsgedanke als Ausdruck für das Suchen der Zeit."

[2] W. R. Inge, *Truth and Falsehood in Religion*, p. 129.

14

Allowing for the development—and also for the occasional
vacillation—of his thought, it may be said that Heim lays
right emphasis on both aspects of the religious experience.
In the first, the soul is aware of the otherness and the
transcendence of God ; in the second it acknowledges His
immanence and kinship. It may be that the second is in
greater need of being stressed. It carries within it the
ethical and personal character of faith. It does not deny
the utter dependence of the soul on God's absolute power,
but it recognises humbly that God asks, not merely for
obedience to a divine imperative or blind assent to divine
revelation, but also for understanding. He desires a new
character in men, and one which cannot be brought about
by irresistible grace, but only in the gift of redemption,
where faith responds to grace. In a striking passage in
Die Weltanschauung der Bibel, Heim says : We can experience the redemptive love of Christ only through conscience—
" it may be in a moment of mortal danger, when we feel
that we are going to face God with all the burden of conscience heavy upon us. There is perhaps only one proof of
Christian faith—the experience of thousands of Christian
people in the hour of death, who take refuge in the work
of Christ, and know that the accuser is silent."

It would seem that the mystics are right in finding the
best human analogy for that unassailable certainty between
the believer and Christ in the love that exists between
husband and wife. It is in possession of certainty because
it is a relation of trust. " I am my Beloved's, and my
Beloved is mine." God trusts me beyond that which I
now am ; I trust Him beyond that which I now see.

Barth's fixed point, his absolute, is revelation, God
breaking through, God's Word. But he is hampered by
the fact that it is not easy to know when it *is* revelation.
Heim's fixed point is that " Fate," " Destiny," which is the
meeting of a man with Christ. Both theologians take their
starting-point from the challenge of Spengler and other
relativists. Spengler's might be called the *horizontal
hypothesis*. There is *no* fixed point. One man's centre is
for another only the horizon. All is a level plain. All

values are equally valueless. Barth's may be called the *vertical hypothesis*. God comes straight down from above. The eternal breaks through into the temporal. Then Heim's may be called the *Bethel hypothesis*. There is traffic between earth and heaven. It would be wrong to ignore the possibility that in the relationship between the believer and Christ man is offered that viewpoint which the relativist denies, the non-temporal, non-spatial, universal. God breaking through is the *only* God Whom we know. The Word from which we must begin is the Word made flesh. The ultimate *datum* of Christianity is a historical fact which transcends history. " In the long succession of historical personalities who rise up majestically like pillars of smoke, and then disappear in a higher stratum of air, leaving behind only the lustre of memory, there is one sole exception. There is One Who can say, ' I am with you alway.' " We attempt intellectually to examine His Person ; we find that He is spiritually examining us. Nineteen centuries have bowed before that scrutiny. Stand outside the personal relationship with Jesus, and Christology is an insoluble problem. Cross the threshold, and it is the solution of all problems. God is the God Who sent Jesus. Given that as an axiom, faith can work out anything.[1]

It appears therefore that the definition of faith that is frequently offered by Dr. W. R. Inge is wrong : " Faith is an experiment which ends in an experience." The truth is rather that we begin with the experience. " Thy love unknown hath broken every barrier down." This means that the real creed of the Christian believer is the prayer uttered in the moment of experience. The " unio mystica " is a momentary thing, but it is a living thing. To dissect it, to ask reasons for it, is to destroy the life and to alter its character. Yet in it is to be found unassailable certainty.

In the realm of Metaphysics, confidence in any judgment is made to rest on that which is not purely rational. To take two broadly contrasted types of theory—Idealism takes the leap of faith in believing that the mind is self-authenticating. Realism also moves *per saltum* by its

[1] Heim, *The New Divine Order* (E.T.), pp. 114-117.

affirmation that appearance and reality correspond. In each case it is a necessary leap. And the leap is no less certain than the ratiocination, in all the course of which it is involved. Once more, certainty belongs, not to the process, but to the hidden order by which the process is sustained.

In Ethics we find the same. The ethical decision is very different from subsequent reasoning about it. It is self-authenticating. A like distinction is rightly drawn between a religious experience and the dogma in which it is enshrined.

The results thus far may be summarised :

1. *Epistemologically.* The Reality which we are endeavouring to apprehend is personal, and is searching for us ; we are so made as to be capable of apprehending, and only as we do so apprehend do we ourselves become real.

2. *In more religious terminology.* The certainty being that of a personal relationship, we can say, with Augustine, " O Thou Good Omnipotent, Who so carest for everyone of us, as if Thou caredst for him alone, and so for all, as if they were but one ! " Our "interest " in the Cross of Christ is intimate and personal.[1]

3. *Homiletically.* The appeal in preaching, whether it be to reason, to imagination, or to the ethical will, is null and void if it does not first lead towards a closer communion with Christ. Revelation being personal and incommunicable, it is possible for the preacher to come between the convert and God. There may be times when a man's soul is best left alone—with God.

The word " certainty " perhaps best expresses this conclusion, for the word has two sides. It is, first, convincing truth, and, second, personal conviction. Only from truth that is certain can we produce certainty about the truth. The preacher seeks a verdict and he therefore speaks urgently, as dying unto dying men. And he is able so to preach only because he can say, " It pleased God to reveal His Son in me."

.   .   .   .   .   .

[1] Augustine, *Confessions,* iii. 11.

The symbolism of Nicolas Berdyaev shows many undesigned parallels with the dimensional philosophy of Heim. He speaks, for example, of the *discontinuity of our thought about God*. When thought tries to penetrate into the final mysteries, it involves a drastic revolution in our consciousness, which brings with it a spiritual illumination transforming the very nature of reason itself. Reason thus illuminated is reason of a different type, belonging neither to this world nor to this age.[1] This discontinuity in our thought about God " consists precisely in the abandonment of concepts in favour of symbols and myths." In the discontinuity of thought we see the equivalent of Heim's Dimension of the divine ; in the reference to symbol and myth (both terms are used with a specific meaning, which Berdyaev carefully defines) we have a parallel to Heim's " paradox." Discontinuity involves a " leap of faith," but this is not a venture, a hazard. Faith leaps because it sees the truth. It does not abandon reason ; it carries reason with it ; but reason is transformed and illumined.[2] Berdyaev is striving after an expression of symbolism which will transcend idealism and realism, rationalism and mysticism.

Rationalism, we have seen, is involved in certain insurmountable difficulties. Reason, for example, cannot prove the authority of reason ; for every stage of the proof depends on the acceptance of that authority which is to be proved ! From this there have followed two fatal consequences in the history of rationalism :

1. It reduced nature to a *mechanical scheme of matter and motion*, and it regarded religion as no more than a body of doctrines about God, providence, and immortality.

2. It failed to realise that *each kind of reality has its own appropriate evidence*, on which must depend the method of investigation ; and thus, having determined the method in advance, rationalism limited its inquiry to that which could be made amenable to the method.[3]

[1] *Freedom and the Spirit*, pp. 73–74.   [2] *Op. cit.* p. 79.
[3] Cf. Oman, *The Natural and the Supernatural* (Cambridge, 1931), p. 103.

On the other hand, mysticism, as we must now conceive it, is not to be confined to that revolt against reason represented by William James, who would reduce religion to the working of non-rational feelings and subconscious impulses ; nor to Bergson's glorification of supra-rational intuition. Nor is it to be narrowed down to Otto's awareness of a *mysterium tremendum*, or awe in the presence of the numinous. We should require to take into account the character of this feeling-experience. On this its *religious* quality depends, for not every form of awe is religious.[1] Our genuine mysticism must be one which takes account also of reason. If, with Berdyaev, we speak of it as symbolism, then we must be sure that we have only the *highest* symbols. Friedrich Heiler has emphasised the weakness of much Christian mysticism. It is a *formless* ecstasy. The soul seeks to lose itself in the death of Christ on the Cross. But the words and the deeds of Christ are only points of support for the soul in its journey back to the ineffable. Mystics can take part in the Mass without hearing any word or seeing anything on the altar. The passion of Christ is not a redemptive fact, but only a symbol of that sacrifice which the mystic must every day offer afresh.[2] If this is possible, then it does not matter which intellectual element has acted as the point of departure. Such mysticism has abandoned its religious character and has become æsthetic experience, pleasurable, it may be, and useful, but quite definitely not religious.

The mystic must meet the difficulties of scientist, philosopher, historian, even textual critic ; and must at least show that the difficulties are non-vital or unreal.

Moreover, the philosopher must take into account the evidence of mystical experience. While checking the experience and restraining it from eccentricities and subjective fancies, the rationalist should be prepared to recognise that the solution of his difficulties, the key to his problems, may lie in this experience. Reason changes its type. It is prepared to deal with new evidence, hitherto

[1] Cf. Galloway, *Faith and Reason in Religion*, pp. 24–29.

[2] Heiler, *Der Katholizismus* (Reinhardt, Munich, 1923), p. 527.

unknown to it or unrecognised by it ; and, because of its illumination, reason now sees this evidence more clearly and estimates it with more justice. " Revelation," says Berdyaev,[1] " is a catastrophic transformation of conscious-ness, a radical modification of its structure, almost, one might say, a creation of new organs of being with functions in another world." " In the basic and original life and in the spiritual will an orientation towards a new world is possible which will create new organs of consciousness." [2]

Remembering that the organ of religious knowledge is a spiritual organ—a mind obedient, illumined, consecrated—we see that two results follow. The first is negative : The transcendence of God has not been rightly conceived. The wrong conception has arisen through the isolation of one side of the relation. Both philosophy and theology must refuse to take either God or man as their starting-point. " The transcendent is only part of the immanent, an incident in the course of spiritual development, a separation of spirit from spirit." " In the process of this antithetical division of the spirit revelation appears to possess a trans-cendent and objective character, but actually in its inner nature revelation is entirely immanent in the spirit within which it occurs." [3]

In this connection it is essential to take most cognisance of that barrier which is presented to divine self-revelation by human unworthiness. We recall the consequences of sin, in darkening the spirit, distorting its vision, and falsi-fying its values ; and we remember that it is not only of the individual transgressions that we take account, but of the mass of human guilt, including, perhaps, *Ursünde*, the Fall as pre-history in the spiritual world. It would be impossible to overstate the consequences of estrangement from God. The disability is not metaphysical, but ethical. Christian certitude begins, therefore, with the experience of redemption through Christ.

Second, we have a positive consequence. The Christian Absolute is not thought out but revealed. It is not accur-

[1] *Op. cit.* p. 96.
[2] *Ibid.* p. 98.
[3] Berdyaev, *op. cit.* p. 96.

ately spoken of in terms of Aristotle's " Unmoved," Plato's ὄντως ὄν, the " Absolute and Unconditioned," the absolute ego, absolute spirit, absolute reason. These represent man's efforts to jump off his own shadow. We must not confuse two things : (i) our active attempt to make absolute something of our own conceiving ; (ii) that passivity by which we find an ultimate wherein we can anchor the soul. This ultimate is beyond our grasp, unless something happens which breaks through the polarity of our thinking.[1]

Faith is not an achievement, but a response. There are those who say that certitude is unattainable ; there can be nothing more than probability.[2] But this statement can then be no more than probable ! When we say, ' Certainty is unattainable,' *ex hypothesi* we cannot be certain of the truth of our statement ! This is said here, not to score a point in metaphysical debate, but to indicate that there is no solution to be had on epistemological lines. The certainty of which we speak is something quite different from that discussed by metaphysicians. It is different in that ours is an inquiry concerning religion, where a particular *character* is necessary for the possession of certitude.

Our investigation is only as deep as our love : our grasp of the truth is measurable by our obedience.

[1] Cf. Heim, *Jesus der Herr*, pp. 33–34.
[2] Cf. John Dewey, *The Quest for Certainty* (Allen & Unwin, 1930), p. 291 ff.

CHAPTER XI

FINALITY OF THE CHRISTIAN GOSPEL.

I. Limits of Syncretism

SUMMARY

Is finality in religion conceivable ? The question may be asked by the sceptic out of unreadiness to believe that any final solution is available. But his own position is (1) is self-contradictory ; (2) questions the general belief in revelation without supplying an alternative explanation of the facts ; (3) fails to take account of the possibility that in Christianity there may be found a guarantee both of revelation and of its absolute form. Or the question may be posed by those who believe in the infinite possibilities of human progress. It is probable, however, that bitter experience has already put too great a strain on this facile type of optimism. Religion is confused with culture. The question may also be asked by the religious man on religious grounds. He may feel that the riches of God are so boundless, and the capacity of man so grievously lessened by indifference, disloyalty, doubt, and sin, that no individual and not even the universal Christian Church can claim to have more of the truth than would be represented by the sip of a swallow from the fulness of a brimming river. But his difficulty arises from a confusion of Divine revelation and human response.

The claim of finality is not made for absoluteness of dogma, nor for the absoluteness of any particular Church. To set either of these in opposition to the finality of Jesus Himself is not a defence but a betrayal of Christianity. As in art, so in religion, there is no inherent objection to the claim that the supreme revelation may come, not at the end of the series, but in the course of it. In religion we may put the matter positively, since we are speaking, not of the response of man, but of the revelation of God. By contrast with those religions which may plausibly be suggested as competitors, we discover those features which differentiate Christianity from all other faiths, and do so in a way which marks it out as the truth in religion. It would be unfair to reject Mohammedanism on the ground solely of its fatalism and doctrine of predestination, for we should then require to include in our condemnation many noble and lofty expressions of Christianity. But we find that in Islam the unity and omnipotence of God are secured at the expense of His fatherhood and His love towards men. In Buddhism, the ideal is not redemption of life, but redemption *from* life. Where Christianity calls for repentance, Buddhism advises illumination. To recognise the illusion of life is to find release from it. Hinduism has developed an attitude of comprehensive charity instead of a fanatical faith in an inflexible creed. But there ought to be two stubborn limits to tolerance—truth and morality. We find here a belief in the unreality of the world and the consequent denial of human freedom and responsibility.

The suggestion is made that we are to seek an amalgam of the best elements in all the known faiths. The difficulties involved are evident in Theosophy, "the amateur side of comparative religion." A religion is an organic unity ; it may not be dissected without destroying the life of those parts into which it is analysed. Some have proposed to claim finality for those doctrines, wherever found, which tend to promote Christian character. They forget that the Christian life cannot be separated from the Christian religion and the Person of Christ.

The determining feature in religion is its idea of God. Because Christians have received their idea of God from the teaching, the life, and the death and resurrection of Jesus, they know that there are definite *limits of syncretism*. The redemption which is offered to mankind by Christ leaves no profound and legitimate longing unsatisfied.

CHAPTER XI

FINALITY OF THE CHRISTIAN GOSPEL

I. LIMITS OF SYNCRETISM

WE read that when John the Baptist heard in prison of the works of Jesus, he sent two of his disciples to ask, " Art thou he that should come, or do we look for another ? " That is the question which we have to ask again in our day. And perhaps it is significant that the answer of Jesus was not a direct affirmative. Then, as now, men were required to reach their own conclusion, though all the evidence for arriving at it is given. " Go and shew John again those things which ye do hear and see."

It is probable that a preliminary question will be raised : *Is finality in religion at all conceivable ?* It may be asked by the sceptic out of sheer unreadiness to believe that any final solution is available. Or it may be asked, for a different reason, by the man of an optimistic temperament, who is prepared to believe in an endless amelioration of the lot of man, not physically alone but morally and spiritually also. It may even be asked by the profoundly religious mind, and for religious reasons. The symbol used in currency to represent the dollar is said to come from an engraving of the " pillars of Hercules " entwined by a scroll bearing the motto " Ne plus ultra," " Look for no more beyond " ; but the voyage of Columbus discovered a vaster world beneath the horizon, and the negative had to be struck out. *Plus ultra !* The believer may feel that it is impossible to say that we have ever beheld the boundaries of God's grace. It cannot be measured ; there is always more beyond.

> " Though thy soul sail leagues and leagues beyond,—
> Still, leagues beyond those leagues, there is more sea."

We do not need to linger long over the sceptical objection. To say that no stable truth can ever be attained is self-contradictory. It requires a great deal of knowledge to be able to say even that knowledge is unattainable. At best this scepticism is a hypothesis, which cannot be proved without the use of at least *some* reliable knowledge—the possibility of which is denied by the same scepticism. Secondly, the sceptic's challenge is directed not alone against Christianity, but against the whole possibility of revelation, and we have therefore the right to ask that he shall submit an alternative theory to explain the facts which call for some explanation, and which for us are adequately accounted for by our belief in revelation. Thirdly, it would be unfair for him to declare roundly that stable truth is not anywhere to be found until he had himself examined this Christian faith in which, it is claimed, that stable truth is offered. His objection, then, need not be taken seriously, since (1) it is self-contradictory; (2) it questions the general belief in revelation without supplying an alternative; and (3) it fails to take account of the possibility that in Christianity there may be found a guarantee both of revelation and of its absolute form.

Next we turn to those who deny the likelihood of a final revelation because of their view of human history and progress. They are impressed by the evidence of evolution. They realise how small is the period covered by the records of history and they look forward to a long course of continued advance in which, as man has in the past progressed physically, he will rise to ever greater spiritual heights. A study of the history of religions appears at first to be in their favour. What we see is the incessant rise and fall of different faiths. As one ceases to command the best that is in man of thought and aspiration, it degenerates and decays, to be replaced by some higher manifestation of the human spirit, and they imagine this process going on indefinitely. To look for finality in religion, they say, is to set limits to the achievements of which the human spirit is capable.

Of this position it must be said at once that its optimism

is unjustified. Of himself, man cannot hope for inevitable, automatic progress in the things of the spirit. That naive faith belongs to an age of material and scientific progress which accepted uncritically the belief in the spontaneous amelioration of man's powers and the extension of his conquests. It may be that bitter experience has already put too great a strain on this facile type of optimism.

This view, therefore, is exposed to two criticisms. The first is a formal one. It is not to be allowed that the principle of evolution should claim absoluteness for itself, while denying it to everything else. " As an instrument of knowledge must not it also, in strict logic, be regarded as limited in application and value, and liable to be replaced by something else ? "[1] The second criticism is that this theory confuses culture and religion. An eminent Dutch scholar in the science of religion[2] was betrayed into this mistake. One of his earlier essays bore the title, " The Laws of the Development of Religion." In his Gifford Lectures, delivered in Edinburgh in 1896, he argued that this title was wrong. It should, he thought, have been " Laws of Development in their Application to Religion." For, in point of fact, he says, " I only meant even then to maintain that the laws which govern the development of the human mind hold true of religion also, though their application may differ in form and in details."[3] He argues for the principle of the "unity of the mind." Culture and religion rise or fall together. Any particular religion must keep pace with civilisation. If it does not, and civilisation gets the upper hand, that religion will suffer and languish ; whereas, if the religion itself gains the victory, it does so at the cost of depriving its adherents of the benefits of that civilisation.

No one would deny the interaction of culture and religion, but it would be historically untrue to claim that the highest levels of civilisation have always coincided with the best periods of faith. The word " highest " is full

---

[1] Alexander Martin, *The Finality of Jesus for Faith* (T. & T. Clark, 1933), p. 32.

[2] C. P. Tiele, *Elements of the Science of Religion*, vol. i. chap. viii.

[3] *Elements of the Science of Religion*, vol. i. p. 214.

of ambiguity. It is true, as Tiele maintains, that all progress is *mental* progress. Even the most materialistic age owes its discoveries, conveniences, and inventions to the mind of man. But civilisation is not to be judged by the mental standard alone. It involves elements, moral and spiritual, which are of far more profound significance. The criterion of any particular civilisation lies not in its technical achievements but in the purposes for which they are employed. It cannot be doubted that our own age will be judged by its success or failure in devoting its wealth of scientific knowledge to the real welfare of mankind and not by what it may do for the trivialities of public amusement or the destructiveness of national armaments.

Culture and religion may have to part company. It may be the fault of either. Culture may lead to luxury and spiritual degeneration, or religion may grow stagnant, concerning itself with the past of dogma instead of with living issues and the clamant needs of man's mind and spirit. But it is clear that there is no argument here for refusing *a priori* the claim of finality in religious revelation. An absolute religion will be such, not because it is congruent with the tenor of contemporary culture, but in virtue of its proving true to itself. " No mistake could be cruder," writes Professor John Baillie,[1] " no ' Idol of the Theatre ' could be more childish, than the assumption that because we know more than our fathers did about the movements of the stars or the inside of the atom or the origin of specific differences in living organisms, or still more that because we have harnessed to our use the forces of electricity and radioactivity and have built ourselves the telephone and the radio and the aeroplane, we have therefore any greater insight into the ultimate meaning of life and the ultimate nature of the Most High God. For it does not take much burrowing in the buried riches of the past, nor yet does it take a very penetrating awareness of our own souls' needs, to make us realise that in the deepest

---

[1] *The Place of Jesus Christ in Modern Christianity* (T. & T. Clark, 1929), pp. 16–17. See also the same author's *The Interpretation of Religion*, chap. ix.

things of the spirit men like Socrates and Marcus Aurelius and St. Paul and St. Augustine had at least as true a judgment and as keen a vision as any of us moderns is likely to attain. When the question is, ' What are the laws of the electrical constitution of matter ? ' or, ' How am I to build an internal-combustion engine ? ' then indeed we moderns have it over all our forefathers. But when the question is, ' What must I do to be saved ? ' or ' What is the ultimate purport of existence ? ' then you and I feel that we can often sit at the feet of those ancients in an almost silent humility." [1]

When the question, " Is finality in revelation conceivable ? " is asked, not by the sceptic doubting the validity of all knowledge, nor by the intellectual with an optimistic faith in the future of the human spirit, but by the religious man on religious grounds, then we are brought much nearer to the heart of the problem. He is chary of accepting any revelation as final, not because he distrusts man's mind (like the sceptic), nor because he places excessive confidence in it (like the optimist), but rather because of his reverence before the deep things of God. God has been revealed to us : we worship Him in gratitude and adoration ; but is not the term " finality," when applied to His acts and to His Word, a claim too majestical to be made by any of His creatures ? Dr. Nicol Macnicol [2] imagines such a question as this being asked : Is not to speak of finality to speak of what is beyond our compass ? And he answers it by saying, " Our right to go as far as to make that claim will probably be questioned by many. In making it we may be reaching out beyond the logical understanding. We have certainly no natural right in ourselves to advance further. In order that we may do so we shall require a reason ' out of nature.' "

Sir Robert Ball once wrote that the sip which a flying swallow takes from a river is as far from exhausting the

---

[1] For further discussion of the relation between culture and faith, see Söderblom, " The Religion of Revelation " (in *The Nature of Revelation*, Oxford, 1933).

[2] *Is Christianity Unique ?* (Student Christian Movement Press, 1936), pp. 164 f.

water in the river as are the planets from using all the
heat which streams from the sun.[1] It is felt, perhaps, by
many earnest believers, that the riches of God are so boundless, and the capacity of man so poor and so grievously
lessened by indifference, or by disloyalty to the truth, or
by wilful doubt and sinfulness, that no individual and
not even the universal Christian Church can claim to have
more of the truth than would be represented by the sip of
a swallow from the fulness of a brimming river. But the
difficulty arises from a confusion of divine revelation and
human response. We cannot doubt that there will be ever
new and fuller apprehension of religious truth. And if we
care to give to this fuller appreciation the name of revelation we may not perhaps go very far astray. The new
discoveries made by saintly individuals and by the Christian Church under the guidance of the Spirit have, for
others who learn of them, the character of revelation. But,
because these do not supersede Christianity but come, in
fact, through new understanding of Christ, they do not
constitute a new religion, but only a better understanding
of that which is given already once for all.

The claim of finality which we are to consider is not one
for absoluteness of dogma, any more than for the absoluteness of any particular Church. To set either of these in
opposition to the finality of Jesus Himself is not a defence
but a betrayal of Christianity. " The watchword of the
Reformation, ' by faith alone,' is but a variant of this
conviction, and perhaps the most unchristian thing in
Romanism is that beside the religious absoluteness of Jesus
Christ it has dared to set the absoluteness of the Papal
Church." [2] We are to discuss the finality, not of any
authoritative pronouncement nor of any individual's faith,
but the finality of the faith as it is given in Christ. For
external knowledge of Him we are dependent on the testimony of the apostles. Without them we should not know
how He taught and how He acted. But the final authority

[1] *The Story of the Heavens*, second ed. p. 68.
[2] H. R. Mackintosh, *The Originality of the Christian Message* (Duckworth, 1920), p. 179.

is Jesus Himself. The response to His authority and the apprehension of His truth have varied in different ways and in different individuals and churches. But that is by no means an indication that the revelation in Jesus is not final and absolute. On the contrary, it is part of the evidence for the defence. Understanding of the Christian message is enriched by every person, every age, and every race which responds to it. And that is what we should expect. Its change is one proof of its finality. It is adequate for the needs of all sorts and conditions of men. Even the apparent failures of Christianity point in this direction. If it is said that the strongest argument against Christianity is the Christian Church, whose noble mission contrasts sadly with its meagre achievement and with the low spiritual temperature of Christian men and women, it may be replied that, even through the fallible human instrument of the Church on earth, men and women are nevertheless converted and sustained. In spite of opposition from without and the weight of the dead hand within, the Church has kept its purity and power. " As the appointed means for realising the kingdom of God, Christianity is a progressive religion. Growth is the law of its life, and this along all lines—doctrinal, institutional, practical." In its power of adaptation " we have not only the secret of its past victories, but also the ground for faith in its continued influence and final triumph." [1]

It may be wise to remember that this situation has a parallel in the realm of art. Rodin declared that " no artist will ever surpass Pheidias—for progress exists in the world, but not in art. The greatest of sculptors, who appeared at a time when the whole human dream could blossom in the pediment of a temple, will remain for ever without an equal." [2] Söderblom (who was an accomplished musician as well as a great theologian, and was particularly conversant with Bach) writes in one of his essays : " Some-

[1] William Adams Brown, *Christian Theology in Outline* (T. & T. Clark, 1923), p. 39.
[2] *Art*, in English Translation, p. 234, quoted by B. H. Streeter in *Adventure*, p. 159.

15

thing of the life of music lives in all of us. But when Bach
and Beethoven arise they become for us, not merely two
persons much more musically gifted than the rest of us but
rather they are revelations of music itself. In them the
spirit of music comes forth to meet us. I am almost as
certain that we reach in Bach, in principle, the highest
point in music, and that Plotinus constitutes the perfection
of the mysticism of infinity, as I am that Christ will never
be surpassed nor even equalled in the history of divine
revelation." [1] In art as in religion, finality need not wait
for the end of time. [2]

There is, then, no inherent objection to the claim that,
in art and in religion, the supreme revelation may come,
not at the end of the series, but in the course of it. In
religion we may go much further. We may put the matter
positively, since we are speaking, not of the response of
man, but of the revelation of God. And of the nature of
God we have more than negative evidence. We learn much
of the divine nature from the best of that long course
of religious development which was the preparation for
Christ, and from the very fact of this organic unity of
the process. It is God's nature to reveal Himself pro-
gressively. And this knowledge of God leads us to expect
that some day, when the time is ripe, He will reveal all.
If there is divine purpose in the world at all, it follows
that there is also a " fulness of time " when God will give

[1] Söderblom, " The Portals of Revelation " (in *The Nature of Revelation*), pp. 123–124.

[2] See also A. C. Bouquet, *Is Christianity the Final Religion?* (Macmillan, 1921), pp. 66–67 : " It is usual to say that the greatest sculptors
lived much more than two thousand years ago, and to point to the Italian
painters as giving us the canons of pictorial art, while to the Romans we
attribute the fixation and definition of the principles of law and government, and to the Western Europeans of the nineteenth century the
application of science to industry, while perhaps Germany may still
keep the credit of having produced most of the great musical geniuses.
. . . These choice flowerings of the human spirit touched by the Divine
Spirit are, however, not affected in value by being ranged in an order
other than chronological. . . . There is therefore, it would appear, no
inherent objection to the belief that two thousand years ago the spirit
of the ages produced a unique human being, who in the words of Augustine
' Summed up in Himself the long series of human life.' "

the final word and accomplish the unique act. Those who believe in limitless progress on evolutionary lines cannot conceive the consummation coming elsewhere than at the end of the time-series. Such an idea of progress, as we have seen, is in spiritual matters out of date. There is no such thing as inevitable advance. It comes only as God grants it and as man is worthy of it. Granted, therefore, the liberty of believing that God's purpose is being worked out in the world, we cannot suppose that the absolute Word is withheld until the end, when we might legitimately infer that it was no longer necessary, since His own people would be seeing Him face to face.

We may pause here to examine one suggested possibility. Our inquiry, it may be said, might be completed at once if it were shown that Christianity, so far from being the final revelation of God, was outrivalled already by one of the other known religions.

How are we to deal with this suggestion ? Clearly it is impossible to proceed by simple elimination. In my boyhood tales were told of a schoolmaster whose habit it was, when a misdemeanour had happened while he was out of the classroom, to ask each of the thirty-six boys individually, round the class, whether he was responsible. If thirty-five boys answered " No," the master proceeded, without further inquiry, to thrash the thirty-sixth. He showed great confidence in the method of elimination as well as in the honesty of his boys, but the method is not a suitable one for our inquiry. There is little doubt that claims would be put forward by someone for every known form of religion, from the most primitive fetishism to the most nebulous theosophy. On the other hand, it would be fairly easy, by examining one or two of the more plausible claims, not merely to show that Christianity is superior— that would fall far short of the claim made by Christianity —but to discover by contrast those features which differentiate Christianity from all other faiths, and do so in a way which marks it out as the truth in religion.

There is one standard ready to hand, as it might appear —that of morality. A religion is judged by its fruits. But it is possible that the ethics of a faith may not belong inalienably to it. They may be borrowed or imitated from another, and may therefore be rather a parasitic growth on the religion than its own natural leaf and blossom.[1] While, therefore, we shall find in morality an indispensable pointer, indicating perhaps that we need go no farther, since a worthy religion is not to be looked for in conjunction with this or that inferior morality, we should require to apply instead a measure which is specifically religious. A faith stands or falls by its idea of God and His relation to men. " What does it profit a man if he possess the most excellent worldly wisdom and knowledge of human nature, the best ethical code, yes, even the most beautiful ideals, if faith and hope collapse, if heaven is closed and the spiritual sun of divine power and love is darkened, so that the spirit is left cold and empty ? "[2] Attention is naturally concentrated on teaching concerning man's salvation. We ask, What is the idea of God presented in each case ? and How far does each faith preserve belief in the distinct existence and intrinsic worth of the human soul and in the reality of the moral life ?

It is true that the Oriental mind tends towards fatalism, but this is perhaps to be regarded rather as a temperamental trait than as a settled religious conviction. In the popular mind, predestination may be limited to the outstanding events of life, and to the coming of death. Even in this restricted sense, however, it is corrected by orthodox theology. The word *Islam* means " resignation," but it may be interpreted as the rightful abandonment of the pious soul to the will of God whatever it may have in store. The words of the Khalif Omar represent the attitude of Moslem theology : " He who is in the fire should resign

[1] It is said, for example, by some Indian Moslem reformers, that the Veil, polygamy, and divorce are not essential principles of the Koran ; that they were occasional, not eternal commands ; that, on a closer inspection, they will be found to point to the *freedom* of women, *monogamy*, and the *permanence* of marriage. That view, however, would probably be classed as Islamic rationalism (Mutazilite). It owes its origin not to the spirit of Islam, but to the permeation of Christian ideals.

[2] Söderblom, *The Nature of Revelation*, p. 1.

himself to the will of God ; but he who is not yet in the fire need not throw himself into it." The doctrine of fatalism has always been expressly repudiated by orthodox Islam, which believes in the free will of man, " although it encounters serious difficulty in reconciling this with the all-powerful will of God." [1]

It would be unfair, therefore, on this ground alone to reject Mohammedanism as inferior in its idea of God without at the same time condemning many noble and lofty expressions of Christianity itself. Though its doctrine may recall the Greek conception of destiny, there is this important distinction, that while Zeus was generally thought of as himself subject to Μοῖρα,[2] Fate, for the Moslem, is identified with the omnipresent will of Allah. All will depend on the way in which God is conceived. And it is just here that this religion is at its weakest. Allah is so remote from the world of men that he becomes almost the equivalent of blind destiny. His will is everything ; man's life is nothing. " Rotten rags and dirt—that is your life." Where God is so far transcendent, man's life, including his moral struggle, becomes trivial and meaningless. The realm of time and sense is emptied of all worth. " In the fierce blaze of Allah's will it shrivels to complete insignificance." [3] Evil as well as good comes from his predestination, his will, his operation. It is inevitable also that the origin even of sin is ascribed to God. He " leads astray whom he pleases and guides whom he pleases." [4] In Islam the unity and omnipotence of God

---

[1] See the article by Baron Carra de Vaux on " Fate (Muslim) " in Hastings' *Encyclopædia of Religion and Ethics*, vol. v. 794a.

[2] See, for example, Pindar in *Pyth.* xii. 30, τό γε μόρσιμον οὐ παραφυκτόν, and *Prometheus Vinctus*, 511–525.

[3] Nicol Macnicol, *Is Christianity Unique ?* p. 47, and the same author's *The Living Religions of the Indian People* (Student Christian Movement, 1934), chap. vi.

[4] It is said that the following answer was once made to the presentation of very strict Calvinist doctrine : " When the first sin was committed Adam put the blame on the woman and the woman put the blame on the serpent. The serpent, who was as yet young and dull, made no answer. Now he has become old and confident and comes to the Synod of Dort and says that God has done it." See Söderblom, *The Nature of*

are secured at the expense of His fatherhood and His love towards men. " ' The most excellent names,' ninety and nine in number, do not contain any term which denotes the relation of God as a Father to His people. The idea is repugnant to the Muslim mind, and so in Islam the relation of man to God must ever be that of a slave, who lacks the freedom and dignity of a son." [1]

. . . .

In speaking of contrasted doctrines of salvation, Professor Heim uses this figure : When we arrive in an unfamiliar city, we ask for a plan of it, so that we may go about independently. But this is not what God offers to us in the world. Instead, He offers a leader. This is perhaps a shock to our pride and our self-reliance. We wish to learn about the world for ourselves. Nevertheless, it is not a philosophical system or a code of ethics which is presented to us in Christianity : it is the Person of Jesus. [2]

In Buddhism, it is the plan not the person that is offered to us. (In its modern guise, Buddhism has definitely strayed from its origin, and offers adoration to the founder.) The need of salvation is acknowledged. Buddhism stands high among the religions of the world in its recognition of the problems of suffering and of sin, and in its emphasis on the community of mankind in facing them. Salvation is presented first as escape from the sorrows of disaster, of death, and, in particular, of life. Life itself, with its constant exposure to the wretchedness of desire, is an evil. But, in addition, salvation is presented as ultimate blessedness and security. It is doubtful, however, whether even here we are in touch with a concept that is specifically religious. Inevitably, Buddhism describes sin in terms of

Revelation, p. 67. Söderblom writes in the same chapter that " Jesus presents no theodicy, no defence for God in the terrible and mysterious trial of sin and misery " ; yet " no one had penetrated further into the problem of evil than He with the words : ' An enemy hath done this ' " (p. 66).

[1] Edward Sell, " God (Muslim) " in Hastings' *Encyclopædia of Religion and Ethics*, vol. vi. 302a.

[2] See Heim, *Jesus der Herr*, p. 214.

its human misery and not as the breach of communion between man and God, for Whose fellowship he was created. The causes of suffering are constantly represented as dangerous because they hold man in bondage now and hereafter, not because they set man at enmity with a god.[1] Since life is regarded as nothing but illusion and the wretchedness of desire, it follows that, for Buddhism, the ideal is not redemption of life, but redemption *from* life. And the method of salvation is correspondingly inferior. It is not through conscience that man is brought to seek salvation, but through knowledge that he achieves it for himself. Where Christianity calls for repentance, Buddhism advises illumination. To recognise the illusion of life is to find release from it. Man is redeemed not by grace but by his own works.

It is not always easy to see what precisely is implied in the ultimate blessedness for which man can hope. Nirvana is described as the blowing out of a lamp, or the quenching of a flame in water, but Buddha himself did not speculate on the nature of the state hereafter. His mission was not to satisfy idle curiosity but to show men how they could escape for ever from the wheel of existence with its round of birth, sorrow, old age, death. Logically, it would appear, there is nothing which can pass over into a new life except *karma*, the predispositions which are the material of a new existence. But, when Nirvana is reached, " the residuum of karma has been consumed, and there is nothing left to continue existence in any form." [2] It is true that the logical conclusion was not always drawn, and the belief in annihilation could be classed as heresy. Perhaps we can go no further than to say that Nirvana is the peaceful end beyond the dread of rebirth ; that Buddha would deny neither existence nor non-existence in Nirvana, because he did not know the unknowable and was concerned only to open up the way of emancipation.

It may be said that Christianity does not attempt to

---

[1] See C. A. F. Rhys Davids in Hastings' *Encyclopædia of Religion and Ethics*, article " Salvation (Buddhist)."

[2] G. F. Moore, *The History of Religions*, vol. i. p. 297.

picture in any detail the life that awaits man on the other side of the grave. Nevertheless, we are sure of this, that each soul is precious in the sight of God—so precious that Christ died for it; and that the life beyond will consist of fellowship with the Father. We know that the life and death of Jesus have raised love from a mere incident of fleeting human existence to the preoccupation of eternity.

Hinduism, it has been said,[1] " is like the Ganges itself, which welcomes waters from a thousand tributaries." When Buddhism appeared, and threatened to be a dangerous rival, Hinduism quietly absorbed it. It is possible for the Hindu, when any new missionary cult appears, to declare that the essence of what is contained in it has long been known to him. In the words of Professor Radhakrishnan, " Hinduism developed an attitude of comprehensive charity instead of a fanatic faith in an inflexible creed."

There ought, however, to be two stubborn limits to all-comprehending tolerance. The first is truth. It is possible to have a mind so open that everything of value falls out at the bottom. The second is morality. A religion which takes ethics seriously cannot be tolerant when morals are threatened. The second consideration is illustrated by a sentence in Mr. Arthur Mayhew's *Christianity and the Government of India*.[2] " To the Hindu philosopher all religions may be equally true; the administrator, comparing a Christian settlement with the pariah village at its gates, has good reason to know that they are not equally effective."

For the deficiency of Hinduism in moral illumination and moral drive, two principal reasons may be adduced : (1) The unreality of the world to the Hindu mind. The intellectual Hindu sees one god, an impersonal being, revealing himself in the innumerable forms and personalities of popular belief, and manifesting himself in all existing things. Individual things and persons may be spoken of as " selves," but their separateness is only illusion (*maya*). Logically, it might appear, Principal Oman has said, that

[1] E. E. Kellett, *A Short History of Religions* (Gollancz, 1933), p. 401.
[2] P. 14 ; quoted by Dr. Macnicol in *Is Christianity Unique ?* p. 67.

Hinduism should be optimistic. " If all things are Brahma
are they not good, and if our soul or *atman* is all Brahma
is it not also good ? But whether we can explain it or not,
the passage from pantheistic optimism to the sense that
all is unreality and all misery has always been both certain
and rapid. Nor are reasons impossible to find. When all
is given by process, there is no real room for human achievement." [1] (2) The consequent denial of human freedom.
This may be seen in sayings taken at random. " Fate I
consider paramount, human effort is futile. Everything
is governed by Fate ; Fate is the final resort." [2] " Fate
binds a man with adamantine cords, and drags him upwards
to the highest rank, or downwards to the depths of misery." [3]
But it may perhaps be illustrated best by the story of the
snake.[4] A snake which had killed a boy was afterwards
caught by a hunter. It protests its guiltlessness ; it was
merely the instrument of Mrtyu, the god of death. There-
upon Mrtyu appears and casts the responsibility on Kala.
" Guided by Kala, I, O serpent, sent thee on this errand.
All creatures, mobile or immobile, in heaven or earth, are
pervaded by this same inspiration of Kala. The whole
universe is imbued with the same influence of Kala."
Kala, in his turn, refuses to accept responsibility. " The
child has met his death as the result of its karma in the
past. We all are subject to the influence of our respective
karma. As men make from a lump of clay whatever they
wish to make, even so do men attain to various results
determined by karma. As light and shadow are related to
each other, so are men related to karma through their
own actions. Therefore, neither art thou, nor am I, nor is
Mrtyu, nor the serpent, nor this old Brahman lady, the
cause of the child's death. He himself is the cause here."
On hearing this, the mother was consoled. Seeing that the
loss was due to Fate alone, she commanded the hunter to

[1] *The Natural and the Supernatural*, p. 416. In a footnote, Dr. Oman
adds, " ' The Western world,' an Indian professor of physics once said
to me, ' plays with pantheism, and perhaps then pantheism may not do
much harm, but the Eastern takes it seriously, and it sucks the blood.' "
[2] *Ramayana*, I. viii. 22.   [3] *Ibid*. VII. xxxvii. 3.
[4] *Mahabharata*, XIII. 1.

release the snake.[1] It is not surprising that, where such a belief is consciously or unconsciously a determining factor in life and conduct, moral activity is strangled and, in particular, indifference to human suffering and disease is everywhere prevalent.

Where the new Hinduism of to-day seeks to inscribe "service" on its banners, it has been said that this is an attempt "to transform into its direct contrary the Hindu tradition and ideal of dispassion and inaction."[2] In Hinduism, the ordinary attitude is passive; the part played by man is reduced to the vanishing-point. There is no moral urgency or impulse tending to regeneration of character. Where Christianity minimises the importance of man's part, in order to avoid the suspicion of relying on man's own works for accomplishing his salvation, it does so because of its rich conception of divine grace. Hinduism, on the contrary, disregards the claim of moral effort, not because the greatness of God seems to make it unnecessary, but because the insignificance of man renders it useless and illusory. Christian people have often erred, and have suffered those things to endure which deeply offend the conscience, but in so doing they have proved false, not always unwittingly, to their professed Christianity. And at its best Christianity has shown to what heights of service and self-sacrifice the spirit of Jesus can carry consecrated men and women. The moral tragedies of Hinduism, on the contrary, are too often found to be inseparably linked with its philosophy of life.

Contrasted with the way of knowledge, which is ideal and metaphysical, is the *Bhakti Marga*, or path of devotion. It indicates the law of the right activity of man's emotional side. Bhakti may be translated "faith," but it is faith which is not dependent on belief. Perhaps "devotional faith" best renders the sense. There is the adoration of that which is regarded as altogether perfect. For this devotion nothing less than the highest conceivable will do. The devotee has a sense of utter humiliation. "In the presence of the ideal

---

[1] Readers of O. Henry will compare his story, *Roads of Destiny*.
[2] Macnicol: *Living Religions of the Indian People*, p. 116.

he feels that he is nothing, and such an utter prostration of the self is the indispensable pre-requisite of true religious devotion. God loves meekness. The individual feels himself to be worthless apart from God." Devotion expresses itself as love for God, or as misery due to the absence of God. Discovering the supreme value of its object, the self must reject itself as worthless dross. Whatever the devotee may do, he does it for the glory of God. His work is altogether unselfish, for it is indifferent to fruits. He is " consumed by an all-embracing beneficent love that seeks not its own or any return for its overflowing. It is like the divine love that brought the universe into being, maintains it and lifts it up to itself. Not the devotee but the power of spirit acts in him in a divine freedom." [1]

We see that bhakti involves two lofty doctrines, that of the grace of God and that of the all-sufficiency of faith. It is probable that the doctrine owes something in its development to the influence of Christianity, but it is certain also that its origin lies far back in the history of Indian religion long before Christianity entered the country. The rapid extension of the system in the Middle Ages and the overwhelming success of a Bhagavata reformation were so phenomenal and the ideas so lofty that scholars were driven to the conclusion that here we had to deal with a new religion outside the bounds of Indian tradition. Lassen and Weber declared that the only possible explanation was that the doctrine of bhakti arose under the influence of Christianity. Since then, opinion has changed in many respects, and it has been established that bhakti, in some form, is indigenous to India. The question remains, How far is it likely that the doctrine was modified by Christian influence, direct or indirect ? The material for supplying the answer is given by Dr. G. A. Grierson in his article " Bhakti-Marga " in Hastings' *Encyclopædia of Religion and Ethics*.[2] It is possible that the Christian student is inevitably inclined to read into the literature more than

[1] Radhakrishnan, *Indian Philosophy* (Allen & Unwin, 1929), vol. i. pp. 558–565.
[2] Vol. ii. p. 548.

is really there, but the nobility of some of its ideas is manifest. Where the deficiency is most evident is not so much in the method of approaching the divine, but in the idea of the nature of God to Whose fellowship and favour the soul of man is to be restored. It is this which determines the quality of a faith. The many gods of the people are tolerated. " In view of the unlimited variety of the habits and minds of men," says Professor Radhakrishnan, " liberty of thought and worship is allowed to the individual. Some love is better than none, for if we do not love, we become shut up within ourselves. The infinite presents itself to the human soul in a variety of aspects. The lower gods are forms or aspects of the one Supreme." He adds : " The philosophical justification of this tolerant attitude is suggested though not worked out. A man is what his thoughts are. Whatever he has faith in, that he will attain to." [1]

There is, however, no doubt that it is the nature of the God who is worshipped which determines the quality of faith. Worship of an abstract deity or of an unworthy "incarnation" does not give that staying power which is essential to religion nor the ability to discriminate truth from falsehood and to reject unworthy elements in worship and in morals. And because it does not give the assurance that salvation is really to be received, it opens the door to the deceitful quest of it by the many other methods which are found in Hinduism. At the best, the result is that which has been indicated by Dr. Macnicol : " What we find, therefore, in the Bhakti cults is a conflict between an instinctive theism on the one hand which craves the satisfaction that comes from worship and from an intuition of the divine love, and an authoritative pantheism on the other which imposes itself upon the adherents of these cults and weakens the confidence and hope that theism tends to bring to them. There is apt, as a consequence, to be a confusion and a contradiction lurking within their spiritual life which weakens their whole religious attitude." [2]

---

[1] *Op. cit.* p. 562.

[2] Macnicol, *The Living Religions of the Indian People*, p. 89.

We may now consider the suggestion that the whole truth is not to be found in any one of the historical manifestations of religion, but in an amalgam composed of the best that is to be discovered in all the known faiths. This eclecticism raises a difficult problem at the outset. How difficult we readily surmise from Theosophy, which has been called " the amateur side of comparative religion," " the attempt of untrained minds to construct an all-inclusive religious philosophy." [1] The difficulty is inherent in the fact that a true religion is an organic unity. It may not be dissected without destroying the life of those parts into which it is analysed.

Quite as serious a problem faces the man who attempts to assemble the parts. It may be, for example, that pantheism appears to solve one set of problems or to explain one set of facts, while personalism is successful in settling other questions and accounting for other phenomena. But we cannot have it both ways. We must choose. Pantheism and personalism cannot be combined.

The possibility of an eclectic religion is suggested also from another quarter. In the report entitled *Re-Thinking Missions,* published by a commission of American laymen, it is hinted that we may have carried Christian intransigence too far ; that we ought to be more tolerant towards the religions of the Orient, seeing in them a common search for truth. " All fences and private properties in truth are futile," says the report ; " the final truth, whatever it may be, is the New Testament of every existing faith." [2] The true religion, it seems to suggest, may be as different from our Christianity as the Christianity of the first century was from Judaism. Buddhism, Hinduism, Islam may yet have their share in contributing to the final revelation.

It will perhaps be sufficient to quote the words of Toyohiko Kagawa in an article on the report just mentioned. " Where can the motive for foreign missions be found, and how can energy for it be expected to well up and overflow, except as proceeding from a sense of absolute

---

[1] A. C. Bouquet, *Is Christianity the Final Religion ?* p. 278.
[2] P. 44.

commission from God ? There would have been no need for
Christ to be crucified merely to propagate humanism !
There are, indeed, many religions in the Orient ; but is
there any that clearly teaches that God loves humanity
with the love of the Cross ? Buddhism propounds abstract
principles, but it failed to wipe away my tears. To this day
Buddhism compromises with the system of public prosti-
tution in Japan. Shintoism and militarism, and Brahmanism and superstition, are closely associated. I do not wish
to attack other religions, but it is useless to be too lenient
with them. Man will not be saved thus." [1] Where truth
is concerned, Christianity cannot adopt a policy of accom-
modation. A better statement of the attitude of Christianity to non-Christian religion is therefore that which
is found in the report adopted by the International
Missionary Council Meeting at Jerusalem in 1928.[2] "We
call on the followers of non-Christian religions to join with
us in the study of Jesus Christ as He stands before us in the
Scriptures, His place in the life of the world, and His power
to satisfy the human heart ; to hold fast to faith in the
unseen and eternal in face of the growing materialism of the
world ; to co-operate with us against all the evils of
secularism ; to respect freedom of conscience so that men
may confess Christ without separation from home and
friends ; and to discern that all the good of which men
have conceived is fulfilled and secured in Christ."

When men and women, of whatever faith, are genuinely
looking for light, there will be inevitably a community of
spirit, but that will be endangered rather than promoted
by compromise of the truth. " The objective differences
between the religions must not be concealed or forgotten,
while the subjective unity of those who are sincerely
endeavouring to exercise faith in the unseen is at the same
time fully realised. If the religions were all of them
humanisms, then it would be proper enough for us all to
produce our spiritual possessions and combine them in a
common store. But we cannot thus use what is not ours
but God's, His gift to us. There is a core of adamant in

---

[1] *The Christian Century*, 1933.   [2] *Reports*, vol. i. p. 491.

our Christian faith that is not anyone's private property to barter or to buy and sell." [1] And, even with the practical aim alone in view, the defence of spiritual values against materialism, it will readily be granted that it is not syncretism which has preserved the supernatural from oblivion. Spiritual values have been saved, not by an amalgam of redemptive faiths but by Christianity itself. When all the modifications of Christian theology, in contact with Hellenistic and Oriental ways of thinking, have been fully acknowledged, one conclusion still stands : " Whatever may be the truth about marginal details, to say that in the Gospel of the New Testament the ideas of Judaism or Hellenism rank as of equal importance with the redemptive significance of Jesus is to put oneself out of court. In the life, death, and victory of Jesus Christ a new standard of reality and value had risen before the human mind, antiquating its predecessors, and it plainly forbade the young religion to be anything so facile or so uninspiring as an eclectic version of paganism." [2]

When we ask, How shall we strengthen Christianity against the threatenings of secularism ? the only possible answer is, By making it more truly Christian.

Three other considerations may be indicated. (1) The amalgam of faiths which is desired can never be produced. For we have to inquire, Who is to decide on the claims of the different doctrines ? The Theosophical Society puts forward the criterion of *catholicity*, but quite evidently the criterion ought to be not catholicity but truth ! Actually, what is " best " in other faiths is decided by referring it to Christ. What is good in other religions is found better in Christianity.[3]

---

[1] N. Macnicol, *Is Christianity Unique ?* p. 19.

[2] H. R. Mackintosh, *The Originality of the Christian Message*, p. 14.

[3] Dr. R. E. Speer, in a paper delivered at the Jerusalem Conference of 1928 on " What is the Value of the Religious Values of the Non-Christian Religions ? " said, " These values are not a supplement to Christianity, as though, to borrow Paul's words, Christ needed anything from any one. We find when we come with Christianity to the other religions of the world, and place Christianity in comparison with them, that Christianity has all the good of other religions. There is good and

It may justly be maintained that those who take up the position now being considered are not required to accept this Christian claim ; but, if they reject it, they are nevertheless bound to suggest an alternative standard of valuation and to indicate wherein, to their mind, Christianity exhibits a deficiency which has been supplied elsewhere. Otherwise, they will be launched on an interminable debate and involved in endless indecision. We shall be offered not merely a series which is never completed but one which cannot even be begun.

The only alternative is to judge by some standard which is not specifically religious. Three of these may be suggested :

(i) Those doctrines are to be admitted which are most successful in the extent of their appeal. This is the standard of catholicity or comprehensiveness in another form. It is in effect to pronounce a verdict on a doctrine not by its truth but by its popularity. This principle might lead us to decide for the truth of Buddhism or Mohammedanism when they were vigorous and expanding faiths and for the deficiency of Christianity because of the ages of persecution and martyrdoms.[1]

(ii) A claim may be made for those doctrines which bring satisfaction to human desires. This also is a fallible standard. Man's desires do not often indicate the truth. We hear sometimes of the emptiness of the churches, but it has been said that, if the Gospel were preached more faithfully in them, they would be emptier still ! It is by their truth that religions are to be judged. Very frequently the first effect of a new revelation is not to satisfy old needs but to awaken men to more worthy desires.

truth in these religions, which we joyfully acknowledge, which has enabled them to survive and given them their power ; but there is no truth or good in them which is not found in a purer and fuller form in Christianity. Hinduism teaches the immanence of God ; Mohammedanism the sovereignty of God ; Buddhism the transitoriness and yet the solemn issues of our present life ; Confucianism the dignity of our earthly relationships and of human society. But are not all these truths in Christianity also ? It is so with whatever of good we find anywhere " (*Reports*, vol. i. pp. 427–428).

[1] Cf. Galloway, *The Philosophy of Religion*, chap. vi.

(iii) Acknowledging that the mere popularity of a doctrine is no indication of its validity and acknowledging also that a belief is not authenticated simply because it makes the believer happier, the exponents of this view may fall back on a criterion which seems to escape these errors. We take our stand, they say, on *character*. Here we have an absolute. (" A character," says Dr. W. R. Inge, " can never be refuted or ignored.") [1] They may even admit that the Christian character is the best that has yet been produced. Let us take this as our standard therefore and hold as true all such doctrines, wherever found, which tend to promote the Christian character. But this is no solution. If they refuse to admit that the Christian character is the norm, they must point to something superior to it and must indicate also the standard (and it must be a non-Christian standard) by which that superiority is determined. Or, if they accept the supremacy of the Christian character, they are faced with the discovery that Christian character always goes back to Christ Himself ; that it owes to His teaching the purity of its ideals and to His love the power to attain them. They cannot isolate the Christian character from the Christian religion.

The desired amalgam of faiths cannot, it seems, be produced. That is the first remark.

2. The second is this : If this eclectic faith is to be a *religion*, then it must be something that man can *live by*. Now you cannot live by an artificial product. It is not simply that the quality of a doctrine is determined in part by its historic setting, though that is true. You cannot tear it up by the roots without changing its nature. But there is more in it than that. A religion is an organic unity. It is as impossible to produce a living faith by selection from the tenets of different religions as it would be to make an artistic whole with scissors and paste out of the fragments of pictures by different artists. Religion implies worship, and man cannot pay reverence to even the most painstaking enumeration of facets of truth.

This difficulty has driven some to hold that the ideal

[1] *Personal Religion and the Life of Devotion*, p. 72.

16

religion may still be hidden in the future. If that view is propounded, we are entitled to inquire what relation such a religion is likely to have to Christianity. The possibility of a higher than Christianity is not ruled out, says Troeltsch. Though Christianity meets the loftiest desires of man and fulfils all the needs of his soul, it is conceivable that a higher faith might yet appear, revealing itself by the discovery of, and satisfaction of, longings and cravings hitherto unsuspected. It is true, he adds, that personal conviction rules out this speculation as quite improbable, and the believer may rest content that at least he is in the right way. All the deepening of spiritual life which has taken place since the advent of Christianity has been achieved by Christianity itself. We may therefore declare that Christianity, though not demonstrably the absolute, is certainly the normative religion.

The distinction is, surely, quite unreal. The two epithets go together, absolute and normative. For Christianity the norm is the Person of Jesus, and only a Person of absolute significance can be normative. We are forced back to a fresh examination of His Person. That may conveniently be introduced by the third remark which should be made in this connection.

3. The determining feature in religion is its idea of God. Because Christians have received their idea of God from the teaching, the life, and the death and resurrection of Jesus, they know that there are definite "limits of syncretism."[1] If the theory before us persists in denying the existence of these limits, it is because its idea of God is not the Christian idea. In other words, it rejects the absoluteness of Christianity because it does not believe in Christianity. H. R. Mackintosh, in a different connection, makes this point : " It is very doubtful whether anyone who understands what Jesus meant by the Fatherhood of God, and who believes Jesus' meaning to be objectively valid in the sense that there is just such a Father in Heaven as He proclaimed, can intelligibly hold that this truth could

[1] These words are the title of chapter vii. of Dr. Macnicol's *Is Christianity Unique ?*

be replaced by something better. Here, then, we have a position antagonistic to the absoluteness of Christianity because it is antagonistic to Christianity itself." [1]

Those who still seek a more comprehensive faith, which will give more truth than is given by Jesus, must first point to the deficiency of Christianity that calls for the incorporation of material from elsewhere. They must indicate where we are to look for something greater than holy divine love as seen in Jesus.

In fact, the redemption which is offered to mankind by Christ leaves no profound and legitimate longing unfulfilled.

[1] *The Originality of the Christian Message*, p. 165.

CHAPTER XII

FINALITY OF THE CHRISTIAN GOSPEL

II. Jesus is Lord

IN Jesus we have a fact which transcends logic. The scientific inquirer does not choose, force, or interpret the facts to fit his theory, but follows them wherever they may lead. Not only is it in Jesus that we see the glory of God, but no other than He can enable sinful men to stand before that glory.

Jesus as Teacher. He taught with authority. He spoke, while the Rabbis stammered. He brought home to men the reality of the spiritual world. God is Spirit, the centre of all the universe, which is the Father's house. He taught men about themselves ; released them from triviality and the curse of littleness. And He taught them about God : that was the theme of His teaching. When Jesus spoke about God, He was speaking on His own subject. In Him the conditions of right knowledge were fulfilled. The most significant fact, however, is the organic relation between the message and the Teacher. Jesus knows no more sacred task than to point men to Himself.

Jesus as Judge of mankind. He knows men's hearts, and will judge, not by hollow profession, but by sincere obedience. The judgment will be universal and final. It follows that the vital matter for men is to come into a right relation with Him in Whose hands is their eternal destiny.

Jesus as Pattern. In Him we have the pattern of faith. He was " mankind's Supreme Believer." And it is thus that Jesus brings the Father near. His communion with the Father was a more fundamental factor than the fluctuations of consciousness. He was also the supreme pattern of conduct. Yet He was far more than an illustration of the character which He commended. His very holiness prevents us from regarding Him as pattern only. His vocation was unique. Christian character would not be produced by the closest reproduction of His life in Palestine, homeless, celibate, untravelled ; His preaching and healing mission ; His sufferings and death.

Of His sinlessness, we have the evidence of those who knew Him most intimately and lived with Him continually. But most important is His own testimony concerning Himself. The Sermon on the Mount convinces all men of sin, but it did not convince Christ of sin. The historical evidence is as conclusive as by its nature it can be. Yet ultimately the decision is one of faith. The salvation of which Christians have inward knowledge could come only through a Saviour Who was such as this.

The finality of the Christian faith is thus found to belong neither to its morals nor to its piety, but to that which is much deeper. Redemption breaks out of the realm of morality and is the pre-requisite of morality. (1) Forgiveness of sin appears in the world as a breach of the ethical system. Forgiveness is a " moral impossibility " which the Divine Love alone makes possible. (2) Salvation must come to man before a right worship can be offered to the God Who is of purer eyes than to behold evil.

Jesus is not only the mirror of His own teaching about the proper attitude of men to their sinful fellow-men ; He is also the mirror of God the Father. We have to think of God in terms of Christ, *sub specie Christi.* Union between the believer and Christ is union between the forgiven and the Forgiver. It is in the offer of forgiveness that the finality of the Gospel is found. Nothing can be conceived greater than divine holy love as it is in Jesus. This finality is summed up in the confession, " Jesus is Lord." The words imply (i) Illumination. In Him we have light on the problems of good and evil, of time and eternity. (ii) Authority. Commands are laid on men which are bound up with their eternal destiny. (iii) Salvation. Through Him there is deliverance from that which opposes the illumination and stands in the way of obedience. (iv) Security. Men find protection in the fulfilment of their vocation and ultimate peace for the children of God through the victory of the right and the blessedness of life everlasting in God.

CHAPTER XII

FINALITY OF THE CHRISTIAN GOSPEL

II. JESUS IS LORD

THERE is one particular question which appears more frequently than any other in those handed in to the speaker in conferences on religious and ethical subjects. A characteristic formulation is in the terms, " Jesus was crucified in Palestine nineteen hundred years ago. What has that to do with me to-day ? "

What is the motive of the implied objection ? Is it an *a priori* veto which holds that, in the nature of things, God cannot become man ? If it is that, then we must remember how little we know of the nature of the universe and the ways of God. We are not able to dogmatise, saying, " This or that cannot be His way." In Jesus we have a fact which shatters logic. The true scientific inquirer does not choose, force, or interpret the facts to fit some preconceived theory of his own as to what is possible and what is not. He follows the facts, wherever they may lead him.[1]

---

[1] The Dean of St. Paul's has brought out very clearly this parallel between good science and good theology. " The modern world is not rationalist in the true meaning of that ambiguous term ; it does not rely on the deduction of consequences from self-evident principles. On the contrary, the scientific method, which is the real distinguishing mark of our present phase of culture, begins from the other end. It sets out from the data of experience, and its general ideas are reached in the attempt to interpret what is given. The modern scientific temper, therefore, has no reason for objecting to a theology which starts from experience. Nor can it safely protest against reliance upon human testimony and records for acquaintance with the data to be interpreted, for science itself is in precisely the same situation. The phenomena with which it deals are known by observation, record, and narration. The researcher must depend on human testimony. If he were confined to principles which are to him self-evident and experiences which he himself has had, he could make no progress towards a science of nature."—W. R. Matthews, *God in Christian Thought and Experience* (Nisbet, 1930), pp. 45–46.

Here we have the Fact of Christ. It was *His* death, and it can be understood only when we understand Him. Quite clearly, the coming into the world, nineteen hundred years ago, of One Who was to know no sin has very much to do with me. And the coming of One Who, free from all human frailties, free from all fanaticism; calm, clear - eyed in all spiritual things, having a knowledge of God which no one else ever had—that has very much to do with us, especially when He comes to us as One Who claims to be the Son of God. In a word, it not only makes a difference, it makes all the difference, if God has once stepped down into His world for men. It is the one vital question for me.

Jesus stands in a special relation to His followers. Alone without sin, He also is alone in possessing the power to conquer sin in men. Having perfect knowledge of God, only He can bring that knowledge to others. Not only is it that in Him we see the glory of God, but no other than He can enable sinful men to stand before that glory. His relation to Christianity is very different from that of Gautama to Buddhism. Whereas Buddhism has become a religion through proving false to the principles of its founder, Christianity is renewed and purified again and again by returning to the Person of Jesus. The centuries have seen many and varied theories of atonement, but the motive of each fresh theory is always a desire to be more faithful to the spirit of Christ. The correction of inadequate theories lies not in human speculation, but in revelation already given in Jesus. There is only one legitimate way of showing that any view is unworthy, namely, by proving it to be unchristian. Yet the Founder of Christianity does not prevent the rightful development of Christianity. Other teachers have been the liberators of their own generation, only to become the gaolers of the generations which follow.[1] It is not so with Jesus. No one ever felt that he had exhausted the truth that comes from Christ, or that men need to supplement it by private speculations.

[1] D. S. Cairns, *The Reasonableness of the Christian Faith* (Hodder & Stoughton, 1918), p. 167.

Jesus as Teacher. " They were astonished at his doctrine ; for He taught them as one that had authority, and not as the scribes." [1] He spoke, while the Rabbis stammered. And men knew the difference at once. He taught men something about the world in which they live. The vastness of the universe is always a perplexing subject. The discoveries of physical science in our own time have brought the problems connected with it more vividly before us, but the problems were always there. They were not unknown to the writers of the Old Testament ; and, in their own way, they solved them. Jesus had behind Him the astronomy of the Eighth Psalm, " When I consider Thy heavens, the work of Thy fingers ; the moon and the stars which Thou hast ordained." Magnitude does not matter, for there is a world where size is nothing. You cannot give the spatial dimensions of love. Jesus brought home to men the reality of the spiritual world. God is Spirit, the centre of all the universe, which is the Father's house.

And He taught men about themselves. Because God is a Father, He loves His children one by one. Jesus was " the great believer in man." He released him from triviality and the curse of littleness. And for His belief in man He died.

Above all, He taught men about God. That was the theme of His teaching. Men, He showed, were censorious of one another, because they had forgotten that they themselves were under the scrutiny of God. They were anxious about food and drink and about what was going to happen to them, but they would not be like this if they believed in God's care for them. " He would have His disciples live shining lives, but the shining is to be traceable to their religion so that outsiders will say, ' This is of God ' and glorify their Father in Heaven." [2] When Jesus spoke about God He was speaking on His own subject. We have all failed to fulfil the spiritual conditions for right know-

[1] Mark i. 22.
[2] W. R. Maltby, *The Significance of Jesus* (Student Christian Movement, 1929), p. 50.

ledge of God. We therefore discern these realities only dimly and doubtfully. But in Jesus the conditions were fulfilled. " Blessed are the pure in heart, for they shall see God." The Beatitude might be an epitome of His autobiography. On the nature of God He speaks with authority, because He has seen Him, has been with Him, is one with Him.

It is not, however, any particular quality of His teaching, such as its note of authority, its concentration on the essential, the inwardness of its moral standard, its attitude to the sinner and the untouchable, which is the decisive thing. All these features are insignificant compared with that of the organic relation between the message and the Teacher. The Gospel of Jesus consists not merely in what He taught but also in what He did—His life and death and resurrection. And the perfect harmony of His words and acts presses us back to ask who He was Who spoke and acted thus, and to Whom these things happened.

It has been said that " For Judaism good conduct is a part of religion ; for Jesus it is a product of religion." [1] When Jesus asks for obedience, it is because of something prior to all ethical commands. The question is simply whether He linked this new consciousness of God as closely with His own Person as the early Christian Church undoubtedly did ; whether, that is, the Christology of the first Christians was a legitimate expansion of that which was already present in the words and bearing of Jesus Himself.

Herrmann has said that Jesus " knows no more sacred task than to point men to His own Person." [2] The reason for our obedience to His unequivocal commands lies in His authority. In obeying, we recognise the right of that authority to command us. Men knew at once that somehow, in His presence, they were being brought face to face with God. His own attitude to the Law is quite conclusive. There was a reason for setting aside even its ancient pre-

[1] T. W. Manson, *The Teaching of Jesus* (Cambridge, 1935), second ed. p. 305.
[2] *The Communion of the Christian with God*, Book II. chap. ii. section 5.

cepts, and the reason was nowhere else than in Himself. In Him moral authority is final. That is the claim which is implicit in every employment of the words, " It hath been said by them of old, *but I say unto you.*" And the claim has been acknowledged far beyond the bounds of the Christian Church. " No man has ever complained that Jesus' will misled him or deprived him of that which is, in the absolute sense, good." [1]

It is only a corollary of this organic relation between the message and the Teacher that Jesus is the *Judge of mankind.* Whereas the prophets could go no further than " Thus saith the Lord," Jesus habitually used the phrase, " But I say unto you." And naturally He in Whom resides the final moral authority is also the One Who judges men as to their faithfulness or disobedience. Even if our conscience should acquit us, we are not therefore vindicated. For it is the Lord who judgeth.[2] It is Christ alone who holds in His hand the balance of God, by which we are weighed. " This Man of Destiny is not simply awaited in the future, as in Judaism and in Parseeism. No ; He is already come." [3] God has committed all judgment to the Son.[4] That judgment begins with His coming into the world.[5] Men are separated out for blessedness and for condemnation according to their attitude to Jesus. " Whosoever therefore shall be ashamed of me and of my words in this adulterous and sinful generation ; of him also shall the Son of man be ashamed, when he cometh in the glory of his Father with the holy angels." [6] " Whosoever therefore shall confess me before men, him will I confess also before my Father which is in heaven. But whosoever shall deny me before men, him will I also deny before my Father which is in heaven." [7] He knows men's hearts and will judge not by hollow profession but by sincere obedience.[8] The judgment will be universal and final. " When the Son

---

[1] H. R. Mackintosh, *The Person of Jesus Christ* (T. & T. Clark, 1923), p. 328.

[2] 1 Cor. iv. 4.

[3] Karl Heim, *The New Divine Order* (E.T.), p. 112.

[4] John v. 22, 27.   [5] John ix. 39.

[6] Mark, viii. 38.   [7] Matt. x. 32-33.   [8] Matt. vii. 21 ff.

of man shall come in his glory, and all the holy angels with him, then shall he sit upon the throne of his glory. And before him shall be gathered all nations." [1] It is particularly significant that the passage in Matthew vii. 21 ff. occurs in a chapter of which the first verse is the warning, " Judge not, that ye be not judged." He Who forbids men to judge one another takes by right the highest place that heaven affords.

It follows that for men the vital matter is to come into a right personal relationship with Him in Whose hands is their eternal destiny. "Even in pagan redemptive religions there is a significant place for prophetic person-alities and guides, such as Plato, Buddha, and Confucius. But their significance consists always in this alone, that they advocate an idea by teaching and example. It may be a truth, as, for instance, the Buddhist teaching on the origin and the conquest of suffering, or it may be an ethical ideal, or a social contract such as that contained in the five relationships of Confucius. With Christ it is different. He is not only the messenger of the Gospel ; He is Himself the message. He is not only the herald of a truth ; He is Himself the truth. He is not only the guide who gives direction to the ethical life ; He is Himself the way." [2]

Jesus as Pattern. Professor Rudolf Bultmann, in his book, *Jesus*, has declared that it is impossible to gather from the Gospels sufficient evidence to enable us to under-stand the inner experience of Jesus, and, in particular, His consciousness of God. Dr. Bultmann adds that this does not greatly matter, since the important evidence for us is concerned not with that which Jesus experienced, but with what He willed. But it is surely impossible to hold that we have sufficient material for knowing what Jesus willed, without admitting that we have considerable evidence also of His inner experience, which is inseparable from His will and His vocation. In Jesus we have the pattern of true

[1] Matt. xxv. 31–32.
[2] Heim, *The New Divine Order* (E.T.), p. 113. Cf. the same author's *Jesus der Herr*, ch. ii. section 7.

faith in God the Father. He was " mankind's Supreme Believer." [1] And it is because of this that Jesus " brings the Father near." Revelation and response go hand in hand. Every right response is the vestibule of a new revelation. In Jesus we see the perfect response, and, because of that, also the perfect revelation.

In the Garden of Gethsemane we overhear the prayer of Jesus, " Nevertheless not My will, but Thine, be done." On one side was the darkness of the night and an easy escape for Him out of the fatal situation. He had only to withdraw from the neighbourhood of the city and He was safe. On the other side, the light of torches gleaming through the trees ; the tramp of soldiers coming for His capture ; the inevitable trial, and torture, and death. Jesus stands fast. The guiding principle of His life is to be found in the words, " I came down from heaven, not to do mine own will, but the will of Him that sent me." [2] For a victory like that of Gethsemane a momentary flash of heroism is not enough. It requires a whole life of courage and devotion. Jesus won His victory at long range. The word " sent " rings through all His life. It was to do the Father's will that He came into the world. It was in the doing of His Father's will that He died. God was the one vital reality in His thoughts. Jesus lived in the consciousness of His Father's presence. We see in the crises of His life how this faith was tested and proved. But it was not formed there, not granted, as it were, to enable Him to meet special emergencies. It was always there, the outstanding characteristic of His life, and we are constantly told of His surprise and disappointment at finding that it was not present in others. It was perhaps this sense that His knowledge of God was not fitful but all-pervading that led the author of the Fourth Gospel to smooth out the crises in the life of Jesus—the Baptism, the Temptation, the Confession of Simon Peter, the Transfiguration, the Agony in Gethsemane. Although it loses

[1] Cf. D. M. Baillie, *Faith in God and its Christian Consummation* (T. & T. Clark, 1927), p. 237.
[2] John vi. 38.

thereby an important feature of the self-consciousness of Jesus—His gradual realisation of what was implied in His holy calling—it recognises that " the deep underlying communion of Jesus with the Father . . . was a more fundamental factor than the fluctuations or crises of consciousness." [1]

Dr. D. W. Forrest wrote in *The Authority of Christ* [2] :— Jesus " dwelt in the abiding consciousness of the Father ; wrought no work without seeking His guidance and receiving His grace ; met every surprise of temptation or disaster as having its appointed place in the wise order of an over- ruling purpose that cannot be taken by surprise and has prepared from of old for the emergencies of every passing hour. The unmistakable accent of assurance with which He spoke of the Father and His claim upon men, the per- petual reference to One that sent Him, whose will it was His ' meat ' to do, the relief and exaltation which He found in prayer, showed incontestably that the life which so humbled and inspired them was grounded in God, and drew from a divine communion its beauty and glory."

Jesus was the Supreme Believer. He has also been called the Supreme Pattern of conduct. Dr. Maltby speaks of the Beatitudes as " fragments of His autobiography." [3] We might also speak of every characterisation of the ideal Christian as a portrait of Jesus. When St. Paul writes his hymn on Christian love,[4] it is surely of Jesus that he is thinking. " Can we have any doubt who it was who sat in the studio of Paul's imagination for that famous little vignette of the ideal man ? " [5] Yet Jesus was far more than an illustration of the character and conduct which He commended. His very holiness prevents us from regarding Him as pattern only. The famous test of conduct, " What would Jesus do ? " is inadequate for two reasons. In the

[1] William Manson, *The Incarnate Glory : A Study of St. John's Gospel* (James Clarke, 1923), pp. 19–20.
[2] Second ed. (T. & T. Clark, 1906), p. 121.
[3] *The Significance of Jesus*, p. 47.
[4] 1 Cor. xiii.
[5] John Baillie, *The Place of Jesus Christ in Modern Christianity* (T. & T. Clark, 1929), p. 81.

first place, when we ask ourselves that question, we frequently realise that we are asking it too late ; that Jesus would never have been in the position in which we find ourselves. Our perplexity is often the result of our own weakness and failure. Secondly, His vocation is unique, and that which is unique cannot be imitated. Christian character would not be produced by the closest reproduction of His daily life in Palestine, homeless, celibate, untravelled ; His preaching and healing mission ; His death. Jesus is not simply an example to men in their struggle to be like Him. For this, Haering has said, " a Paul, with his experience of mercy, is more suited in his way." [1] Nor did He leave an ethical code for the guidance of men in all the details of their life. He was rather, in the phrase of Lactantius, a " living law," a law that breathes and speaks.

Nor was the holiness of Jesus that of a fugitive and cloistered virtue. Tempted forty days in the wilderness ; tempted by Simon Peter, His trusted friend, to avoid the death of the Cross ; tempted at the last to doubt the very presence of God—the " best will in the world " could not remain untempted.[2] He has been tempted like ourselves, yet without sinning.[3]

It has been the custom of late to lay all the emphasis on the positive aspect of the sinlessness of Jesus and to minimise the importance of demonstrating, or even believing in, the historical fact of our Lord's freedom from all moral fault. Thus, for example, Professor A. C. Knudson, of Boston, in *The Doctrine of Redemption*, refers to the " traditional " method of approaching the subject, and quotes in illustration the statements of two Scottish theologians. The first is from the late Professor H. R. Mackintosh. The actual words as written by Dr. Mackintosh will be found in *The Doctrine of the Person of Jesus Christ*.[4] " Faith cannot acquiesce in the thought that conceivably the Divine redeeming plan might have been frustrated ; yet frustration would have been had Jesus yielded to temptation even

---

[1] *The Christian Faith*, p. 626.
[2] Cf. J. M. Thompson, *Jesus according to St. Mark* (Methuen, 1910), second ed., p. 143.　　　[3] Heb. iv. 15.　　　[4] Pp. 412–413.

once." The second quotation Dean Knudson gives thus from Dr. D. W. Forrest : " A single moral fault committed by a hitherto stainless soul, if we can imagine that, alters its entire relation to God." And the author objects to the whole tenor of these statements. They are, he thinks, untrue to the facts of the moral life and overstrained. Sin is not all of the same magnitude. That which matters is not fidelity to an abstract standard of right but complete devotion to the kingdom of God. " Whether He met all the demands of an abstract moral perfection does not matter much, but that He was unswervingly faithful to His divine vocation is of vital concern." [1]

It may be readily admitted that the emphasis is rightly laid on the positive aspect of the sinlessness of Jesus ; it was at the opposite pole from that virtue which practises fastidiousness and calls it holiness. But when Dr. Knudson speaks of " the demands of an abstract moral perfection," is he not forgetting for the moment that there was really nothing abstract about it, since, considered even as pattern only, Jesus Himself is the standard ? To be untrue to that would have meant being untrue to Himself, and therefore disloyal to His vocation. It is inconceivable that the vocation of Jesus could remain what it was in the face of any moral lapse, for then it would have been possible, even inevitable, for men to say that there could be a greater than He. The attitude represented by Dr. Knudson must always come perilously near ascribing to Jesus either hypocrisy or fanaticism. Certainly it makes Him less than many saints, who have always been instant in warning others against their own mistakes. But indeed this possi-bility, which Dr. Knudson thinks may be granted without endangering the value of Christ's ministry, is negated, as far as historical evidence alone can conceivably carry us, first by the evidence of those who knew Him, or were very near to those who did, and second by the testimony of Jesus Himself. In the first place, such an opinion concern-ing Jesus could never have formed itself or flourished in

[1] A. C. Knudson: *The Doctrine of Redemption* (The Abingdon Press, New York, 1933), p. 383.

the minds of the early apostles unless it were a true opinion ;
and in the second place, had it been a false opinion, Jesus
would have checked it at the outset.[1]

To the objection advanced by Strauss that the apostles
meant to express no more than was affirmed by Xenophon [2]
of Socrates, that he had never seen him do an unjust action,
or heard him speak an unholy word, Ullmann replies
conclusively : " Jesus was to them not merely what Socrates
was to his school—a noble, truth-seeking man, one inde-
fatigably striving after wisdom—He was, in their eyes,
Himself the truth, the Son of God, the sole Mediator between
God and man ; and when, in consequence of the impression
they had themselves received, they attributed sinlessness
to One whom they viewed in this light, such a statement is
undoubtedly one of far deeper and more serious import
than that of a disciple of Socrates, when he says that he
had never seen him do an unrighteous act, nor heard him
speak an unholy word." [3]

The disciples were with Jesus in all the varied circumstances of His ministry ; in the busy, overcrowded days,
and in the hours of relaxation ; in times of fatigue and
danger ; in His popularity and in bitter hostility. They
lived with Him in a genuine human friendship, with every
chance to see weaknesses.[4] It is true that their companionship with Him was at the most for three out of thirty
years, but then moral character is not a patchwork ; perfection is not displayed over three years of mature manhood
if its previous development has not been of a piece with it.[5]
The testimony of the disciples is therefore of great significance. " They saw Him live in the tempting, defiling

[1] That is, assuming that the opinion was already being formed in His
lifetime. It is possible to question this. But those who do so would have
to account for the facts, (1) that such passages as Hebrews iv. 15 and
1 Peter i. 19 show no signs of awareness that a *new* opinion was being put
forward ; (2) that in any case Jesus could not but be conscious of the
inevitable conclusion to which men would be pointed by the claim of
unique Sonship which He made.   [2] *Memorabilia*, i, 11.

[3] Ullmann, *The Sinlessness of Jesus* (E.T.) (T. & T. Clark, 1901),
seventh ed. p. 65.

[4] Cf. T. R. Glover, *The Jesus of History*, p. 81.

[5] Ullmann, *ibid.* p. 65.

17

world, facing allurements, enduring hardship, ignoring flattery. Plainly there was a struggle ; to keep His integrity was a real conflict. More than once they caught His anguished voice as He prayed concerning His difficulties, and at such time they could do little more than stand far off, guessing at the pain. Eventually they reached the irreversible conclusion that His soul had never once been touched with evil. They said to each other that this Man was not, like them, a sinner. He had never felt an evil conscience or had to speak the bitter words of self-accusation due from all the rest." [1]

Nor must we forget the testimony of His enemies. Ullmann thinks that the action of Judas Iscariot is considerable evidence. He had the same opportunities as the other disciples of intimate fellowship with Jesus. If he had detected any flaw in the character of the Master, would he not certainly have brought it forward after his treachery, in order to palliate his act and to quieten his conscience ? Yet, confessing that he had betrayed *innocent blood,* he took his own life in a paroxysm of despair.[2] It is doubtful, however, whether this evidence can be used. It is impossible to say what might have been the effect of a pure life on a man of the nature of Judas. The story as given in the first Gospel is difficult to reconcile in its details with that of Acts ; and the term $αἷμα\ ἀθῷον$ (cf. Matt. xxvii. 4 with xxvii. 24) means no more than innocence in the legal sense, guiltlessness of any conduct which might have justified such a condemnation and such a sentence.[3]

More important from the side of His enemies is the fact that in the trial of Jesus no evidence was led and no charge made that would indicate any suspicion of His moral rectitude. Notorious wrong-doing they could never have thought of suggesting ; but we should naturally expect (from the hints of " false witnesses " in Matt. xxvi. 59 and Mark xiv. 55–56) that no chance was missed of blackening

---

[1] H. R. Mackintosh, *The Christian Experience of Forgiveness*, p. 87.

[2] Ullmann, *op. cit.* pp. 42–43.

[3] Cf. Deut. xxvii. 25, " Cursed be he that taketh a reward to slay an innocent person."

the character of the accused. They knew that there was no
hold even for insinuations, nor was any suggestion made by
His accusers of any inconsistency between His teaching
and His conduct. Again, the prosecution must have
realised that they could not now, with any hope of success,
revive the charge of gluttony and wine-bibbing, or con-
sorting with men and women of evil reputation. In their
own courts the charges are those connected with opinion—
heresy and blasphemy ; and in the Roman court they are
purely political. It is in Luke that we have the latter
in some kind of official form. The charges are three :
(1) Stirring up the people, or inciting to disaffection ;
(2) instigating the refusal of the imperial tribute ; (3)
treason—pretensions to political leadership.[1]

Of supreme significance is the testimony of Jesus concerning Himself. First we have to recall a point already
indicated in passing. In the words of A. S. Peake,[2] the
disciples " could not have been in such familiar intercourse
with Him without it coming to light, over and over again,
that Jesus thought of Himself as sinful, if that had really
been His inmost conviction. Jesus could not have allowed
the impression of sinlessness to be created if He knew
that it did not correspond with the facts." Again, just as
it is inconceivable that Jesus should warn men against
judging others and then name Himself as the Judge of all
mankind, unless He were aware that this was indeed His
destiny, so it is unthinkable that He should so earnestly
and urgently call men to repentance and Himself refrain
from confession of sin, unless He knew that for Him there
was no need to confess. Yet on His lips there is no word
of contrition. The Sermon on the Mount, says Principal
Cairns, " convinces us all of sin. But here is the strange
thing. It did not convince Christ of sin. It was with this
standard in His soul that He steadfastly refused to confess
sin, asserted for Himself spiritual lordship over all men and
women and children, and said that the day was coming

[1] See *The Expository Times*, April 1935 : " The Third Gospel : A Hidden
Source."
[2] *Christianity : Its Nature and Truth* (Duckworth, 1922), p. 215.

when all mankind, living and dead, would stand before His judgment seat." [1]

The historical evidence is as conclusive as historical evidence can ever be. Yet ultimately the decision on this matter is a judgment of faith. The sinless perfection of Jesus follows from what He has done for us. The salvation which Christian men and women have inward knowledge of, could come only through a Saviour Who was such as this. " If faith knows the task fulfilled ; if it is assured of God indeed brought near through Jesus, of His fatherly forgiveness and love made available and eternal life itself brought within reach, then faith apprehends also a sinless Christ. Not—a sinless man, therefore the world's Saviour, is the order of their thought ; but rather this—the Saviour, therefore sinless." [2]   Because He is Saviour, we know that His character is of one piece. It may be a very small portion on which the light of publicity has fallen, but the Christian knows that no one part can contradict any other. What is hidden is of the same texture. Sin—that is, antagonism to God—is unthinkable in Him. Whatever interpretation is placed upon the cry of dereliction from the Cross,[3] none is valid which sees in it any alienation between the Father and the Son. God and Jesus were never more closely bound together than in the moment of the atoning sacrifice on Calvary.

It is clear that the Christian religion is not to be confused with the religion of Christ. Instead, it is a faith which has its centre in Him. It is possible that we have in the Epistle of St. James a document belonging to some circle which thought otherwise. There may have been some who regarded Jesus as above all a teacher and an example, and believed that His will for them was to imitate His life and to practise His faith. Lessing in the eighteenth century declared that Christianity had mistakenly given up the " Testament of John " for the " Gospel of John " ;

[1] D. S. Cairns, *The Reasonableness of the Christian Faith*, pp. 149–150.
[2] Alexander Martin, *The Finality of Jesus for Faith*, pp. 134, 131.
[3] I have written more fully on this in a book, *The Seven Words from the Cross*.

all that is needed is the love of mankind which was shown in Jesus ; real Christianity consists in love, and all opinions concerning Jesus are devoid of religious importance. Christianity as presented by its adherents, he argued, is incompatible with the religion of Christ. The latter is the true religion. Men are required only to practise that which Jesus Himself as a man recognised and practised. And this all men may have in common with Him.

Whatever it may be that is here advocated, it is certainly not historical Christianity. As we have seen, the " Gospel of John " (and the Gospel of Paul too) in laying all the emphasis on the Person of Jesus, is only making explicit that which was already in the mind and words of Jesus Himself. We may rightly say that He was the Supreme Believer. In Him revelation met the full and adequate and right response. But all along we have seen also that His response is not of the same type as man's response. He is not only the Supreme Man of Faith, but also the Supreme Object of faith. It is true that every right response to divine revelation is itself in turn a true revelation of the divine. The saints are those who make it easier for others to believe ; those in whose faces men see God. But the faith of Jesus is different because it is *His*. The uniqueness of the Person gives uniqueness to the faith.

The finality of the Christian Gospel is thus to be found neither in its morals nor in its piety, but much deeper. There is that which transcends these. It breaks out of the realm of morality and it is the pre-requisite of piety. (i) Forgiveness of sin appears in the world as a breach of the ethical system and *catena*. (ii) Salvation must come to man before a right worship can be offered to the God Who is of purer eyes than to behold evil.

(i) Divine pardon means the contravention of the logical result of a world law ; it must involve " a process more vast and profound than we could even imagine, a change far more vast than the suspension of the laws of nature. For the laws of nature are laws of the Divine Creation, external laws. But the law of penalty is the expression of the personal Will of God, of the Divine Holiness itself. Forgiveness, therefore, would be the declaration of the non-validity of the unconditioned order of righteousness which requires penalty." [1] In taking up this position there is no need to fear the charge that forgiveness is immoral. It is religion which takes the grave view of sin, and none ever took a graver than He through Whom salvation comes. The thought of Divine pardon is not unethical but beyond ethics. Forgiveness cannot be won by obedience, works, sacrifices. Nor can it be regarded as a right to be claimed; it is the free gift of God. Forgiveness is "a moral impossibility" which the divine love alone makes possible.

(ii) Salvation is also a pre-requisite of worship. The normal re-action of the sincere soul to the majesty of Divine holiness is that of Simon Peter, "Depart from me, for I am a sinful man, O Lord." Fellowship with God is the offer of divine grace to man. It is right to take account of human volitions, instincts, and aspirations, but, as Professor James Moffatt writes, in doing so we "do not penetrate to the secret of the religious hope. One saving merit of any presentation of Christianity which retains the truth of grace, however crudely it may be expressed, is that it prevents the faith from lapsing into a form of natural religion. . . . 'Grace' is an excellent touchstone for determining whether the mysticism which constantly claims a place within the sphere of Christianity is authentic or exotic." [2] Even adoration of God is impossible unless first there is restoration. In all worship we are conscious that we come into the presence of a gracious God; that we should not be coming to Him unless He had sought us undeserved.

This salvation, which transcends morality and is the pre-condition of worship, was not simply proclaimed by Jesus as a fact in the divine realm; nor was it merely pronounced by Him in the name of God. Instead, it was offered by Him in His own right. Christian awareness of this is summed up in the title which believers accord

[1] Brunner, *The Mediator*, p. 447.
[2] *Grace in the New Testament* (Hodder & Stoughton, 1931), p. 393.

to Jesus. He is the Son of God. And this title has a unique significance. It will not do to say that Jesus is no more than the supreme believer, the ideal pattern, the spiritual zenith of mankind. That is not what Christian people mean by the words, and it is not compatible with the unique place which Jesus assumed for Himself.[1] The revealing medium has an absolute and exclusive harmony with that which is revealed. All others become children of God by way of debt to Jesus ; in His case alone Sonship is the constitutive factor of His being.[2] Jesus is not *a* son, but *the* Son. That He Himself assumed this place, not as one which others might attain to, but as one which was unique, for Him alone, we see clearly from the effects of His references to it. For this He incurred the charge of blasphemy. Being a man, His enemies said, He made Himself equal with God.[3] " I and My Father are one," He said ; and therefore the Jews took up stones again to stone Him.[4] He is to God what no other has been before Him or can be after Him.[5]

Discussing the originality of Jesus, Dr. Claude Montefiore writes that we must consider His teaching as a whole. Then we may rightly call it original, even though Rabbinic and Old Testament parallels were to be found for every verse. It is possible, for example, to match every

[1] In refutation of the charge that Christians claim for Christ what He never claimed for Himself, Stalker pointed to the answer of Jesus to the high-priest (Matt. xxvi. 64). " This great statement, made upon oath, must impress every honest mind. Every effort has, indeed, been made to deplete its terms of their importance and to reduce them to the lowest possible value. It is argued, for example, that, when the high-priest asked if He were ' the Son of God,' he meant no more than when he asked if He were ' the Christ.' But what is to be said of Christ's description of Himself as ' sitting on the right hand of power and coming in the clouds of heaven ' ? " (*The Trial and Death of Jesus Christ* (Hodder & Stoughton, 1894), pp. 23–24. And, as we have seen, the matter does not depend on any single text but on the whole attitude of Jesus throughout His life. See William Manson, *The Incarnate Glory*, pp. 63 ff.).

[2] H. R. Mackintosh, *The Doctrine of the Person of Jesus Christ*, p. 28.

[3] John v. 18 and x. 33.   [4] John x. 31.

[5] Cf. A. M. Fairbairn, *The Philosophy of the Christian Religion*, pp. 446, 543.

one of the Beatitudes with a Rabbinic quotation, yet, considered together, they present a glow and intensity which is new and distinctive. The same thought applies to Christ's teaching on the Fatherhood of God. That conception was already known, but with Jesus it was no accidental, sporadic figure, but essentially the symbol of the divine nature. " This regular conception of God as Father, in proportion to the intensity and vividness of the feeling which suggested it, was something which may fitly be called original." [1]   When, however, we come to consider the salvation of men, we find something which has no parallel in the Old Testament or in Rabbinic teaching. The Rabbis indeed attached no less value than Jesus to repentance. They welcomed the penitent sinner. " But to *seek out* the sinner, and, instead of avoiding the bad companion, to choose him as your friend, in order to work his moral redemption, this was, I fancy, something new in the religious history of Israel. . . . It inaugurated a new idea : the idea of redemption." [2]

In the rescue and deliverance of the sinner through pity, love, and personal service, we find a new method and a new work. But, in fact, we find something far greater. This way of redemption implies that God is of such a nature that it must also be His way. And the truth of this conviction about God is authenticated for us by the Person of Jesus. He is not only the mirror of His own teaching about the proper attitude of men to their sinful fellow-men ; He is also the mirror of God the Father. We have to think of God in terms of Christ, *sub specie Christi*.[3]

Yet this truth was set by Jesus in the framework of the strictest monotheism—the Jewish. It will not do to say bluntly that Jesus is God, just as the Father in Heaven is God. Jesus was a man, though He was different from all other men. Nor will it do to say that Jesus on earth was

[1] See an article in *The Hibbert Journal*, October, 1929.
[2] Montefiore, *Some Elements of the Religious Teaching of Jesus* (Macmillan, 1910), pp. 57–58.
[3] Cf. Pringle-Pattison, *Studies in the Philosophy of Religion* (Oxford, 1930), p. 252.

identical with God in Heaven. If He were, He could not
have talked about God and prayed to God. And God did
not die on the Cross.[1] Wise emphasis has recently been
laid on a point which is too readily forgotten. The question
of the Divinity of Christ must be approached from the right
end. To ask, Is Jesus Divine ? seems to presuppose that
we know already what the Divine attributes are. The
truth is just the other way. Christ came to reveal, not that
He was like God, but that God was like Christ. The right
question is therefore, What is God like ? And the Christian
answer is that He is like Christ. There are no hidden tracts
of His being which can be incompatible with holy love
as we see it in Jesus. We cannot assume that God is known
and then inquire whether Jesus is in every respect like Him.
What we do know is the life of love and the sacrificial
death of Christ. In our desire to know God and to worship
Him it is always with God revealed that we must begin.
He is transcendent ; His nature is unfathomable ; every
doctrine is false which does not leave Him in the end *Deus
absconditus*. (God *has* revealed Himself. Man is nowhere
left without a witness of Him. But every revelation, even
the supreme and final revelation in Jesus, is of One Who is
ultimately incomprehensible, since man is not God.) But
because He is incomprehensible, He is not therefore unknowable. If He were, it could never have been said that " God
is love " ; Jesus could not have said, " He that hath seen
Me hath seen the Father." [2]

" To ask whether Christ is Divine," says the Archbishop
of York,[3] " is to suggest that Christ is an enigma while
Deity is a simple and familiar conception. But the truth is
the exact opposite to this." We cannot begin with God
transcendent ; we must begin with God made manifest in
Christ. Thence we learn, not all about God, but all that

[1] See Professor D. M. Baillie's illumination of a boy's perplexity,
How did God look after the world while Christ was in Palestine ? *Asking
Them Questions* (Oxford, 1936), pp. 76 ff.

[2] Cf. W. R. Matthews, *God in Christian Thought and Experience* (1930),
pp. 136 ff. and H. R. Mackintosh, *The Christian Apprehension of God*
(1929), *sub init.*

[3] In his essay in *Foundations* (Macmillan, 1912), p. 214.

ature is able, and we are worthy, by the grace of
know.

essor John Baillie [1] indicates that the question,
you believe that Jesus is God ? " so often put by
nervous defenders of tradition as a test of orthodoxy, is
one which no Christian should be willing to answer in the
affirmative. " The statement that ' Jesus is God ' taken
thus by itself, is not orthodox, let alone true." Such a
formula " if indeed it says too much for our comprehension, says also too little for our salvation. . . . The
Christian Gospel is rather that we must radically revise our
old conception of deity in the light of the new predicate of
Christlikeness." [2] " Jesus is God incarnate, God the Son,
God manifest "—this we may say and must say ; or, with
St. Paul, " God was in Christ, reconciling the world unto
Himself."

The last is the best formulation in one important respect.
For in Christianity we have not only the supreme revelation
of God but the *act* of God. We believe in the love of God,
not primarily because in Jesus was love matchless and
immeasurable, but because in Him God was actively at
work. It is in Jesus that we behold God, but it is God
Whom we behold in Jesus. The sacrifice of the Son is the
sacrifice of the Father. God proves His own love for us in
this, that while we were yet sinners, Christ died for us.[3]

In the New Testament, union with Christ is almost a
synonym for salvation. Henri Barbusse in his war-book
Le Feu,[4] tells of a conversation overheard in a dug-out
full of wounded men. One of them knows that he is dying.
He cannot last out long enough to reach hospital. And he
says to the other, " It can't be long ; I'm going to die.
Listen, Dominique, you've led a bad life. There are no
convictions against me. There's nothing on my name.
Take my name. Take it—I give it you. Straight off, you've
no more convictions. Take it. It's there in my pocket-

---

[1] *The Place of Jesus Christ in Modern Christianity*, chap. vii.
[2] *Op. cit.* pp. 144, 147.
[3] Rom. v. 8.
[4] Translated as *Under Fire* (Everyman, 1926), see p. 289.

book. Go on, take it, and hand yours over to me—so that
I can carry it all away with me."

Salvation means that the old personality is gone for
ever. " If any man be in Christ, he is a new creature ; old
things are passed away ; behold all things are become
new." Yet this term " union " is easily misunderstood.
When St. Paul says,[1] " I am crucified with Christ ; nevertheless I live ; yet not I, but Christ liveth in me," he does
not mean that his own identity has vanished. But he does
mean to express two fundamental convictions of the
redeemed soul, first, that he has no part in his own salvation ; it has all been done for him in the sacrifice of Jesus ;
yet nevertheless it was all truly for him and as personally
as if Christ had died for him alone ; second, that the consecrated life which he now lives is possible only by the
grace of God as revealed and conveyed to Him in Jesus.
The term " union with Christ " is thus regarded by some as
liable to an unduly mystical interpretation and therefore
to be sparingly employed. (1) Ritschl felt that those who
made use of it were in danger of minimising the importance
of faith in the historic Christ.[2] But this danger threatens
only if the term is used in what is a very haphazard fashion.
For union with Christ means union with the exalted and
living Lord, Who is the same with the historic Jesus now
risen and alive. (2) Others object that the conception
is in danger of minimising the ethical aspect of salvation.

[1] Gal. ii. 20.

[2] Mysticism " which claims to lead men to the attainment of essential
union with God, is quite different from the Evangelical doctrine of justification by faith ; and its sentimental communion with Christ as the Bride-
groom is quite different from trust in Christ as the Bearer of the Divine
promise. The mystical communion of love with Christ, it is claimed,
transcends trust in the merits of Christ. . . . The whole mystical scheme,
in fine, lies outside the spiritual horizon of the Reformers ; it has no
point of agreement with their doctrinal standards ; it stands in contradiction to both the direct and the indirect estimate of the value of the
community of believers and the public preaching of the Word of grace,
which the standards attest ; and, judged in its own special character, it
is no improvement on the Reformed type of religious life, as certainly as
it is derived from the practice of Monasticism." Ritschl, *The Christian
Doctrine of Justification and Reconciliation* (English translation by H. R.
Mackintosh and A. B. Macaulay), pp. 112–114.

Whenever it is used in the epistles, they say, it refers simply to ethical union with Christ. Hence our own use of it must always conform to this pattern. It is fairly clear that the objection, while providing a useful safeguard against any form of mysticism which is ethically indifferent, is itself in danger of misrepresenting the Christian experience by robbing it of an essential element. As before, it should be an adequate safeguard simply to take seriously the phrase itself, "union *with Christ.*" And there is, in a passage quoted by H. R. Mackintosh,[1] an indication that the bare terms of ethics are not in fact sufficient to express the experience of which Christian believers are aware. "When two persons, two moral natures, are to enter into union with each other, then their union, no matter how intimate and profound it may be, must at the same time be personal and moral." It is true that personality lives only in a moral world, but the employment of the two adjectives, "personal" and "moral" suggests that there is indeed a certain uneasiness in defining this union in ethical terms alone. The relation which the words seek to define is one which transcends morality. Even in the case of human friendship this is plain. Its presuppositions are ethical; its effects are ethical; but there is something precious left out if we stop there. And in the relation between redeemed and Redeemer there is the sense of trust and peace and blessedness which cannot be exhausted by description in terms of the ethical. That something additional is best expressed by words which speak not of the human task, but of the grace of God. " Those who plead for the word ' mystic,' and are dissatisfied with the word 'moral,'" said H. R. Mackintosh, "feel, I think, whether consciously or not, that to describe Union with Christ as moral, and no more, makes no provision, or only a quite insufficient one, for the fundamental truth that the Union is initiated on *His* side and sustained at every point by *His* power." [2]

---

[1] From Denney, *The Expositor*, February 1904, p. 156. See H. R. Mackintosh, *Some Aspects of Christian Belief*, p. 109.

[2] *Some Aspects of Christian Belief*, p. 111. Cf. *The Doctrine of the Person of Jesus Christ*, pp. 333 ff.

It is perhaps true that the word "union" is open to ambiguity. It might suggest complete identification of the human and the divine, a kind of absorption which the term "communion" would avoid. But, since "union" has won its place, it is sufficient to note the insistence of writers like St. Paul that the human personality is not expunged. The old is not removed altogether. It may even be said that sad memories of the past have their place in making the glory of the new life. Paul remembers that he was the chief of sinners.[1] Mr. J. S. Stewart quotes the very different words of Philo, "When the divine light blazes forth, the human light sets; and when the former sets, the latter rises. The reason within us leaves its abode at the arrival of the divine Spirit, but when the Spirit departs the reason returns to its place." There is no hint of this absorption in any words of St. Paul. Least of all may we find it in his life. "Study the record of that amazing career, mark the impact which this God-filled and Christ-mastered soul made upon the life of men and Churches and nations, and then declare if he was lacking in individuality! No, it was anything but a blurring and obliterating of personality that resulted from the Damascus experience."[2] The truth is that real self-knowledge comes to a man only in so far as this union is actual. It is by the help of Christ alone that a man is enabled to judge himself fairly. St. Paul writes of winning Christ and being found in Him "not having mine own righteousness, which is of the law, but that which is through the faith of Christ," and a few verses later he adds, "I count not myself to have apprehended; but this one thing I do, forgetting those things which are behind, and reaching forth unto those things which are before, I press toward the mark for the prize of the high calling of God in Christ Jesus."[3]

Nevertheless, the union is one between the forgiven and the Forgiver. It is here, in the offer of forgiveness, that the finality of the Christian Gospel lies. Nothing can be con-

---

[1] 1 Tim. i. 11–16.
[2] J. S. Stewart, *A Man in Christ* (Hodder & Stoughton, 1935), p. 167.
[3] Phil. iii. 9, 13–14.

ceived greater than divine holy love as it is in Jesus. Of fundamental importance is the declaration of Jesus Himself. He knows of no task more sacred than to point men to Himself. He offers to men perfect fellowship with the Father. The coming of the Kingdom is closely linked with His own Person. " All things are delivered unto Me of My Father ; and no man knoweth the Son, but the Father ; neither knoweth any man the Father, save the Son, and he to whomsoever the Son will reveal Him." [1] His own claims make it abundantly clear that either Jesus is divine, or He comes between men and God. If He was no more than a prophet, worship of Him is heathenism.[2] Jesus never suggested that any new revelation was still to come. *He* could not say, " I must decrease." He completes the history of revelation. In His name the disciples were to go out to conquer, and in His name they did conquer.

The finality of Jesus for religion is summed up in the confession of the early Christian Church, " Jesus is Lord." These words imply (1) *Illumination*. In Him we have light on the problems of time and eternity, and of good and evil. Christianity refuses to deny the reality of the temporal, and it insists on the centrality of the moral struggle. (2) *Authority*. Commands are laid on us which are bound up with our eternal destiny. Obedience is the condition of further illumination. Christ is the Judge of all mankind. (3) *Salvation*. Through Him there is deliverance from that which prevents us gaining the illumination which He brings, and from that which stands in the way of our obedience. (4) *Security* ; protection in the fulfilment of our vocation and ultimate peace for the children of God through the victory of the right and the blessedness of life everlasting in God.

[1] Matt. xi. 27.
[2] Cf. Heim, " Krieg und Heilstatsache " in *Glaube und Leben*, p. 198.

INDEXES

INDEX

Absolute, The, 119 ; in History, 146, 216.
Absoluteness in religion, 146 ff.
Adam, 229 n.
Adam, Karl, 57 n., 89, 131 ff.
Adler, A., 34 n.
Æsthetics, 179.
Agnosticism, 25, 106.
Alanus of Lille, 117.
Alastor, 8.
Allah, 229.
Amos, 195.
Andrewes, Lancelot, 190.
Anthropology, 87.
Anthropomorphism, 25, 100 f.
Aquinas, Thomas, 135, 195.
Aristotle, 72 n., 83 n., 135, 183 n., 195, 216.
Arnold, Matthew, 4.
Art, Greek, 101.
Assurance, 178 ff.
Assyria, 159.
Atman, 233.
Atonement, 248.
Augustine, 153, 163, 195, 212.
Authority, chap. iv, 117 ff., 250, 270.

Babylon, 159.
Bach, 195, 225 f.
Baillie, D. M., 87, 146, 253, 265 n.
Baillie, J., 39, 49 n., 95 n., 222, 254, 266.
Balfour, A. J., 81.
Ball, Sir Robert, 223.
Baptism of Jesus, 253.
Barbusse, Henri, 266.
Barker, Henry, 177.
Barth, Karl, 98 ff., 100, 101, 130, 135 n., 158, 160, 186 ff., 201, 209 ff.
Beatitudes, 250, 254, 264.
Beethoven, 34, 195, 226.
Behaviourism, 29 ff.
Belief, and desire, 9.
Berdyaev, N., 22, 118, 135, 213, 214 f.
Bergmann, E., 13, 23, 23 n.
Bergson H., 57, 58 ff., 76, 214.
Bethhoron, battle of, 126.
Bhakti, 234 ff.

18

Bible, 124 ff., 158, 186.
Biology, 75 f.
Blake, Wm., 110.
Böhme, J., 136.
Le Bon, 83 n.
Bosanquet, B., 175.
Bouquet, A. C., 146 n., 226 n., 237.
Bradley, F. H., 119, 198, 200.
Brahma, 238.
Brahmanism, 238.
Bremi, W., 184 n.
Brown, Wm., 29 n., 35.
Brown, W. Adams, 121 n., 225.
Browne, Sir Thomas, 54 n., 97.
Brunner, E., 7, 46 n., 50 n., 56 n., 98, 106, 159, 160, 167 n., 170, 183, 185, 186, 188 n., 196, 262.
Buber, Martin, 201.
Buddha, 252.
Buddhism, 33 n., 148, 230, 237 f., 248.
Bultmann, R., 164, 169 n., 252.
de Burgh, W. G., preface, 77.

Cairns, D., 98 n.
Cairns, D. S., 46 n., 248, 259.
Calvin, 177.
Camfield, F. W., 160 n.
Carlyle, 34.
Catholicity, 239 f.
Certainty, 71, 73, 117, 134 ; chap. ix ; chap. x ; logical, 176.
Certitude, psychological, 175.
Character, 48, 197, 216, 241.
Chesterton, G. K., 67.
Christ, authority of, 208, 209 death of, 214 ; person of, 127, 143, 147 f. ; preparation for, 226 ; union with, 266 ff.
Christianity and the Crisis, 5 n.
Christian Faith, The, 12.
Church, 122 ff., 166, 171, 185, 199, 224, 270 ; authority of, 130 ff.
Columbus, 219.
Communism, 22 f.
Confucianism, 239 n. 3.
Confucius, 252.
Conscience, an authoritative ghost, 22 ; 47, 210.
Consciousness, 29 f.

INDEX OF BIBLICAL REFERENCES

INDEX OF GREEK TERMS

THE KERR LECTURESHIP.

THE " KERR LECTURESHIP " was founded by the TRUSTEES of the late Miss JOAN KERR of Sanquhar, under her Deed of Settlement, and formally adopted by the United Presbyterian Synod in May 1886. In the following year, May 1887, the provisions and conditions of the Lectureship, as finally adjusted, were adopted by the Synod, and embodied in a Memorandum, printed in the Appendix to the Synod Minutes, p. 489.

On the union of the United Presbyterian Church with the Free Church of Scotland in October 1900, the necessary changes were made in the designation of the object of the Lectureship and the persons eligible for appointment to it, so as to suit the altered circumstances. And at the General Assembly of 1901 it was agreed that the Lectureship should in future be connected with the Glasgow College of the United Free Church. From the Memorandum, as thus amended, the following excerpts are here given :—

II. The amount to be invested shall be £3000.

III. The object of the Lectureship is the promotion of the Study of Scientific Theology in the United Free Church of Scotland.

The Lectures shall be upon some such subjects as the following, viz. :—

A. Historic Theology—

(1) Biblical Theology, (2) History of Doctrine, (3) Patristics, with special reference to the significance and authority of the first three centuries.

B. Systematic Theology—

(1) Christian Doctrine—(*a*) Philosophy of Religion, (*b*) Comparative Theology, (*c*) Anthropology, (*d*) Christology, (*e*) Soteriology, (*f*) Eschatology.

(2) Christian Ethics—(*a*) Doctrine of Sin, (*b*) Individual and Social Ethics, (*c*) The Sacraments, (*d*) The Place of Art in Religious Life and Worship.

Further, the Committee of Selection shall, from time to time, as they think fit, appoint as the subject of the Lectures any important Phases of Modern Religious Thought or Scientific Theories in their bearing upon Evangelical Theology. The Committee may also appoint a subject connected with the practical work of the Ministry as subject of Lecture, but in no case shall this be admissible more than once in every five appointments.

IV. The appointments to this Lectureship shall be made in the first instance from among the Licentiates or Ministers of the United Free Church of Scotland, of whom no one shall be eligible who, when the appointment falls to be made, shall have been licensed for more than twenty-five years, and who is not a graduate of a British University, preferential regard being had to those who have for some time been connected with a Continental University.

The Kerr Lectureship

V. Appointments to this Lectureship not subject to the conditions in Section IV. may also from time to time, at the discretion of the Committee, be made from among eminent members of the Ministry of any of the Nonconformist Churches of Great Britain and Ireland, America, and the Colonies, or of the Protestant Evangelical Churches of the Continent.

VI. The Lecturer shall hold the appointment for three years.

VII. The number of Lectures to be delivered shall be left to the discretion of the Lecturer, except thus far, that in no case shall there be more than twelve or less than eight.

VIII. The Lectures shall be published at the Lecturer's own expense within one year after their delivery.

IX. The Lectures shall be delivered to the students of the Glasgow College of the United Free Church of Scotland.

XII. The Public shall be admitted to the Lectures.

THE KERR LECTURES

PUBLISHED BY MESSRS. T. & T. CLARK

MORALITY AND RELIGION
  By JAMES KIDD, D.D.

THE CHRIST OF HISTORY AND OF EXPERIENCE.
  By DAVID W. FORREST, D.D. *Seventh Edition.*

THE RELATION OF THE APOSTOLIC TEACHING TO THE TEACHING OF CHRIST.
  By ROBERT J. DRUMMOND, D.D. *Second Edition.*

THE SACRAMENTS IN THE NEW TESTAMENT.
  By J. C. LAMBERT, D.D.

THE TESTS OF LIFE.
  By Prof. ROBERT LAW, D.D. *Third Edition.*

THE RELIGION OF ISRAEL UNDER THE KINGDOM.
  By Prof. ADAM C. WELCH, Theol.D.

THE RELIGION AND THEOLOGY OF ST. PAUL.
  By Prof. W. MORGAN, D.D.

THE WORLD TO COME AND FINAL DESTINY.
  By JOSEPH H. LECKIE, D.D. *Second Edition.*

BYWAYS IN EARLY CHRISTIAN LITERATURE.
  By Prof. ADAM FYFE FINDLAY, D.D.

RELIGIOUS EXPERIENCE: ITS NATURE AND TRUTH.
  By Prof. KENNETH EDWARD, D.Ph.

FAITH IN GOD AND ITS CHRISTIAN CONSUMMATION.
  By Prof. D. M. BAILLIE, D.D.

THE GOSPEL AND ITS TRIBUTARIES.
  By Prof. E. F. SCOTT, D.D.

OUR HERITAGE IN PUBLIC WORSHIP.
  By the Rev. D. H. HISLOP, D.D.

REVELATION AND RESPONSE.
  By Prof. E. P. DICKIE, M.C., B.D.